# What Happened To Paul Carter?

The very true story of love, passion and a Hitman.

VOL I

## Katherine De Bois

Katherine De Bois LLC
**2017**

Other Works by Katherine De Bois

What Happened to Paul Carter VOL II Collateral Damage

Copyright © 2017 by Katherine De Bois

All rights reserved. This book or any portion thereof may not be reproduced or used in any manner whatsoever without the express written permission of the publisher except for the use of brief quotations in a book review or scholarly journal.

First Printing: 2017

ISBN 978-0-9992339-0-0

Katherine De Bois LLC
16192 Coastal Highway
Lewes, Delaware. USA

www.whathappenedtopaulcarter.com

# Dedication

For all the loves in my life, and
my son, whom I love more than he will ever comprehend.
To the moon and back, and all the stars in the sky.


And for all the women who have loved and been loved,
and for all those that haven't.

# Acknowledgements

I would like to thank Paul, for without him loving me, this book would never have been written. I would also like to acknowledge my beautiful son, for he is the motivation that kept me focused to finish it. I am forever grateful to my wonderful friends and clients who have shown extraordinary kindness and empathy as I travelled this journey.

As a reader, please forgive me. I am no professional writer.
I did my best.

# Chapter 1

*Being deeply loved by someone gives you strength,*
*while loving someone deeply gives you courage.*
**Unknown**

March 9th 2015

I'm driving in the dark without my glasses, trying to figure out exactly where I am, which is a challenge considering I can hardly see the road, let alone the signs.

'Where am I?' This is ridiculous and under the circumstances, I don't need to be adding anymore stress. I need to look and feel truly calm, not flustered and panicked. My stomach is churning.

It isn't everyday you arrange to meet a hitman, and my grasp of the unfolding situation is a few feet distanced from reality. I'm terrified that my knowledge of exactly what is happening, may be a few months behind where I should be. I'm petrified that I have done the wrong thing, and that I'm probably walking straight into a trap.

Tonight I need to be in the moment.
'God I wish I had gone to the loo.'

I'm not lost, just navigating towards another meeting with more strangers in the middle of nowhere, but at least the road is 3 lanes wide and relatively straight. I glance down at my phone's GPS and scroll the map forward. The blue line goes forever. Another 20 minutes before I need to turn. I put it back between my legs, safely nestled in the voluptuous folds of the tulle skirt that

I chose for this auspicious occasion, and lightly laugh at myself. Only I would have stressed over what to wear.

Before leaving home, I had texted George, a trusted friend.

*'I'm going to 1 Stantham Court. East Morang. If I have called this wrong, all my money is under the bed. Give it to Oliver.'*

The response was valid.

*'Are you kidding? I don't want you going there. Katherine, that's crazy. It's just too dangerous. It's a trap. I know they say they need your help, but who cares. They are nobody to you. Don't be stupid.'*

*'George, it needs to be sorted and if it helps bring that asshole to justice then I have always said I am prepared to be the sacrificial lamb. You want your money don't you? I want answers. I need information. I want proof. I need it finished and I'm just so over everything. I'll message you when I leave, but if you don't hear from me, then call the police, you know what has happened.'*

*'Katherine, just keep this call on. I'm not happy. I think it's a trap. I'll be around the corner. Did you tell the police yet?'*

*'No, I don't have enough evidence yet, and you don't have to be involved.'*

"*Katherine I am so invested in this. I will be around the corner. Any trouble, I will be there before it happens. Don't hang up on me. I feel sick.*"

He feels sick. Know the feeling. My chest is pounding in my ears. Adrenalin is coursing. My head feels empty. Numb. Overloaded to the point of nothing. The veins on my hands are thick welts running towards my fingers. It's sort of fascinating watching my body react, and objectively, it's distracting.

The evening shadows of trees and houses blur and my chest is forcing long calm breaths. Chestfuls.

How did this happen? I'm not even meant to be in Australia still. I'm meant to be married and happily living in New York. That was our plan, right?

Man of my dreams, Paul. Paul Carter.

6 ft 2, eyes of blue. All the romance and fantasy, that I didn't think I had been looking for. There it was on a platter. Paul. Perfection on a plate. Yes, that is exactly what it is.

I was happy because I had it all. We were both so passionately in love with everything about each other. It had been perfect. I want it to stay this way. So much of me wants to sort this all out and have him come and sweep me off my feet.

He always said. "You make me a better man, Katherine. I hope I am worthy of you."

I used to struggle comprehending that sentiment. I felt that I brought nothing to the table. I was not in his league. He was everything.

He was the life of the party, could handle every situation, always made people feel at ease, while I stumble over my words and freak at meeting strangers. He is fiercely loyal, protective, strong, funny, loving and super intelligent. As if that wasn't enough, he is good looking, charismatic, charming and clearly generously wealthy.

A large man, in size and stature. Dark hair, light olive skin, with pale blue eyes framed by thick black lashes and a smile that would light up an entire room. He's a head turner and boy, do those girls turn. For that matter, so do the men.

Seriously what did he see in me?
Something. Obviously. He adored me. I knew it. Everyone knew it.

What the hell? How can everything have changed so much? Why has he been taken away? What has happened to the perfect man I love? I feel like I'm being punished. Why was I allowed to be with him in the first place? Are the stories true? I cannot reconcile how my world went from paradise to this nightmare of thugs, lies, thieves, cons and betrayals, let alone living under the shadow of a 'hit.' I just don't understand why I got thrown into it. When am I going to reach the bottom, so I can climb over and out? When will any of this make sense?

Hopefully tonight will provide the answers and I can put it all behind me, but I know my Paul will never be found, no matter how many people try.

I glance down and realize the turn is ahead and start to concentrate on the road. The side streets of East Morang are narrow and windy. I feel uncomfortable by the mere fact that I can see gumtrees on the nature strips. Suburbia. This one, in particular, was the back of beyond breeding ground for sleeve tattoos, mediocrity and thugs, specifically known for it's bogun population. I do not belong out here.

My heart is pounding in my throat.

The polite voice of my GPS announces. "In 20 meters, turn right. You have arrived at your destination."

I pass by the house and turn back around at the end of the court, parking on the exit side of the street. If it gets bad and there's a chance to get to the car, I'd like a clear escape route. This being said, I'm in stilettos, so I'm doomed already. Whatever happens tonight, I'm doing it in style.

I leave the car unlocked and walk across the road, taking a breath of bravery that is so large it moves my shoulder blades, and steel myself for all the possibilities of the evening. I stop, look down at the tips of my shoes and let my eyelids deliberately close. It's not even half a second, but long enough to become a more centered and courageous version of myself. My congenial facade is flashed on and a shiver goes down my spine. I raise my head, opening my eyes and stare forward. What have I got to lose? It's this way or the slow way. The rational part of my brain doesn't believe any of this is real anyway. My life is too average for this drama level.

I feel nothing. I'm on autopilot. I am ready.

Another deep breath, then I delicately navigate my heels up the cobbled driveway towards a tall, young man standing at the top of the stairs near the front door.

Dark haired. He is coming down to greet me. "I heard you pull up. Thanks for coming." He sounds sincere.

"Hi Tony." I lean in and kiss him on the cheek. Let the bizarreness begin. This face, I have at least seen before, but as he leads me through the foyer, I wonder whose side he's really on.

Keep your friends close. Your enemies closer. Never a truer word spoken.

Until recently, he used to work for Paul. Yes, the hitman's son worked for Paul, and I had met him briefly, once at a BBQ 10 months ago. He knew the truth then, and never felt the need to tell me. He has certainly betrayed me before, allowing me to be surrounded by all the lies. At the same time, I also think he may have inadvertently protected me. What were his motives then? Where are his loyalties now?

He smiles and guides me inside. It's awkward and tense. I'm trying to get my bearings, and feel the vibe of the house.

His mother, Filomina, is standing in the entrance. I have never met her, but she has been a Facebook "friend" for a couple of months. Same height as me. Only 5'4." Bleached, blonde hair in a sharp cut, and a warm smile. I lean in and give her a gentle hug and a kiss.

Then there is Kara, Tony's sister, and apparently a client of my beauty salon at some point in time. I only know this fact as her name is in our data base and comes up on my phone. Her mother's daughter in looks. Striking red lipstick across perfectly shaped, pouting lips. Dark hair. Maltese. They bred well.

I walk towards her. "You must be Kara. It's lovely to finally meet you." She and I give each other a genuine tight hug and I whisper in her ear. "Thank you for telling me."
I feel the threat of an emotional tear try to glaze my right eye.

She gently pulls back and looks me straight in the eyes. "You needed to know. As a woman, I would want to know."

Behind her, in the kitchen, I see a grey headed man approaching. He is balding and the hair he has left is pulled back into a thin plait. Tall, big and strong. He is older than me, maybe late 50's. Eyes of a poker player, giving nothing away. I can't decide if he looks more like a Vietnam vet, or a biker. Either way, I'm dead if this goes bad.

"You must be Vito." We walk towards each other, our hands mutually rising for a handshake. His politely. He expected this greeting. It was respect. Personally, I can't stretch far enough away from my own hand. I want distance. There will be no hug here. I'm terrified, and at the same time, proud of my stupidity, or is this courage? Add it to the list of things I don't know.

I can't read faces very well but I look him in the eyes as we shake. They are impenetrable. I am scared. I am polite. I call the bluff.

"Thank you for not killing me yet."

"That's OK love."

The lack of denial hits the pit of my stomach. The casual acceptance of what I just said was mind fucking. This is actually happening. He has really been hired to kill me. I am in his house and he may still carry the deed out. This is so ridiculous. Epitome of surreal. I know that these are the facts but I can't compute them. Clearly, none of this is normal.
I cannot believe the reality of the situation.

Hopefully, I am now worth more to him alive than dead but I suppose it depends on a fair few things. Firstly, does he really need my help? Or is this just a setup? What about all the stuff I don't know, and what is it that they hope I do know? Am I going to be able to be of help to them and what if I can't? The incessant chatter in my head questions whether I'll be leaving this house tonight. Walking or body bag? Another reason to dislike the 'burbs.

I'm ushered into the kitchen and we sit down at the grey, marble counter. Filomina offering me a coffee, which I accept, joking that under the circumstances, maybe something stiffer would be more appropriate.

Before I had left home, I had debated about whether to bring Scotch as a peace offering, but wasn't sure whether you brought gifts to your potential killer's home. Someone should write an etiquette book on the subject. They'd make a killing. I smirk inwardly at my silent repartee. Nothing feels real.

Vito is sitting on a stool at the far end of the bench, leaning against the wall. There's a mounted phone beside his head. I realize I have to ask.

"So he really hired you to kill me then?"

His voice is heavily accented, European, and his demeanor genuine.

"Yeah."

WHAM. It was like being hit in the face, chest and stomach simultaneously. Body blow of destruction. An eyebrow raise and a non comprehending slight shake of my head, as I try to accept the finality of my reality.
Emotional heartbreak stabs through my chest crushing my very being. The desire to be dead, crumples my brow and my eyes drop shut, taking me into the safety of blackness.

I immediately force them open to face these facts. That's what I'm here for. Knowledge. Knowledge I leave with and use, or I die trying. Literally.

Nearly too exhausted to care. 'Be brave.' The self talk is incessant. I have become a Nike ad. 'Just do it.'

Filomina leans across the counter and hands me the freshly made coffee as she asks. "So how did you find out?"

Fair enough question, I suppose. We all have our concerns. This is all so blase, it's as if we are discussing grocery prices. "I first knew about the threat, the day after I found out about Paul. It was a lot to take on board in a short time."

She looked at me.

"You know, the 10$^{th}$, Filomina. The 10$^{th}$ of September." Even as I said it, I felt my heart hankering for the simplicity of the nightmare as it was, back then. As horrendous as it was at the time, it was plain and simple. This was now just the universe's arse's act.

These people needed to know I was being honest. Or at least think I was. I suck at poker. I glanced towards Vito, aware that tonight required a lot of direct eye contact. Then I stared at him. I was hurt and angry.

"Vito, that man cold heartedly told me that you had called and asked if I was a problem. He informed me, that if I was, then you were going to sort me out. That you were concerned as to whether I was now a threat to your mutual business projects and that you were happy to solve the issue by putting me through a tree shredder at a pig farm."
"You understand this right? The night before I had just lost my partner and I wake to this. The beginning of the end.
 All I had was that shattering phone call the night before and everything changed. As you know, Kara, that changed my life."

She looked at me and gave everyone, (there were now two more teenagers in the kitchen), a surprised innocent, confused look. I took it on board. Oh my God, she just publicly denied that she had made that first anonymous call to me. Yet, didn't she just admit it in my ear when I arrived. Tread carefully Katherine, these people are not your friends. They aren't even loyal to each other.

"Obviously that was a pretty ghastly night all round and this is what I deal with the next day. That now *I'm* viewed as the problem. I still can't get my head around this. ME!. …. I'm now the problem?"

Vito didn't flinch.

But then my focus moved abruptly. I was suddenly aware of the presence of yet another person.

Shivers.

Casual side glance and a toss of my hair so I can subtly look over my shoulder. A solid, big, cumbersome man, coming up from behind. I took half a breath.

"Gerry." Vito's smile was warm and inviting, as they shook hands like mates catching up at a summer's day BBQ. Honestly what have I walked into?

"Gerry, this is Katherine. Katherine, this is Gerry, works with Paul."

Another face to another name.

I take a large lungful of air, accompanied by an electric shiver down my spine. The hairs on my arms lift and then immediately subside.

"Nice to meet you, Gerry. I believe you're not necessarily a fan either?" Over the last few months, I had acquired a bit of background knowledge on a few random people. Every new face implicating and incriminating another person. Tattling on each other. Divulging separate secrets that when put together were slowly making a simple story into an unimaginable suspense filled drama. I was aware my life had become a film. A John le Carre epic. It had begun as a romance.

This didn't mean that anything I thought I knew was true. The layers continued to unfold.

"No, love. No. That bastard has cost me millions. Sorry 'bout what's happened to you though. Better now than later. You'll be alright in the end and we will find Paul, OK?"

That was a matter of opinion. What would be better, was that none of this had happened. What would be best, was that I had been allowed to happily marry Paul, and be living with the man that loved me. Happily ever after, in New York. That would be the better and best scenarios. Not any of this. This is what is referred to as the beyond worst scenario for one's life. I just wanted Paul back.

Vito obviously was going to control the conversation and drive the message home. "Yeah, Gerry, we were just talking about how Katherine has become a bit of a problem."

"I can see that." Gerry smiled, settling himself in behind my chair, with his hand resting across the back.

I'm back to shitting myself again.

Filomina laid her hands open, palms down on the bench in front of me. "Well, the man IS an ass. He is cold hearted and will do anything to get the job done. You should have seen him, storming around here, when he didn't get the money.

The kitchen erupted into laughter from everyone. Tony interjected. "Yeah. He was marching up and down the family room right there." He pointed to the TV area behind me.

Filomina laughed. "He was swearing and cursing. Saying it wasn't fair. He only needed another week and he would have got it all. All that effort organizing everybody. Bribing. Threatening. It had all gone to plan. A total waste of his time now she knows. Oh my God, he was furious that you had got in the way."

What money?? What bribing? What plan? Are they talking about things I already know? I'm here to negotiate my life. What are they now talking about? Are they in on something more than I know? Oh god, probably. Clearly. I know nothing. Shit!

They were still all laughing, oblivious to my confusion.

Kara and Filomina looked at each other. There was something between them. A secret. Do I need to know? Is it, that Filomina really knows that Kara is the one that caused this? Is she covering for Kara?

She continued. "He really wanted you dead then, that's for sure. He'd put all that effort into getting your money and now you had accidentally prevented him. He was crazy angry and switched from his initial plan of conning you, to having you killed, right there. Stood in front of the TV and swung around facing Vito.

'Kill her Vito. Just kill her. Her and her bloody ungrateful son.'"

They all were all talking at the same time. One over the top of the other, repeating what he had been yelling.

"It was suddenly so much easier. Less effort."
"Wished he'd done it earlier. Less fucking around."
"It made no difference to him."
"He said that he knew you were both there just waiting for the Carter inheritance."

A cacophony of wounding words.

"He had a contract with you." She distracted herself. "Why would you sign anything with that man? Did Paul think that was a good idea? I mean no one in their right mind would go up against him. They are all formidable business men. What? What was the contract? Were you selling him your business? Did you become partners? Did you sign something without reading it?... He never went into that detail but he said 'it' would hold for a little longer. So you must have agreed to something. Suddenly, he didn't care how it was done. Just wanted Vito to fix it."

My mind flicked to the amount of legal documents I had signed in the last year. 'Was I paying attention to every single one? There had been so many meetings with so many solicitors and business men. Regardless, and more to the point, I hadn't *accidentally* prevented anything. It was Kara who contacted me. I still have the texts. Kara, Ash, Tony and the rest of that millennial group. They caused this landslide, not me. Not me at all!'

She interrupted my thoughts. "But, after everything you had been through, with the rape, and your son and the burns." She slowed for a second as she saw the look on my face, "Yes, Paul told us about your past. Sorry love. You've had a really horrid time, so I told Vito not to do anything. You realise Vito didn't make that call. It's the other way around. He was asked to kill you, but I didn't think it was fair. Enough is enough for one life time don't you think?"

"I couldn't agree more." I replied.

Inwardly, my mind just caved in on itself. I could hear an external buzz weirdly inside my head. Out of body. Of the few things I expected tonight, this hadn't been one of them. That was my past. My personal, revolting past. Casually thrown in to conversation. Rape! Burns! Skin grafts! My son! Casual, as if we are best friends with the right of knowledge, full disclosure, trust and shared secrets, but this isn't the case. I haven't told them my story and I feel it has been used against me, and yet she is saying it's what kept me alive.

I feel my brain whirring through all this. Blurring. Refocussing. Fogging.

Yay, that she felt I had had enough shit for one life time, but what the fuck? Yay, she deemed me worthy of living. WOW. There is no holding back here. No editing for my benefit. Well, no, let's rethink. There is no editing for the benefit of *my* feelings. I am very clearly still viewed as expendable and they are only telling me things they want me to know. The only editing here will be for their benefit.

My mind drowning in it's own thoughts. The way I just took hit after emotional hit.

The words were circling, uncaught in my head.

'Was conning me for my money.'
'Happy to just kill me if it was easier.'
'I'm so dispensable?'
'I'm alive because I was raped?'

'Who drops this into conversation?

A hitman and his family, that's who. This is their life. They don't care that I'm reeling. They want that.

But this isn't all true. I'm not alive because she took pity on me. It may have been months ago, but not now. Even I know that. I'm alive because they think I can help them recover $500,000 that the asshole who wants me dead, conned them out of.

Ah the irony.

The hitman betrayed by the very person who hires him, and so now the tables have turned.'

Regardless I'm still not safe.

Filomina looks me in the eyes and I try to refocus as she says. "How did Paul allow this to happen? He is normally so in control. This is, um, what does he say?"

"A cluster fuck" Tony helped fill the gap.

"Yeah," Gerry drawled. "Pretty sure Paul has just done a runner. Safer away from all of this. He hates drama. His life has always been too easy. He'll return when it's calmed down. Not that he should have left you with this mess. We can't make sense of it. Let alone with the threat of danger."

Filomina interjected. With a caring, sisterly look on her face.

"True though, if you're viewed as a threat, imagine how some people may now see Paul. Although he has just angered them more by disappearing, leaving us to all pick up the pieces. I bet he surfaces when he thinks it's safe."

Is she trying to reassure me everything was going to be ok? I'm not convinced.

Vito gives me another encouraging look and asks me to explain how I knew about him.

"Well, I was coming in from the garage. I had been getting ready to leave and he was suddenly just sitting at the dining table, looking vaguely familiar, but obviously not anyone I knew, and as it turned out, you two were talking on the phone. Clearly I had no idea it was you. I was still shocked and scared that he was sitting there. When he realized I was near, he hung up and said.

"That was the 'Toe Cutter' on the phone. You know…, Vito. Vito Falcone. He has that name for a reason Katherine. He solves problems. I'm pretty sure, you have always known that."

At the time, my scared and panicked brain had tried to filter the news. Deep down, yes, I had known something. I'd heard conversations that were never muted, they were out in public domain between business men. Various things. That 'the Toe Cutter had been used to sort a problem' or that someone may have to 'get the toe cutter to go fix an issue.' It had never been exactly spoken as to how, but I had got the gist, that the Toe Cutter solved problems by force or coercion. To be honest, I thought it was just a tough nickname, not a lifestyle. I had never asked. I had pretended not to hear. I hadn't known that this was Vito's moniker. At the time it was new news.

I looked at Vito. He raised his eye brows in acknowledgement and nodded his chin forward, as a sign to keep talking.

"I asked him if he was threatening me? And he said, 'No Katherine, just thought you should know. I'm just the messenger.' I told him that I wasn't too scared of dying as I had had a fairly shitty life, and he assured me that, 'I'd end up begging for mercy. They all do.'"

"Go on." Vito wanted to hear more.

"Well, He told me, 'that you said I was already an issue that needed to be solved, and would definitely be a bigger problem if I kept asking questions and that I needed to remove all evidence of being in a relationship with Paul and the photos. Best if I no longer existed really.' He told me that, 'you and he obviously just felt the need to make sure I understood' and he reminded me that 'I was a mother and you weren't to be trusted as you go off the handle.' He made sure I understood that 'you wanted to remove me by using a tree shredder and that I shouldn't put my son in danger.'"

The kids were all quiet but smiling. A collection of knowing smirks spread around the kitchen. I was completely outnumbered here. Gerry was silent, breathing behind me.

Vito and Filomina both looked a bit flushed; A bit put out.

I was sick of this shit. This game that I had no idea how to play. "What? Isn't that what you two discussed?" I blurted it, clearly annoyed.

Everyone in the kitchen knew this was true, except, maybe, Gerry. Again Filomina answered. "Firstly, no one would ever touch your son, Katherine. He has nothing to do with this. It's not what's done. I wouldn't allow that. God if he had said that to me. OMG. I would have killed him on the spot with my bare hands. No one threatens my family."

In my head, I thought. 'Yes, you're right Filomina. No one threatens my boy either. But, I've done, and am doing, everything I can to sort it.' Why did they think I was there, if not to try and ensure my son's safety. I certainly wasn't there altruistically. I looked at Vito questioningly.

"No, love, that's right. If there's a problem it would get sorted but not your kid. No, I'm just surprised he was stupid enough to use my name. He shouldn't have told you my name. That's just wrong. Disloyal, you know. That's his problem. No loyalty. I told you on the phone the other day. Wild angry rogues are more of a danger than professionals."

"Yes, but that wasn't about him. You were talking about someone else who also wants to kill me." Who knew I was so important?

"Same blood type, Katherine. Desperate, conniving. Ruthless. That man has done some terrible, terrible things in his time."

I was trying to stay with the conversation as my mind pieced things together. 'You aren't so loyal, or predictable either, are you? Any of you. I'm here at your invitation. You were going to kill me only weeks ago, until you realised I may be of use to you, because now you have been conned like everyone else, and I may have information to help rescue the situation. I have literally been in hiding for months, enduring a campaign of belligerent intimidation, but now you say you have turned on the very man you were working for. You want to use me for what I may know, to help get your own justice and revenge.' From our previous phone calls, I think the tree shredder is going to get used one way or the other.

Time to clear the air. "So that's how you would have done it then? In a shredder at a pig farm?"

"Yeah, it's pretty clean."

WOW! This reality just doesn't have any soft landings.

"So you were really going to do it then?" He just looked through me. I felt his lack of conscience spear my body. He would have done it without a care in the world. This is so real, it's bordering on ignorant that I ever doubted it. I have been in legitimate danger for 6 months probably more, and yet I've only told a few close friends, because I don't want people to think I'm crazy.

"So, um, exactly how much would that cost, you know, to remove me as a problem." I suppose I want to know how much I was worth dead. Also how much it might cost to counter offer the deal. What has my world become???

"Well, I took the first $5,000 and the other ten went to The Hells Angels. He had to come with me to hand it over."

Total shock. A million thoughts machine gun across my brain.
'So cheap. Who knew?'
OMG. Really? He is being so brutally honest. Is this how murderers and hit men talk? Even in the Soprano's they kept the women out of it. It was hidden.' My knowledge of the underbelly of society is limited to TV. This is just so casual. The kids are here.
In films they only ever tell their victims the truth before they kill them.
Why? Why would he admit this?

Of course. I'm either not making it out of here, or he doesn't care as I have no witnesses. Fuck, I hope George can hear this. It's not as though I can check.
And now The Hells Angels are involved?
What the hell? Literally!

I still had my sense of humour. Sort of. Twisted. Ironic. Disbelieving. Naive.

So payment has already been exchanged!

This isn't a hypothetical. I'm really wanted dead. I'm hated that much. I'm such a danger. To what???? It was a whine. A pathetic, confused whine. Why on earth am I needed dead?

I'm sitting with a hired killer who has been paid to carry out the job. My stomach is turning. I can hear it. I want it to stay silent. I'm still trying to feign being nonchalant. I have spent six months trying to gain information, dig up evidence and stay alive at the same time. I'm obviously outnumbered, outmaneuvered and out played. I have only a few things protecting me. Long term, I'm relying on my ability to research and write. The other is my friends. And mostly on fellow victims. Not much protection under the circumstances.

"Alright then, if we are going to be this open, I need to be honest and say, I'd be stupid to pretend I don't still think I'm at risk. Huge risk. Apparently there's more than just one person after me. I'm shocked to think that I'm so important, so hated and I suppose, that I'm considered such a threat, and that you have accepted responsibility to do the task. That you have recently also warned me that I'm better off with you than the 'angry rogue' also after me, doesn't make me feel any better. A bullet is a bullet."

I remember just feeling sick in my stomach. Exhausted. Part of me egged on the bullet. Bring it on. Finish this pain.

"Because you are on my Facebook, you know I've written a book and although it needs to be edited, right now, my solicitor has a copy, and there are several on USB sticks stored with people. I just need to be clear, that if anything happens to me or my son, that your names have not been changed. So it reads like an enormous police statement. Dates, times and your identities. Just so we are clear. I may still be killed but they will come straight to your door. If we are here tonight to strike a better arrangement for me and you to work together, then that book has a better use for all of us and I'd change your details as you wish. I will do what it takes to finish all of this, once and for all. This all needs to stop. Paul needs to be found. I want to have him come back home to Melbourne, and I personally wouldn't mind being allowed to live my life quietly and safely."

Bluff or fact? Even I didn't know anymore.
Writing? - Yes. 175,000 words worth.
Did my solicitor have it? - Yes.
Were there USB sticks and emailed copies? - Yes
Anywhere near finished? - No. Because more stuff kept surfacing.
Useful? - Perhaps.
Weapon? - Maybe if I were to throw it.
Threatening enough to keep me alive? - I'm about to find out.

Tony was sitting on the counter top beside the sink. He laughed.

"No, Keep our names. I want to be famous and I want him to know, that I helped bring him down., but to do any of this, we probably need to figure out where Paul is. Sorry Katherine, but what a coward. Leaving you like this. With all the questions. He obviously has all the answers."

In the corner of a quiet part of my mind. 'Am I going to get through this? If so, when? Am I going to get the answers, that I need to walk out unharmed, satisfied, sane and exonerated? Or have I just walked into the easiest setup?'

I hate that I am having to deal with this. This can't be how the nightmare ends, with me voluntarily meeting the hitman, hired to kill me and him actually doing it.
That would be anti climactic and I feel in my core, that it's not how I want this game to be played out. I'm not quite sure of the rules yet, but I am risking my life that this isn't how it ends. Not tonight at least. Perhaps.

Vito got off his chair and walked towards me. The hackles on the back of my neck again stood up and I saw the hairs on my arm raise on top of goose bumps. Fight or flight in action. I had no physical fight in me. I looked defeat in the eye. Let it be. So this is how it ends. I felt beaten but strangely calm. I'd been on the run for four months: and scared for a lot longer.

"It's all good love. Let's see what can be done to sort this, one way or the other. Come on, we should all go outside and have a glass of wine.

I followed him out to the courtyard. Into the dark, aware of the instability of my ankles, and the twitching of my knees. I am not safe here. The backyard flashed with lights, revealing a gazebo and BBQ table.

Filomina followed out with glasses and a bottle of red wine, as Vito sat across from me. He gave me a compassionate look and suggested I take a seat opposite him. "What a mess. So much money. So many victims. Katherine, you'll need to tell us what you know about the missing inheritance. That's where we will find our compensation. No one messes with my family. But, first, tell me, what do you think has happened to Paul? Has anyone found his car yet?"

Vito has to appear like he cares, he wants information from me. I highly doubt it's genuine concern for my broken heart: My grief: Obviously not for my fear. I had a feeling that Vito actually really knew the answer to his own question, but then again maybe he didn't. I knew nothing.

"Don't worry, Katherine, we'll find him. There's so many people out there looking. You know, I'm sure he's doing just fine."

'Is Paul fine?' I wondered to myself. 'Is he ok? I don't think so.' I miss him so much it hurts to be alive. Am I ok? Personally I believe my beautiful Paul is gone forever. My best hope is that they at least find Paul's body and allow me to mourn all I have lost. As for the new asshole who wants me dead, well that's a whole different story. Two different people. Two very different feelings.

I am so heart broken.

# Chapter 2

September 11, 2014

What has just happened?

I'm sitting in my shop, the curtains are drawn and I can barely move. I have some type of flu. Breathing in, I am aware of the effort. I am acutely aware of my body. The tingling in the tips of my fingers, the tightness of my throat, the buzz in my head.

I lost my partner last night.

The fog, I feel it coming through my eye balls, hazing my thoughts. The furrows on my forehead crushing down as I search through the memories, trying to make sense of it all.

I woke this morning to be told someone wanted to put me through a tree shredder.

I think last night was the worst night of my life, and this morning was just unnecessarily random and cruel. Why, would the universe do this to me? Where is Paul? He is meant to be my protector, my partner. I need to feel the safety of his arms around me. I want to hear him tell me that everything will be all right. I want him to come and fix this quagmire, this disaster, this, oh, so obviously a parallel reality, for it is not mine. He fixes everything. Where are you? What has happened to you? My mind just swirls in panicked disbelief. I am more shocked than scared. I'm aware, that I obviously know nothing. Nothing except, I don't deserve this.

If karma is a truth, I must be the most evil person on the planet. I don't want to believe I am a bad person, let alone deserve this. No one deserves to feel this. Nothing makes sense. Something will make it all right again. I just need to be still. I need to breathe.

I want my bliss back. I know that's just a state of mind. Temporary at best, and finely reliant on the synchronicity of the universe. The kindness of timings. Once experienced nothing else will do. Paul is my bliss and I am certainly his.

Sitting, staring, unfocussed, I'm suddenly painfully aware of the fragility of too much happiness. Three weeks ago, I was celebrating my engagement with the man who adored me: the man whom I adored. We celebrated our love, our future, our happiness, our fortune at finding each other. We rejoiced with family and friends at our good luck to have found each other. Since the day he met me, he had proudly announced that I made his life complete.

Now. Nothing is the same.

He spoke of electricity, of breathing as one. I was happy. We were happy. We were besotted with each other. Whirl wind love and passion. The stuff of romance novels.

"Oh my god, how lucky are we? To both love like this. To feel the counterpart to your own being in the eyes of another." He was forever telling me how lucky he was.

The depth of his sincerity, over rode his passionate corniness.

As numb and slow as I currently feel, these flashbacks are comforting, and I want to immerse myself in them, but, just as I shut my eyes and retract into the past, I'm suddenly jolted out of the warmth of my memories as a loud, over revved car flies past the shop, startling me back from the past and hurtling me into the ugly present of the now.

The "now" that I don't want.

There's an irony. Suddenly I want the solidity of the past or perhaps take my chances with the hopes of the future. I definitely don't want this moment, where the pain and shock are so great I can't even comprehend them. Speed this up. Get this over with. Get me to the tomorrow where I may feel better. I have become Paul wanting to rush through the present into a better future. I smile at the irony.

My body is incapable of anything but sitting. I physically ache. My eyes flicker through the memories like a broken film roll. If I can pull it together, it may make sense. Maybe I can understand, undo, unhurt. Maybe I can fix this.

Stop threatening to feel, Katherine.
Don't hurt.
Just remember.

The overriding feeling about the past year, is one of awesome love. The big love. The one. My memories are filled with passion, love, laughter. Enormous highs, hugs and reassurance. Safety and security. Of being able to breathe. It was social and fun. Extreme and surprising. Fast paced, but worth it.

And challenging. It was definitely challenging. I had made it harder than it needed to be, just to fall in love and be happy. My bliss. I will always think of this year as the time I loved, and was loved like no other. We were one. Paul's life had consumed me, and I now needed him to breathe.

How could the universe do this to us? Separate us? Put me, and my son, in so much danger. I don't understand, but I will.

I open the laptop and go to Facebook. Yes, it happened. I'm engaged. I feel the massive solitaire on my left hand. It doesn't seem real but there's the evidence. It wasn't a dream. The first 11 photos, that the photographer sent through to Paul, who immediately uploaded them on to our shared Facebook page. Our happiness. There for the world to see.

Everyone was thrilled for us. You can see it on their faces. I was so, all encompassingly, loved. We were clearly both inordinately happy.

The engagement was August 23rd and the wedding was booked for the 29th of November. Everything on speed dial. Paul rushing head long into his future, and me always a few steps behind trying to catch up. A honey moon in Bora Bora and a permanent move to New York, before Christmas. We would take nothing and start complete afresh. All Paul's choices. He would tell me all the time, how perfect our lives were going to be.

"You're going to love it, Princess. You deserve everything, because you ask for nothing."

I agreed. Being with him was wonderful. The rest a bonus.

He was literally bursting with excitement. Planning our future. Listing goals. Like an impatient, enthusiastic teenager, just wanting to get on with his life, on his terms. He wanted the engagement and wedding to be bigger and better than any of my suggestions. The size of his love. He told me all the time. 'I want you to have everything you ever dreamed of. I want you to feel how much I love you, and know how important you are to me. I want everyone to know that you're 'The One."

I struggled with the speed; the intensity. His devotion was overpowering and I couldn't believe I deserved it. I'd said I would be happy marrying in a Registry office with just our immediate family. He was horrified, yet I had tried to convince him.

"But your Dad is about to marry Grace in a civil ceremony, and it keeps it pure; Purely about the marriage. Lovely and simple."

"Katherine, they are old. Marrying there is a sign that they are over everything. Finished with joy, excitement and passion. I think I can do better than that. I want to celebrate and I want everyone to know that finally I have found my true love, my happiness, my bliss."

He got his way and as a result, our engagement was over the top. Nothing was too good. He was completely involved in the planning. He would only accept the very best. He wanted me and everyone to know that I was what he had waited for. He told me time and time again. He told everyone.

I ran everything past him. The choice of caterers, Dj's, photographers. Music, furniture hire and the venues. He chose the bigger option, the more decadent, expensive choice each time. If the engagement was lavish, our wedding was going to be an opulent extravaganza.

"Princess, this isn't just a wedding. It's a celebration of a marriage forever. I want to be with you till the day you die. I want the world to know, that you will make me happy for the rest of my life and I want you to always know that too. I want you to feel your worth. It is my job to make you happy and that in itself will make me the happiest man in the world. We will be amazing."

It was excessive and effusive. It was constant devotion.
I loved him back. I hoped I deserved him. Could I really be this lucky?

Paul and I at our engagement August 23rd, 2014

Paul's mother Jan & partner Jim. His brother, David & Anna Carter.
Bruna Albanti and husband, Bruno

The lovely Grace and John Carter.

# Chapter 3

The engagement night was elegant and sophisticated. Just as Paul described our future life.

Sitting in the shop, now, I just stare at the photo of us entering the foyer. Mesmerised. There's other photos of his family: my beautiful son; my precious friends. We all bare witness. I was the luckiest girl alive.

And now my beautiful Paul is missing and I'm wanted dead. I self talk my way back into my memories. Where the answers should be.

I saw everything Paul wanted, but I just wanted him. For us to be together was more than enough.

We celebrated with more than 100 family and friends. Dancing the night away with a DJ in The State Library. Everyone looked amazing. Dressed up. The whole night was a statement of love. Paul was the epitome of James Bond. Just as he liked to think of himself. Extremely handsome, debonaire, and totally the man of the night. His face beaming. I was dressed in a flame red ball gown with a beaded, corseted, bustier. For all intents and purposes, it was a wedding dress, just red. It was epic in size and commanding of attention. Paul had chosen it. I had steered more towards figure hugging black, my traditional dress code. He had insisted I stand out. We had spent days looking for it. Finally we ended up in bridal heaven, Brunswick St, a mere week before the engagement.

"It's your night Katherine. I want everyone to see how special you are. I want everyone to remember this night. That I did it. That I got you over the line, and then we will both be gone." He laughed. "You can wear black any day. But, in this; This dress. Only someone as beautiful and elegant as you, can pull it off. You will stand out. It's stunning, as are you. When we move to New York, you will be able to wear it again at the openings, and charity galas. It's perfect. When we are on the red carpet, I will be so proud to stand beside you in this dress. You will be a crowd stopper."

He leaned forward and sang in a whisper the Joe Cocker classic. "You are so beautiful to me."

"Ok, ok! I don't know if I can carry it off, but the dress is gorgeous."

"Of course you can. Anyone who can wear the wedding dress we just designed, can wear this. I can't wait till we get married. When Aldo finishes that couture dress, it will be in the papers. You in that dress. It embodies everything we want in life. It is the epitome of elegant and sophistication. God Katherine I want to be married to you so much. You deserve this. I deserve this."

Paul, always in a rush. Here we were, literally still in the shop, paying for the engagement dress, to be worn in a week, and yet, without stopping for a breath, he was already moving on to the excitement of the wedding. Weeks earlier, he had taken me into Aldo Terrato, so he could design a haute couture dress. It was spectacular. My son, Oliver, had been with us and as Paul signed off on the massive deposit, out of sight, I heard him telling Aldo, that Ollie was his sole hope for the future of his little empire.

"All my dreams now rest with him. He is a great kid. Sadly my two are a bit hopeless, but now I have the chance for someone to groom. Couldn't be happier. New wife. New life."

I couldn't believe how lucky and spoilt, loved, and in love I was. That Paul loved, and accepted my son was crucial.

I could hear Paul in the other room, still chatting away, while I got out of the sample dress. "Aldo, I'm going to change their lives. They have certainly changed mine. I cannot tell you how lucky I am. How much in love I am. Look at them. I'm blessed to have found them both."

A month later, and now we were choosing this dream piece for our engagement party and he was just so full on, bursting with excitement and dreams, already impatient for the wedding. I was constantly pressing the brakes.

"Paul, I know. I know they are both beautiful, but slow down. Please enjoy the journey. Let me breathe."

"Princess, once we get to New York, then we can relax. The quicker we get there, the sooner our lives start for real. I know there's been a lot to do and you have had to do most of it. You need a break. I just can't wait. That's all. I want our lives to start. Don't you?"

To me, I already had all I wanted. More than I needed. My life with Paul had started the day I met him. To Paul, it would begin the day we got married.

"Yes, gorgeous man, I'm excited to move and start our adventures together. I love you."

The memories flooding in, calm my frayed nerves. Its not all reminiscing, I know the answers must lie hidden in the past. I need to relive every moment. Thankfully they are mostly wonderful, happy memories. With this awareness, I realise, that's where the pain will be found, because it hopefully ends with me understanding why I'm now wanted in a tree shredder, at a pig farm. There must have been signs. People. Conversations. I light a reassuring cigarette and breathe in smoky courage. I let my mind wander back. Back to the engagement night.

I want Paul.

# Chapter 4

The engagement celebration was epic. Eighty of my dearest friends, clients and of course, my son. Paul's whole family came. The Carter Clan. Both his parents, in their late 70's with their respective new partners. Jan, his mother, and Jim, and John, his father, with his new wife Grace. Uncles and Aunts. His brother and new wife, Anna. His friends.

His two boys, both in the bridal party, were missing. There had been a disaster occur on the football field that morning and both had been hurt. Paul didn't want to worry me with details and was calm about it. He was very apologetic to me and the rest of the bridal party. Paul's parents were disappointed and worried about their injured grandchildren, but everyone assured me, they would be fine.

"Nothing we can't sort tomorrow, Princess. They will be all right. Boys bounce, you know. I don't want to dwell on it. Shit happens. Tonight is our night."

It was sad that they were missing out on the party, but at least they would be ok. Worse can happen. There were plenty more nights and obligations for them.

The evening was full of congratulations, kisses and hugs; Meetings and introductions. I had only met a few of his family previously, so this was a night of first impressions. They were so happy to meet me. Everyone was polite and light.

"Welcome to our family. Another Carter!"

Congratulations everywhere. Air kisses. Chatter. Clinking of champagne flutes. Polite giggles, small talk and large laughs. Excited plans for the future. Dancing, and escaping outside for cigarettes.

When will you get married? Have you set the date? You must come round for dinner. Everyone was happy. Some were pleasantly shocked that the wedding was so soon, but Paul happily explained how impatient he was to make me his. Small talk: His business. My business. The topic of the impending government acquisition of my shop for the new tunnel, was a huge conversation with his family, as it was all new news to them. I understood. It was a fascinating tale to be one of the very few, impacted by the upcoming development. Everyone wanted to know about our plans: My son, and his plans: My red engagement dress. I hoped his family knew him well enough, to know the dress was all him. Over The Top.

I think they approved of me.

Everyone met my son, Oliver, and his lovely, quiet girlfriend, Sarah. They all said he was beautiful and charming. Naturally I agreed. He is. I'd introduced Paul's father John, and his new wife Grace to Ollie. We tried to talk about their wedding, the cruise they had just returned from, and Ollie joked about the influx of new Carters. They looked at us blankly. They were hard work, and I realised, I must have confused the parents, and this was infact Jan and Jim. Awkwardly Ollie and I retreated, laughing at my lack of facial recognition.

Ollie thought it was hysterical. "Mum, you're meant to be making a good impression. Jeez. Fail!"

As I had predicted and catered for, most of Paul's side, being elderly, sat together for the majority of the night and struggled to stay much longer than the speeches. Anticipating this, we had specifically order oversized, luxurious, wing back chairs and poofs so they would be comfortable when they spent time sitting. I hadn't quite envisaged them making a bee line for them the moment they arrived and not getting back up all night. All I could do was try to encourage my bridal party to mingle with them, and Paul was by their side for most of the night. He literally seemed to be everywhere. Larger than life, as always, with that enormous loving smile. Whenever I was chatting with his family or meeting his friends, he stayed by my side and made me feel comfortable, then he would be off, host with the most. Between us, I hope we managed time with everyone.

Family, friends and clients celebrated with us. All of them over the moon with happiness for me, for Oliver, for Paul. I was aware that I held the fragile hearts of every single girl I knew. To them, I represented the idealistic fantasy that fairy tales do come true. The fact that I had been perused so relentlessly and wooed by the illusive Prince Charming now meant all eyes were on me. We would laugh at work about it. The clients in my beauty salon would tell me, that I had to have the happy ending so I could give them the hope that they could too. Prove that you can have everything!

The images caught by the photographers were magical and candid. Dancing, laughter, love. Everyone was genuinely thrilled. Love was literally in the air. It was a magical night.

It was just after the guests had finished arriving that he pulled me to the side of the reception area.

He produced a small delicate box and opened it to reveal large, heart shaped diamond earrings. He proceeded to put them gently on for me. I was shocked at their size. They were individually nearly as big as my solitaire engagement ring.

"Katherine when are you going to realise your value to me. You are worth this. In fact the truth is, you are worth so much more. Treat them as preciously as I do you. They will match your wedding ring. I love you. I can't wait to be married and start our life."

He escorted me back inside and proudly showed our guests the earrings, which emphasized my sparkling necklace and engagement ring. I was ridiculously spoilt.

"My Princess is worth it."

Paul spent the evening, as with every other opportunity telling everyone how lucky he was.

"When you know, you know. It took a bit to convince her, you know what's she's like. I sometimes feel like I have had to drag her kicking and screaming into this relationship. Then she realized. But I knew from the moment I met her, that we are meant to be. She is so obviously part of my destiny. I have honestly never felt this way before. Knowing she wants me for me, not my money and loves me, and my faults, makes me love her even more. She makes me a better person."

He made people tear up with his utter devotion and happiness. His love. His gratitude.

"My heart physically hurts when I am not near her. She is like a drug to me. My heroin. I want her that much."

I glowed in the shadow of his attention and loved how he made me feel. How he made everyone feel.

He had made a speech, thanking our guests for sharing this special night with us: That we would see them all in November for our wedding, which would also be our goodbye as we were moving to New York to start a new adventure. His guests, family and mine stood around the dance floor. They all clapped. So many good wishes. Excitement. Yes, that is how some found out. A circle of well wishers. His dad, John, hugging me and wishing me well. His eyes sparkling like Paul's. His mum, Jan, holding him by the elbows, leaning back and looking teary.

"You sure you know what you're doing? That this will work out?"

I obviously wasn't meant to hear, but it was a fair question from a concerned mother who had only just met her son's fiance. Both his parents, and their new partners, had been away in Europe on a 2 month cruise together, and this was the first opportunity to meet, me, his girlfriend of only five months, now fiance. It wasn't as though my friends hadn't all asked the same thing. I had been standing behind her, with Louise, one of my dearest girlfriends and bridesmaid. She glanced at me questioningly, before we both heard Paul's reassuring response.

"Of course mum, I have the right one this time."

"You'll be back though?"

"No, no mum. This is it. It's my time to be happy. I want to start afresh. You can come visit my beautiful wife and I, but I won't be back. I'm sorry. I have to look after number one. I deserve to be happy. I've done everything I can to set my life up. I don't want to wait any longer. This is my final hoorah!"

His father, reaching around and hugging Paul tightly. "He knows what he's doing, Jan. Have faith." He turned to Paul. "I love you, son. I'm so proud of everything you have become."

Dave, his brother grabbing him by the shoulders. "So you're really doing this then? Going to leave us. Glad you found someone that can give you what you have been looking for. You've tried hard enough." He laughed. "You and your wife better keep a room for us to visit then. You both owe me. You owe me big."

"Sure, if we are ever home, you can visit." They both laughed, standing shoulder to shoulder as brothers, lovingly teasing each other.

His family wished me well with the upcoming government acquisition of my shop.

"Hope you get a record price for your business. Paul loves a win."
"Welcome to our family. Come have dinner next week."
"You look stunning. It's a shame more people won't get to see you in this dress."
"He has found what he is looking for. We are so happy for him. At last."

Then, I saw Oliver's face. My beautiful, angelic looking son. Even though he knew of our plans, perhaps suddenly it seemed real.

"No Ollie, no! It's not forever. It's a mere flight away. You and Sarah, are meant to be joining us for Christmas. I'm not leaving you. I'm just moving a bit further away. Both you and Sarah will be fine. If anything, anything at all, goes wrong, you can always just get on a plane. Paul has promised me that you will always be welcome and that he will pay for you. We still have the wedding in 3 months. It's plenty of time. I'm not disappearing tomorrow."

Ollie and his beautiful girlfriend Sarah were both in the bridal party and had been on host duty all night. Doing the work of six people. Sarah was one of my bridesmaids and Oliver was not only giving me away, but Paul had also asked him to be his best man. Paul had insisted because he wanted extra time to bond with his future son.

They both did me so proud. They brought their "A" game. A level, that one of my girl friends had literally said at the time, she didn't know they had to bring. We laughed. I agreed. Those two had done such an amazing effort, I had no idea they were capable of it either. I couldn't have been more proud of both of them. Felt the love. Oliver had greeted and chatted to absolutely everyone. Introduced himself and Sarah to Paul's family. Sarah, who hardly says boo to anyone, was seen introducing groups of people to each other. Greeting some of my friends that she recognized, as long lost blessings. I was amazed. They had ensured our side, and Paul's had mingled. Sarah looked gorgeous. We had brought her a baby blue chiffon Princess line evening dress. She worked the guests all night with him. Dancing, chatting, eating and drinking.

It was late. Some of the ladies' shoes were coming off subtly, and so, at this point of the night, Ollie, very politely, said they were tired and asked if they could go home.

"Yes! Totally fair call. You arrived an hour early. You were amazing. I love you both."
Kiss, kiss. I cherished every second of my son's long tight hug.

"Thank you. Seriously, thank you, Ollie."

At the end of the evening, with dancing still going on in the background, a group of us found our way onto the floor. In elegant ball gowns, we were now sitting on the carpet. Glorious happy night. I was exhausted, but happy. Content. In love. Loved.

Paul lent in towards me.

"Perfect. Tonight was perfect. You are perfect. We are perfect, and our lives will be perfect once we get to New York. Get ready, for now we have a wedding.
You make me so happy. I will love you forever, my future Queen."

"I love you too Paul. You are my everything."

# Chapter 5

But that was 19 days ago and life changes in the blink of an eye. A car driving too fast, wrong place at the wrong time, an overheard comment in a restaurant bathroom, a missed call, a slip and fall, a lie. One action, one second and everything is different.

I light another cigarette, the shop is filled with a putrid, grey cloud of smoke. The ashtray, a floral Wedgewood saucer, is overflowing with the carcasses of smoked memories. It's dark outside. I haven't moved from the chair in 10 hours. It's nearly midnight. My eyes focus on the cold, marble floor, as my hand strokes firmly along the left side of my nose and across my eyebrow, as if by doing so, it can release the cause of tension knotted there. I blink. I take a breath. I try to make it a deep one, but my chest gets caught on an emotion, ragged and raw. I gasp an involuntary suck, and my body slumps back into numb. My eyelids sting as if I have been crying. I haven't. They are swollen and heavy. I want to shut them and sink into the black. Forever.

I don't. It's not that easy. I just sit and remember.

The night of the engagement was something we planned in a little less than two months. Simultaneously with the wedding. It wasn't that hard really.

"Why wait Katherine? We could date for years and then…. What? Just live together and grow old? Be boring and plain. Live in the suburbs of mediocrity. Then in ten years finally decide to get married. That's not us. Why not do it now, while we are passionate. Start our life now. Neither of us will be happy, till I make an honest woman of you, so don't make us wait. You're literally procrastinating about being happy.
Princess, you know I literally breathe in and absorb every cell of your goodness. I'm totally addicted to you. How much do want from someone before you realise they belong together?
You are part of my life's plan. Everything that's happened before I met you, means I've earned the right to be with you; to deserve you. Princess, you will make everything in my life right. God, you certainly deserve me. I'm

offering more than you ever dreamed of, and you're worthy of that world because you are so pure. I know you will do good with what I bring into your life. I have faith that you will step up. One day you will look back on everything that happens because we met, and I just know, you will be a different person. I want to help make you an even better person. Help you to help others.
Katherine, at the end of the day, we simply have to announce that we have both finally found our soul mate. That we are going to be happy till we die of old age, together, like the couple in the photo. Curled up around each other dying at the same time. We need to get married, so all our friends and family know this is real. This is it. You are the one to turn my life around.
And I'd like Ollie to think of me as a stable father figure. He needs that in his life. I know I don't have to marry you for that, but I think he would feel the security. I think he needs to know you are finally safe.
I want to marry you. I can see myself getting old with you, but it needs to start sooner not later."

He was Chinese water torture. There was no denying it. Paul was determined and fast paced. I was forever telling him to slow down. He was forever telling me to catch up.

Organizing both events, focusing on the end result of a marriage for life, was instantly a full time job. My biggest whinge was that I had managed to mess my email accounts up, and four out of five stopped working, and I needed to cc everything via friends or Paul. I didn't have time to sort the issue with my provider, so just struggled along, knowing that by the time I was married, the accounts wouldn't be needed anyway. Utterly first world problems.

If co-ordinating invitations, addresses, seating plans, order of service, suits, bridal parties, hiring companies, wedding planners, venues and all the minutiae involved wasn't enough, Paul also decided to pull the pin on all of his Australian business ventures. He wanted to make a new life in America. He would liquidate his Australian interests and focus entirely on the American side. This translated apparently, as to become entirely a man of leisure. We would make home in New York. He had suggested the West coast for the sun, but if I was moving, then it was to New York. I'm a city girl. I wasn't prepared to move away from Oliver and then have a life I didn't want. I'm not really a sun type of girl.

"That's ok, my business is based in Boston, so it's only an hour flight away. I can pop over there whenever needed and you won't even know I'm gone. Not that we need to be involved in that, it's self sufficient and sustaining. The person I now have in charge, is totally under my control." He laughed.

"And they have my business interests totally under control. Just doing their job making me money. So sure, we can buy a penthouse in Manhattan, if you want, but I'm telling you, Princess, you'll last one season and hate the cold. I'll buy you something with a stunning view of the Park, to keep you happy, and then you'll feel guilty because we will always be traveling. You'll never stay there. We have the time and the money now to enjoy ourselves, and you will have the means to do whatever you want."

In my head and to my friends, I had said, that infact *he* had no idea how much time we *would* be spending at home. I like to travel, but I just wanted to be still. I needed the calm and to be able to breathe. This was a whirl wind romance and I felt the ground spinning way underneath. Added to that, was the mounting pressure of my shop. I desperately needed a break. Time out. Too much romance, attention, movement, action and business stress. Too much of everything.

All good, he has his plan, and I'm a woman who has hers. He wanted biggest best, and I was happy with less, less, less. Anything more than I was achieving on my own was a bonus. I was aiming for normal. I was craving it. His dreams would surely slow down. He was such a home body here, now. We went out twice, three times a week, and that was only with my friends, so I figured, it would more likely be the same life, just different geography, albeit, somewhat grander. The engagement, as Paul created it, was an indication of just that. It was lavish, and clearly over the top. I took on board this was a precursor to a lifestyle that was more than enough. It was, if anything, going to be too much....but it came with Paul.

# Chapter 6

September 12. 2014

I can't eat. I'm grateful that I still have the flu. I've had it four days now. Since the day before the call.

Exhaustion gnaws at my very being and I hope that eventually at some point in the later hours of the morning I will finally succumb to sleep again. But for now, I just sit. My bones ache. I'm cold and hot, and I have no idea if I feel this way from what's happening or because I am sick. I light another cigarette and stare at the laptop. It will have answers. My phone lying beside it, indicates 78 unopened texts. It's on silent. The constant ringing, voice mail, and Facebook posts and threads are too much to deal with right now.

What has happened to my wonderful Paul? I need him here beside me. Where are you? My heart is crushing under the pressure, making my chest feel physically heavy.
How much do I need to know? I can't fully believe anything. I can't comprehend what has just happened, let alone how. Do I really want to? Isn't this enough already? I can't seem to make sense. I am not functioning. I'm fixated on finding an explanation that I can accept. I think it will save me and find him. Then everything will right itself.

It's not even logical to even think it could get worse. Because it just can't. There is nothing left that can happen now.

1 day since I was threatened with a tree shredder and a man named Vito.
2 days since I lost my beautiful Paul.

3 days since my world came crashing down.
3 days since the phone call.

But, before then. February. A different call. The first of two that would change the direction of my life.

# Chapter 7

February 12. 2014

It's 8pm and I have just given a stranger my number. My phone rang immediately. That threw me a bit. I thought he would wait a bit, even if only to play the game. The 'I am not desperate game.' Instead, he dove straight in.

Two of my closest friends had been nagging me to get my act together and start going out with age appropriate men and settle down. I put a profile on a dating site. It read.

*Black and white*
*Looking 4 that initial potential 4 a future wonderful*
*Need my coffee*
*No smokers*
*Genuinely believe its better to b the nicest u can just because!*
*Live w laughter & love first*
*I'm scruffy, elegant, compassionate*
*No one's fool*
*Marshmallow encased in concrete*
*U hav mates 4 huntin fishin campin*
*Im a girl*
*Painfully shy w strangers - we all have our thing*
*Logic & reason not hormonal irrationality*
*No casual 1nighters*
*Players-i'll out wait the game*
*Dinner not couch*
*Real gentlemen only*

They say put it out to the universe. I think I did. A specific profile for a change. I'm told it culls the extreme inappropriates and undesirables who don't meet the criteria. That being said, I have met some genuinely beautiful friends through dating.

So with my experience, rules and preference for freedom, I did not see Paul coming. I was definitely not desperate, instead I had been happily single for years. I preferred men who were honest and transparent. Safe. No possibility of hurt. Respectful. "Mature" men like to be players and talk about relationships they have no intention of pursuing beyond getting you into bed, worried about you getting your claws on what's left of their garnished wages. I have no interest in that game. I prefer carefree.

I had prided myself on my rules; my ethics. I could pretty much say them by rote. They kept me safe. My poor clients. I would tell them. "Stick to the rules." It kept things easy to handle. They helped sort out players from the men who were genuinely interested. I had found Paul because I refused to settle for less, only for him to be taken away. Why did I wait for the right one? What was the point. All the wise adages. Better to have loved and lost than not at all. Blah, blah. Better to curl up in a ball.

I have so, so many, many rules. Some, once broken, are instant deal breakers, some are accumulative. Three strikes and you're out.

- Do not be forward or disrespectful towards me.
- Do not send cock shots. In fact, I'm not even interested in your chest. If I met you organically in a bar with friends, I wouldn't know what your chest looked like unless I was about to sleep with you. So no, I just don't want to see it.
- Be single. Not married. Not separating, not separated, divorced and after a rebound then you can call me.
- Be honest, transparent
- Live a policy of do no harm.
- I will not accept second best.
- Do not live in hope. Never, ever live in hope. It either is or it isn't.
- Never ever chase. If he wants you, he will come.
- Do not want someone who does not want you.
- Never ask a question if you really don't want to know the answer.
- NEVER EVER play the "why" game. Why did he do that, why did he leave, why wasn't I enough. This is a guaranteed slippery slope to pity party land. None of your friends want to play this with you. DON'T EVER USE THE WORD WHY? You can take a fun afternoon and wreck it in seconds playing this game. It is for losers, whiners and tears.
- Never be involved on any level with another girl's man. If he wants to cheat on his woman just to be with you then he doesn't have a moral compass. If you get with him, you get what you deserve.
- I will not tolerate abuse, manipulation or power play.

And then there are my beliefs

- How it starts is how it ends
- I am a woman. That does not make me stupid.

- I hold the power. The power is the word "No."
- There is no power in the word yes.
- A man must value add. This is not a monetary thing. This is as, apposed to bringing grief into my life. My life brings enough drama and shit randomly. I do not need to have a man do it.
- Once penis meets vagina, they generally want to hang out more. True perception goes out the window so take your time on that one.
- If I choose to sleep with you early, It's because I do not see a future with you, and there will never be a future with you because I chose that path. This isn't up to you.
- Me NOT sleeping with you, is up to you though. If you are disrespectful, uncouth, sleazy, plain stupid, racist or do not try to flirt with my brain, then you will be finishing that drink on your own and sleeping with Mrs Palmer.
- I may sleep with you in a casual arrangement if you are honest. If you are not honest, I won't sleep with you at all.
- I applaud players. Very few are any good. The two that have put in that much effort just to get me into bed, I have had the privilege of giving a standing ovation to. I'd also like to note that neither were that good in bed.
- I do whom I want, when I want. This may mean you are in the queue for years. It also means I may not get any for ages as well.
- Many of the best men I know are my friends. I value them to much to risk losing them. I hope they realise that.
- I am master of my own destiny within the parameters of the randomness of the universe.
- "The One" is not the one who just broke your heart. - clearly.
- You are not spontaneously available. You are a desired plan worthy of effort.
- Your first date should be your best foot forward. Let's face it, I do not want you burping at the table or having road rage on the way to dinner. If you can't try to put your best face on for a few hours, I do not want to know how bad you can actually be.
- Respect!
- First impression / gut reaction will always be true.
- I am happy on my own. I do not need a man. Period. You are sometimes nice to have around like puppies or grandchildren. Best when you can return them. I believe there are a few exceptions. We call them the keepers. They are like unicorns.
- Do not waste your time. There are plenty of friends, people you chose not to hang out with, acquaintances etc out there. Why add another one? If they don't measure up, then…. NEXT!

Needless to say, "NEXT" is my most common expression. I really don't want to settle for less than what I want. I'd rather be on my own. It's not an arrogance. I use my rules to keep safe. Safety and security are my cravings.

We all need rules, especially nowadays. The internet has opened up the opportunity to meet people, but it also meant there are just so many frogs to meet before finding your Prince. When I met Paul, everyone was excited with me.

My friends, Dianne and John, had been constantly ear bashing me about settling down with an older man. They wanted to see me happy. I thought I was, but to humor them, I went home and limited the age parameter to 38 - 55 years of age.
I rejected copiously and swiped right on four.

One was a picture of a stunning beach side house. I love property. Nothing to lose. Swipe right. He was a developer. We messaged for a bit and knew mutual friends. For no reason, it didn't progress further.

Next was a doctor. Cocky and far too flirtatious.

Another was a father to three young ones. In the suburbs. I've done this. I love my son and he is enough for me. I'm not prepared to contemplate it. Know your own limitations. Next.

There was a man leaning back in an office chair. He looked familiar. His profile said he was a gentleman looking for his Princess for a fairy tale ending. Well travelled. Self employed. It was his time.

We exchanged a few inane messages over the next few weeks.

Hi, how was your long weekend?

                                        Good, caught up with friends
                                        & hung out in St Kilda. You?

Yesterday had lunch in Williamstown
with friends and later a dinner at
Vue d'Monde to celebrate the
completion of a 70 property housing
development.
Too many Louis Cristal magnums!
Exhausted.

Going for a jog around the tan
before brunch in Sth Yarra.


I remember my head registered, "sure, ah huh….. whatever…. Pretentious, name dropper.

Most of what is said online is over exaggerated, enhancements and embellishments of an average life. Not many have the courage to be honest or post ugly selfies, or status updates, which reflect a life that isn't always perfect. It can be a fake world, so I take what I see and hear with a grain of salt. No one really knows anyone. We only know the version of others as they wish they were.

Then he and I so happened to both be online at the same time. Messaging banter, witty one liners, light flirt, followed by complicated ideas and emotions. We began to regularly catch up online. And then it became a month , and the conversation had morphed into lengthy conversations and personal disclosures. Literally hundreds and hundreds of messages. He still only had my attention if I had nothing else to do.

"Katherine, I'm stuck in a hotel in Bendigo after a big day checking my properties and sorting some contractor issues. I think talking to you, not messaging with your crazy typos and corrections, should be my reward and it will finish off my day beautifully."

He asked for my number and as I felt his frustration at my incessant text fails and bizarre auto corrects, I couldn't think of a tactful avoidance so I gave it out and now we finally heard each other talk.

His name was Paul. His voice was deep and commanding, with an Aussie twang.

He was easy to talk to and seemed open. I quickly confessed that I thought we perhaps had met before. His photos seemed familiar. He assured me it wasn't likely.

"I only just got online the week you and I matched. I've been single for a long time now; 8 years and my son, Andrew was sick of me moping around. So he loaded tinder on to my phone. He said it was the best way to meet someone. I was about to delete it, to be honest. It wasn't working. I told Andrew it was a waste of time and he gave me that look. You know the one where they roll their eyes at our technological incompetence."

I laughed. "Yes, as a mother, I do know that look."

"So, apparently you have to swipe." He chuckled.

He laughed at himself easily. "I was really hoping you and I would match. I don't normally go for blondes but your smile; I wanted to meet the woman of that smile."

I checked my own profile pics. I don't like my smile at all. It would be the last thing I would be attracted to. "Well, you haven't met me yet, but you have my number now and to be honest, I have a bit of work to do before I finish tonight, so maybe we can chat again another time?"

He took the hint, but before he said good night, he asked me out.

"Come on Katherine, grab life by the horns. I must meet the charismatic and talented lady behind the smile. How about this Sunday for lunch? I'll pick you up?"

"Sure." I'd replied. "I can meet you somewhere local. How about Polly's on Brunswick St?"

"Done 12.30. I'm not a serial killer Katherine. You will be safe if I picked you up."

"No, It's all good. For all you know I could be the psycho axe murderer. See you then."


Yes, this was the start. In hind sight, I think I owe Diane and John a bottle of something to drink, as a token of my belated gratitude.


I remember how strangely excited I was before our first meeting and how I was aware that it was unusual for me to even remotely care about someone that I hadn't even met. How had that happened? I never get excited about meeting guys. Ever! It defied my logic. Why would I care, and yet, I had gone shopping with a girlfriend and spent money on a wardrobe. Not just an outfit, but options. Casual. I don't do casual at all and I was all over the place trying to figure where this guy fits. Why did I even care? Slacks, genie pants, tops, a few dresses. What the hell? I spent $250 in a chemist. How had that happened? Tan, lipsticks, Apparently my brain was aware that each optional dress code required a different shade of lipstick.
It continued…

Brow pencil, mitt, two foundations. Where had I gone? I don't even wear make up. My skin is flawless, and I hate the feeling of congealed crap on my skin, caking into my pores. The piece de resistance. Hair dye. My roots needed some high lightening. The assistant assured me the color would match.

I was shocked at the total as I handed my card over. I parted with, how much? For a guy I didn't even know.

Now curled on the mattress, propped with a plethora of cushions from the reception chairs, to keep me warm, I pull back from the realization, that I lost myself in Paul, before I even met him. It shocks me to realise that his charisma, his intellect and desirability had seeped down the phone line and begun morphing me into his dream woman, before our first date. It was a fascinating observation. Was it power and weakness, or souls finding their counterpart, as he said?

I realise it's getting light, and admitting defeat on finding answers, and still aching from the centre of my bones, I pull the blankets over my head, and shut my eyes, managing only a few hours unpleasant rest before I woke. Disturbing dreams. Half fog thoughts. A million questions.

Sleep is eluding me so I angrily sludge my way slowly to the little cafe table by the window of my shop. Normally the curtains are pulled back, but now they hang heavy and dark. I'm motivated purely for the cigarettes sitting there. That's what my body wants. Genuinely scared, I'm too sick to leave and I don't want to tell anyone what's going on. I'm afraid they will think I'm crazy. I feel alone.

I need to figure out what's happening so I can protect myself from it. I need to understand so I know how to feel, so I can start reacting and coping with everything. I don't know whether I have the tools in my skill set for this. I don't know what I'm dealing with.

# Chapter 8

Wednesday 26th March 2014

We hadn't managed to meet for that planned first date. An hour beforehand, he had messaged that something had come up and he would explain later. Awesome start. I had wasted money buying clothes for a casual lunch that didn't even happen with a guy I didn't even know.

He rang me in the early evening nearly a fortnight later. I was not impressed. I didn't really care, and it was obvious by his behavior, he didn't either. We both knew there is no excuse for no communication with mobiles phones and internet. End of story.

"Hi, I'm back. Can I make up for my inexcusable neglect by taking you to dinner? I'm sorry that I let you down, but I had to retrieve my son from the police station for drunk driving."

Paul went to great lengths explaining how he had to literally bail him out. As a result there had been unprecedented family drama and a fight with his ex. She should be more strict. He had given both the boys brand new BMW 's and this is how they repay him. Teenagers could be a handful and John was lucky that his father had enough resources to get him back home and avoid further charges. Unfortunately he then had to fly to the USA to sort some business things out.

I understood and without this explanation, had proceeded to live my life. Regardless of whether it was the truth or not, I didn't know this man to care enough. My main annoyance was that I had bothered to spend money on getting ready for a date that hadn't eventuated.

But regardless of my indifference to this man, I'd had a rotten day with solicitors. I was frustrated that the impending tunnel development was going to plow straight through my new shop. It was heartbreaking, watching what I had worked so hard to create, be systematically destroyed by an entity, just so in the end, they were obligated to pay me less.

I was happy for any distraction. "Sure. When were you thinking?"

"Awesome. I know it's short notice but how about tonight?"

"That suits me to be honest. Same place as before? Pollys?"

"Perfect. See you at seven?"

I had walked to the bar. I loved it's cheese and antipasto platters. The cocktails were delicious as well. Ironically, after wasting so much money on improving myself, I had ditched all the new dress options and thrown on a daggy hot pink, over sized jumper paired with black jeans and plain stilettos. I wasn't in a particularly good mood and couldn't motivate myself to dress to impress. Nor did he deserve it. I was no longer interested. I just wanted a drink and distraction.

Remembering back, even feeling the way I do now, dying in the shop; no shower in four days, filthy hair pinned up and wearing the same blue jumper dress the whole time; even as this smelly, half shadow, Gollum version of myself, the memory of how I presented myself that day, still makes me cringe. God it was awful. What an ugly first impression. It wasn't the exceptionally scruffy clothes, it was my hair.
Trying to dye my hair had been a disaster and had taken my blonde hair to a dull orange auburn. It was like straw in color and feel. But, at the time I didn't care.

He was already there and stood up to greet me with a congenial kiss on the cheek. He leant forward in his chair all night and his knee brushed mine. His body language was the study of a man interested in getting to know me. A man happy with his choice. By nature, I moved away each time.

He asked leading questions, listened, probed politely and in return gave in depth answers openly and honestly back. We had a lot in common.

There were areas of our life that over lapped. My son, now 18, had Aspergers and Paul had worked in the disability area. He understood the demands. I didn't mention I was Aspergers too.

"Wow, you did it tough by yourself." He showed compassion and understanding with a full appreciation of the special needs and challenges of autism in particular. He even knew some of the charities and associations.

He was happy to disclose about his life.

"I understand the challenges, I have two adult boys just a bit older. I shared custody until recently. It's always been extremely amicable between me and their mum. Now they are old enough they do as they please. They stay sometimes with me, sometimes with their mum. It depends on whether they want to be with their girlfriends. I admit, I let them sleep together but their mum doesn't, so it sort of encourages them to visit."

He laughed self depreciatingly again. I frowned and he noticed.

"I suppose it is sort of bad of me, but we have a more adult, mate like relationship now they are older. They have reached an age where they're more of a hand full now, more than ever. Pushing boundaries, meeting girls, driving. I gave them new BMW's at the start of the year so I knew that they had safe wheels, not some dangerous beaten up old thing. I wanted something reliable. You know what it's like. I love my kids. I'd die if something happened to either of them. Hardest part of divorce was not seeing them every day. You know, I'm not actually prepared to rule out having more. I'd love to try for a daughter. I feel I have missed out by not having one. I think with the right partner it would be a blessing. You know, to be with someone you love and raise a little girl. Do it right, together for forever."

At 47 that's not in my top 3 desires, let alone top 100, I mused to myself. Although I realise some guys think it's what we want to hear.

"Perhaps," I replied, very non committedly.

"Both boys work with me. We are close. I used to hate it when they went to their mums, now they are young men so it's natural they fly the coup. I try to think of things that will make them spend time with me and then I have to try and not spoil them too much."

I inwardly groaned at the obvious disparity between our disposable incomes and the effect it had on raising our children. My son was definitely not spoilt. I wish I could have given him treats more often, but I literally didn't have the money. I think we had a good life within our means. I listened to Paul continue, oblivious to my situation.

"Hopefully they will take over the business one day. Well, the property development side, anyway. That's what I'm grooming John for. Andrew is a good kid, but he doesn't have what it takes. Not yet. Maybe he will when he is older. Their mum hasn't encouraged them academically to be honest. Let them be lazy. Because they are spoilt and know they are going to inherit so much. I think the knowledge has ruined them to be honest. It's hard for me to watch. I had to work for everything I have, and I put myself through university twice. Education is important. It broadens you. Like travel. Grounds you I think."

He had liked what I said in my profile about being kind and honest.

"It's what I'm looking for. A love based on honesty that makes your soul pine when you're apart. I want to meet someone who makes me want to be a better person.
Honesty. Katherine, it's my corner stone belief. Without it, the world would be anarchy. There is just no need to lie or cheat. If you want to see other people, if you have lost interest, then just leave. Show integrity. Even in my business, I practice this. You know, you don't have to be an asshole to be rich. Treat everyone openly and fairly. That's actually how I have got to where I am now.

I remember, I knew a guy about 18 years ago. He worked as an account manager and then was promoted into sourcing finance for an expanding company. At that point he had been happily married with two kids. Everything going along smoothly and then he changed. Started misappropriating the company funds and buying flash cars. Began an affair with the ditzy hot secretary. Spent more time taking her away on trips and splashing money on her than at work or with his family. I heard they were partying hard; using recreational drugs. She thought he was rich. What an idiot. I warned him it would all unravel and it did. He justified the sudden affluence to an imaginary inheritance. He even got bank loans using that story. Can you imagine the pressure this guy must have been under with all those lies. No vagina is worth it. No wank factor of pretend wealth. All a farce. Oh my God, talk about stress. Obviously, he ended up being caught. But not before he had destroyed everyone he knew, including his family, by convincing them to put money into this company, which because of his thieving, also went under. The guy should be in jail. Begged me to help. Honestly Katherine, what could I do?
He had shown his true colors. What a selfish idiot. He had to declare bankruptcy. Left his wife, who was actually pregnant with his third child at the time, and married the bimbo. Obvious that wasn't going to last. But she had a house. Chasing a dream. Total disaster upon disaster. Idiot. Liar. Destroyed so many people. I learnt a lot from him. He still contacts me from time to time. Begs me to help him fix the situation. Hasn't changed. Still all fake life with no money, no friends and a queue of people wishing him dead.

Awful way to be remembered don't you think? I want to be remembered for doing good. This guy and I are chalk and cheese.
Why lie? It just destroys everything. If you want to leave just leave."

Music to my ears. Perhaps being autistic myself, I literally can't lie. Maybe it's just me, regardless, I have joked for years that I wish I could learn to lie. There should be a "lie" school. Learning to lie is a skill that I have literally craved for. It's hard to defend yourself against it, if you can't match it. I can only spot someone lying, when it doesn't make sense. One of my biggest weaknesses and in relationships, it's my biggest deal breaker. You need an honest foundation so you have an even playing field. Where everyone gets to make informed decisions based on truth and reality.

He told me all about his marriage, when he was 21. It lasted 12 solid years but they grew apart. They both knew it. His ex wife arranged a weekend away in a hotel, without the boys, and they discussed how, as much as they loved each other, they were no longer 'in love.' Better to part now while they were both still young enough to find love again. They had had a good run.

Paul admitted he had changed. "Katherine, I had been working for a Jewish entrepreneur, since I was 21. He was my mentor and I owe a lot of my success to him. He was an old guy and he sent me to Solomon Islands to check his properties out when the civil unrest started. I flew in, and it was suddenly an all out war. I barricaded myself in the hotel room, absolutely terrified for days. I mean people were being shot and gutted in the street in front of me. Never been so scared in my life. I saw things I want to forget. I was unprepared for the brutality. It's not in my make up, that senseless violence. There I was only 25, in the middle of a war, defenseless. I threw all my money down at the airport and got one of the last private planes out with some embassy people. Seeing that, changed me, from a carefree spirit to a closed, wary one. Maggie didn't know how to help. I never got counseling, I was too arrogant and just struggled through. Seems stupid but it drove a wedge between us. She didn't understand the change in me.
I just wanted the security of money. It became my focus."

He had managed to build up a successful backpacking business, and then expand into other profitable ventures. The properties he had invested in had been solid performers. They'd done really well. They discussed the terms of separating. He would leave gradually bit by bit, so the kids weren't shocked and he would set up another house.

They had assets, so it was not going to impact him to give her the house. She got $10,000 per month maintenance. I remember being horrified in a jealous way. I had never got a cent until Oliver was 13. Then it was $5 a month for a year. I used to joke to my friends that it wasn't even a good loaf of bread. It went up to $13 for three months before it stopped. I couldn't fathom $10,000. How lucky were these boys? How lucky was she? She would have assets that would look after the whole family for the rest of her life.

I felt a bit of a loser as I confessed my son's father walked out when I was 8 and a half months pregnant. He simply changed his mind. One second he seemed happy and we were going to get married. The next he was gently guiding me backwards out our front door, saying. "I've changed my mind, Katherine. I don't want to be responsible for you and a baby. I want to hang out with my mates."

We were 30. My life changed in the instant I had to turn and walk down the road to the pay phone and call my parents. Crushed. It finished my university degree. I struggled for the first year and then Oliver got sick. Enough! I wasn't the priority. He was.
I had bought 3 small ex commission houses when he was born. It was a gamble, but ignorance is bliss and I just thought I was doing the right thing. I soldiered on and rode the economic wave of the late 1990's. I worked hard but it set Oliver and I up so that although we never had a lot, we did have a roof over our heads, an income, and an appreciating asset base.

I was aware that I didn't need to say much about anything. Paul understood me. He could finish my sentences which was disarming. He laughed when it happened. "Being with you is so comfortable. It's like I know so much about you already. I think there's something here Katherine."

"Yes, too many expresso martinis." I agreed, but as usual remained rational.

Apparently the opposite of my ex partner, Paul loved being a dad.

"I get that from my family, Katherine. My parents loved us unconditionally and ensured we came first. Ridiculously, they stayed together until my brother and I were in our 30's, and then Dad invited us around to calmly explain that they had drifted apart and were getting a divorce. They had stayed together all those years for us. It's funny now. We were grown men and my parents were worried about how their divorce was going to affect us. Like really?"

He laughed at the silliness of their action. His warmth and love for them displayed in his smiling eyes. "Anyway they were, and still are, the poster faces for amicable divorce. Both of them have new partners. In fact they are all leaving together, on a two month European cruise in a few weeks. Crazy I tell you.

My mother remarried a few years later to a lovely guy named Jim. She is an uppity, conservative woman. I don't see her very often, maybe once a week. Too much name dropping and silver ware, tweed skirts and pearls. I know I come from a privileged background but I hate the way my mum flaunts it."

I nodded. "Ah huh." The closest I got to that sort of wealth was at my senior school and it was extreme, but I wasn't from that class so I only saw it from a distance.

"My mother belongs in Toorak that's for sure. Born and bred. She's of Italian heritage, and worked hard on her chain of hairdressing salons. It was something she was extremely proud of. Her first salon was down in Toorak village. You know, the Trak."

I nodded. I knew the area. My school was down the street.

He continued. "But she also loves the life that Dad gave her. He is from old English money and so naturally doesn't show it. A quiet gentleman. I get most of my characteristics and my blue eyes, from him. He met Grace about 8 years ago and totally changed. Sold his huge house in South Yarra, on Darling St, and moved in with her. God, that was a gorgeous house, backed on to the river. My brother and I have great memories growing up there. Anyway, his new place is still all dark wood and book cases lined with dusty tomes that no one reads, but he and Grace are easier to be around. He has become less rigid and she is a hoot. She got rid of his suits and now he wears cardigans. Always laughing, but he has become old suddenly. I see him at least a couple of times a week as he likes to banter about the stock exchange, what I'm up to and gossip about mutual business colleagues. He likes to stay abreast of what his old board members are getting up to at Harvey Norman. I used to look up to him and fight to get his respect. Now I have his utmost respect and he just looks beaten, as if he is shrinking."

"Um, I think that's literally what happens as we get older." I interrupted with a smirk.

"I don't want to get old, Katherine. I have too many things I want to do still. I haven't got to 200 yet. There are places to see. Fall in love. Maybe have another child. So many people to meet. Adventures and things to experience. Finish my latest projects. I literally just started actioning one today, and I want to see that completed. The list is endless. I can't afford to get old. It's for the weak." He laughed.

I looked at him quizzically. "200?"

"One day I'll tell you. Maybe when I achieve it. Meantime, I think, my Dad is now living vicariously through my business ventures, although he has become risk adverse and we face off all the time over the projects I'm prepared to invest in. Katherine, I'm old school Italian. All my values come from my parents and my Nonna. They will do anything to help me succeed, and they demand I take life by the horns and make the most of everything I can. You know, die screaming, 'that was a great ride.' They have my back 100%. Seriously Katherine, they are genuinely loving, caring people and they expect I treat people the same way they do. So you can see why the divorce between Maggie and I was so civilized."

Yep, that IS how it's supposed to be. No wonder he was so rational about his own separation with Maggie.

"I could hardly be an ass to her and go home to see my parents. They would have crucified me. 'That's not how we raised you.' My father always said, 'Treat your woman like a Queen and you will be a King. After 5 pm is family time. Leave work at work and love your wife whenever you are with her.' My father is so respectful about all women including my mother. It's beautiful to watch. I want that."

So naturally, he and Maggie co-parented. "It was smoother that way, without defined times and weekends." Paul had told me.

I was aware of how little support I had raising Oliver. I would have loved just one hundredth of what Paul's ex had got. Quite simply it would have gone a long way to putting a smile on both Ollie's and my faces.

"Being inflexible just doesn't work for anyone really. You should just want to be there for the kids as much as possible. We both created them and they are pretty cool. I suppose it's easier that I have two boys, I get to muck around with them. Not sure what I would have done with a daughter. Spent even more money on make up and dresses."
He laughed, "I mean, it would be awesome to have a little girl, but time is running out. I'll see."

He seemed pretty obsessed with having a daughter one day. I noted it as a future intention that I didn't share.

He coached Andrew's football team every Saturday for years. Both boys would come and stay at his house in Malvern and up until recently they would all jet ski together and go out on his boat. Reluctantly, he had just sold both as they never helped look after them and he needed to teach them a lesson.

"Well the boat actually went, because it was 90 feet of luxury house on water, that hardly ever gets used and the boys just wanted to party on it, now they are at that age. Plus, I'm the only one that can captain it and I need crew each time. A money pit on water those things."

The conversation bantered back and forth. Mostly forth.

His boys had trust funds. Obviously, it's a bi-product of dispersing money. He had insisted on sending them to Scotch college because it was a family tradition. He had gone there and so had his brother and his father. It's good to keep that network of old boys together. They lived local to the school. He didn't begrudge that neither decided to go to university. A well connected smart man will always be successful over an unpopular educated one. The boys have me, and my friends, so they will land on their feet regardless."

I understood the old school network theory, but I'm not such a snob as to think "wealth maketh the man." I'd rather a poorer, average, nice man than a rich arrogant one, any day.

I had gone to St Catherine's which was sort of a sister school to Scotch. It was extremely privileged and exclusive. I was surprised we didn't have any mutual acquaintances. I had gone on an academic scholarship. He was so bright he never studied. I used to pull all nighters to ensure my grades were acceptable to my parents.

He would sneak out at night and hang at the Jam Factory in Toorak, with the St Cath's and MLC girls. I caught the train and got home to Wheelers Hill, an outer suburb, exhausted already, and then studied until I fell asleep. He got A's in everything without effort and went on to get an engineering degree and then an MBA. He was in a position that he could be well educated, so he took it.

"I love learning, Katherine. I went to Japan and loved it so much, that I leant the language. I'm now fluent in Japanese and Russian. Powerful languages."

This man was pretty impressive.

Chatting was pleasant. We covered so much personal history and our thoughts on multitudes of topics were exchanged, explored and expanded upon.

He had been single all this time since his divorce at 33, with intermittent dalliances, but nothing of any note.

"Katherine, it's hard when you know that the person you're dating has to be suitable for your children as well. It's a tall order and if you get it wrong, you create a nightmare for everyone, for life."

So for 15 years he had been looking. He really wanted to find the one. He loved marriage. The routine. The kids. Maybe he had made a mistake in getting divorced. He thought he had found it once but in a cruel twist of fate it was taken away from him. His last girlfriend had died. They were only together 2 and a half years. He was totally fine about it, now.

"When I first met her, I had thought, that she was the one, and that being with her was going to drastically improve my life. You know what I mean: Love, happiness, health, wealth, leisure, travel and all that, but I realise now, that it wasn't actually her that did it. It was coincidental circumstances and outside influences that made my life better at the time.

I'm not one to dwell on the sad or negative, it is a waste of energy and time. No, Katherine, trust me, I've got no baggage. The only thing I want to take from her death, is a new found appreciation of living. Her death actually opened me up to live a better life.

We cling to this notion that we have to remain miserable after someone's death, out of respect for their memory. In truth, her 'leaving' allowed me to grow. It opened my eyes. I am able to take bigger risks, enjoy life more. You aren't allowed to say it, but I am going to. My life is better now with her gone. She left all the good things behind for me to grow with, and all the bullshit got buried with her in Boston. In my mind, it's like her death allowed me to fully embrace life, and I am. I'm not wasting this opportunity."

I felt my head physically pull back. A subtle recoil. To me, they were harsh words. Perhaps they are the truth, but no one ever says it out loud. Do they? I've never met anyone who has gone through what he has, so maybe this is true.

He continued telling me that it was a long time ago. Eight years and he had gone to counseling for a short time just to ensure he could deal with it. He learnt some things are just not meant to be. For quite a while he didn't want to put his heart on the line again, but he realized it made living meaningless.

"Katherine, you have to take the positives out of life. I learned that I'm fiercely loyal. I love being in a relationship and I'm a stayer to the end. I think these are good things. Please don't think I've been moping for all those years. Trust me, I've been looking. I want to find my Princess. I just haven't found her yet."

He stared at me. I could feel him ascertaining my reaction to all this. I tried my blank face.

Perhaps that puzzled him, and he changed topic. "I know I said I don't smoke, but in truth, I'm giving up and this whole evening is just made for a cigarette out there in the courtyard. I don't want to offend you and I'm so close to quitting, but if you don't mind, I would love to sit outside for one puff of nicotine. Would you join me?"

I looked at him out of the side of my eye.

"Sure, I have to be honest myself then. I did put in the profile that I was only interested in a non smoker because I am trying to give up and I know meeting a smoker will not help. So yes, unfortunately I'd love to join you on that bench beside the sweet fountain, It is gorgeous here." We laughed at the mutual fail.

We wandered out with our drinks and twenty minutes later came back in. It was a leisurely night.

"Katherine, we have been so honest about everything so far and it helps you understand where I come from I suppose. I'm really a stand up guy, just a bit bruised like most of us at this age, I suppose. That all happened years ago though, and it's time for me to be happy. I'm just getting on with my life. Seeing the kids grow up, catching up with my family, friends and running a few companies. Keeping it real."

The conversation returned to more general banter.

We bonded over property; my love of buying, renovating and flipping, which I explained, I had done since Ollie was born in '95, until I was injured on my own work site. Skin grafts and time out, leading to a change in career; To the beauty salon I now owned, and which was being purchased by the government because it was in the way of a future tunnel development. We brushed across the surface of it all.

He had quite a large, property management and development company. I gathered part of which was overseas. It was obvious he was quite successful.

He showed me photos on his phone of two properties he had just bought while he was over there. One in LA which was modern, wall to wall glass and oozed new money. He had included the furniture and the corvette in the deal. The other was a brownstone in Boston. It seemed to be the basement of the building. Odd choice, but clearly he knew his business. Then there was a construction he had recently completed here in Melbourne. It too was modern. Lots of open plan and good use of glass. It was edgy. He was proud of the work his company did. The last photo was from his website and it was an amazing courtyard with a decked swimming pool. I was impressed. He looked across at me, and pointed out the placement of the deck chairs and the bamboo balls, telling me that it was this attention to detail, that keeps his company a step above the rest.

"Those bamboo balls are what sold that house." He laughed. "Paying interior designers to come in and place the right furniture, until a property is sold, is worth its weight in gold. Katherine, I can't believe more developers don't do it here."

In comparison I told him vague details about my little positively geared properties that I had bought for $25,000 and flipped for $60,000. The most I'd ever made on a deal was a quarter of a million. I was proud of the two times I'd managed that incredible achievement, but obviously I wasn't in his league. I felt like a silly school girl in comparison.

He assured me it was hard work and it had taken him a while to get to the level of turnover he was now at. "Most of the times thing run smoothly, but there have been some purchases which are above the General Manager's limit of approval for autonomous decision making. That's why I had to suddenly fly to America. Ensure we were heading in the right direction. Off loaded some, approved other purchases. I'm thinking of moving over there and partially retiring at the end of the year.
You know I only just flew back in from USA this afternoon. I had to get one of the boys to pick me up in his work ute. Well, it's one of my fleet. I have a collection of cars."

I gave him my warning look of please don't talk about caaaaaaarrrrssszzzzz. Snore.

He took it the wrong way.

"Yes, I have quite a few cars: A Maserati, 2 Porches, a few BMWs, 2 Ferraris and of course, a Lamboguini, oh and the fleet of work cars. They used to be parked in the garage underneath my place in Malvern, but because I just sold it, now I have to store them all over the place in my friends' warehouses. So like me, they are homeless until the penthouse in Camberwell is finished."

Since he hadn't taken my impending boredom look the right way, but had seen it as encouragement to continue name dropping cars. I now had to interject. "Ok, would you like to talk about sports now?"

He was confused. Clearly not the reaction he was expecting.

"Paul, I have below zero interest in cars or sports. I can feel my eyes glazing over. I don't even currently own a car because mine died, and I don't really need one at present."

Again he missed the point. "What? What? Wait. You don't have a car? Katherine. Borrow one of mine. Look. I'll drop the Maserati off tomorrow. I have enough choices and they are all just sitting there doing nothing. A lady like yourself can't be walking around here. You need to be in a car. That's ridiculous."

"Oh my god! Seriously? Firstly. Do you drive that car to Cafe Sienna on Chapel St, and park out the front?"

"No, I park out the back."

"Same, same." I tried to soften my derision with a half smile. "And secondly, hell will freeze over before I get in and drive your Maserati. It's seriously not my thing. I identify cars by the following classifications. Daddy car, station wagon, 4WD, and sporty. Then by color. I.e. Black sporty thing. Green station wagon thing. Don't be a wanker, seriously. No, just NO. What sort of crazy man offers a Maserati to a stranger to drive?"

"This sort of stranger. The one in front of you. Katherine, I plan on getting a McLaren this week anyway, so that's another car just stored, doing nothing. I'm seriously giving you the Maz to drive."

I must have looked horrified. I certainly wasn't impressed. As a result of the uncertainty caused by my shop's impending government acquisition, I wasn't prepared to commit to move anywhere, nor buy a car, and here he was, reeling a list of them off, to the equivalent of the national debt. I was just aghast. Yay for him.

"I'm seriously thinking you are crazy."

"Katherine, don't look at me like that. Cars are a passion. A hobby that I can afford. Without someone sitting beside me though, they are rather empty.

You know, you amuse me. I find you fascinating. You present as this classy woman, yet you fly in the face of pretension. One second, sophisticate, next second, swearing like a sailor telling me about your power tools, then arguing about genetically modified seeds. It's rare to find someone with the same passion as me, about everything, let alone the drive and mental ability. I can tell by the way you talk, we need to hang out more.

So let's talk property. It's your fire. Clearly cars are not. Property, that's where you should be. I have an interior design co-ordinator position going. Like an office manager that oversees all my projects and ensures the staging and fit outs are stunning. I think you should give it some thought. Maybe just come and work for me. You would be perfect. The pay is amazing. $100,000. I have it advertised, so the timing is perfect. You never know, maybe you could end up replacing the general Manager in Boston, take over the US operation. Property. That's what makes you tick. Clearly, it would make you happier than what you're doing now. When you spoke on the phone, you certainly didn't have the same passion for your beauty salon as you do for property."

He'd finally managed to navigate out of the boring, pretentious waters and lead us back on to a pleasant and successful path. Property; my passion. I was happy to chat about this. "Yes, well, I can't disagree. The sound of a nail gun makes me salivate. That, shoes, milo and the right house. As for working for anyone. It's not my thing to be honest."

"Seize the day. It would be awesome! Honestly, I'll give you the job right now. You know your stuff better than my current GM in the US. At least think about the offer. Seriously, have you ever thought of living in America, maybe you could eventually take that job, over there. Come on. The shop is going, and that will give you a sizable payout. Your future is ripe for the picking."

Had my date just turned into a job interview? "Sure, I'll think about it." I didn't really mean it though. I heard the offer, contemplated it and rejected it in the time it took to answer him. I was just trying to be polite.

"To be honest Paul, my shop is being bought out by the government. It's in the way of the East West tunnel project. The process of the compulsory acquisition destroyed my business ages ago and I'm just killing time waiting for the payout. I'm not even allowed to buy until the process is over, so its frustrating. Hence my lack of commitment in purchasing a new car or signing a new lease. I'm just treading water, biding time, and don't get me wrong. I love, love my clients. I only have beautiful girls as clients. Beautiful on the inside where it counts."

I admit that I got into the beauty industry by default, after I was injured at one of my own work sites, and the resulting concrete burns left me with some sexy skin grafts. Life's battle scars. So no. "I'm not a beautician. I'm not anything. I learnt to do lash extensions while I was recuperating and bizarrely I turned out to be really good. Like really, really, obsessively good. I've been doing it for 8 years and only a year ago, consolidated two outlets into one."

He wanted to know why I had down sized.

I didn't want to discuss that yet, so I cut the conversation off, saying I was tired and that it was a topic for another time. In truth, the story was just too big to tackle that late in the evening.

He drove me home. The car was a white work ute thing. It was dirty and smelled of cigarettes. He apologized. "It's not mine. Sorry. I told you, this is Tony's work ute. It was the only way I could meet you. He had to pick me up from the airport and then I dropped him back at East Morang and circled back here to meet you. Good kid. He'd do anything for me. Bit stupid, but also really loyal." He laughed. "Apparently an intensive smoker in the car though. Might have to have a word with him about cleaning it up a bit too."

My place was around the corner and as he pulled up, I leant in to kiss him on the cheek and got out.

"Thank you for a lovely evening." I was shutting the door.

"Katherine, wait. I want to see more of you. Dinner? A proper dinner. Next Wednesday? It the earliest I'm free I'm afraid, but, I would like to take you somewhere nice to make up for neglecting you. Especially as I now know you're worth so much more. So be prepared to dress up."

I hadn't even answered affirmatively. He just presumed I would.

"Yes, I think that could be nice. Just tell me when and where."

I was barely inside when my phone pinged. A message. *"I would have come in had you asked."*

'Cocky.' I thought with a frown. 'Of course you would, you have a penis.'

"*I know, but I didn't ask.*" I texted back.

To myself I thought. 'Yes, but I would never have invited you in. Not quite sure yet, but you maybe a unicorn.' There was certainly something. An old friend once said, "You know it in your waters." I don't know about that, I was certainly feeling it somewhere though. There was something about the man.

That was 6 months ago. So much has happened since then. I'm exhausted. From there to this nightmare. To whatever I am now part of............ I don't even know. I know I have to relive our life. Our conversations. Who I met. Where. Put it all together, objectively. I know it must all be there. It would have been there all the time, I just didn't notice, but I will understand, and from there make sense of it all. Then I can defend myself.

When it comes to what I do know. I've got nothing of very little.

Nothing except pain. My eye balls hurt. I am completely miserable. Where are the cold and flu tablets? The pain killers are at least stopping my toes from hurting. The drugs required to keep me at this dulled level of misery are at least numbing the shock factor of the other night. I cannot believe what has happened; That I've just had someone stare coldly into my eyes and tell me that I'm being hunted by someone who wants to put me through a tree shredder; That my beautiful Paul is gone.

Where are you? Why is this happening? How could you leave me like this? Why, why? Why would you or the universe do this? Oh, god! My friends will realise I'm hiding from reality in the shop soon.

Now back in the uncomfortable reality of the present, I needed to grab the waste bin and again throw up. I couldn't believe I was so sick and dealing with everything else as well. It seemed extraordinarily cruel.

I used to sit in here for different reasons, with my clients and friends. We liked hanging in the back of the salon. It was like a cozy, mini home. It was warm, decadent and inviting.

I remember waiting for Paul, for the date that took forever to happen.

# Chapter 9

Thursday, 17th April. 2014.

It was 5 o clock and I was sitting in the back of the shop in the lounge area with one of my favorite clients. We had finished her treatment, and now Jaquie and I were catching up on gossip. One topic. Paul.

"He had better turn up. Do you think he will?" Jaquie was pouring wine which she had brought.

"Well, his track record hasn't been so good really has it. I mean we were meant to go out to dinner 3 weeks ago and twice since. All I've had is intermittent texts and calls. I understand that he is a high powered business man and it's just all been bad timing. USA twice equals two cancelled dates." I looked at Jaquie as her eyes requested me to correct my terminology. "Ha, yes. I know he used the words, 'postponed' and 'Rain checked.' Regardless. If he doesn't show tonight that's it. I turned down Phil, to free myself for this man. I'm really over it. You know me, Jaqs. I don't wait around."

She looked at me and gave a fresh look. It said, Reaaaaalllyyyy! Really? What do you call this?

Without a word, we both laughed.

"I know, it's ridiculous. It's like a spell." I admitted.

He had definitely captured all the girls interest as well, and Jaquie was firmly on his side most of the time. "Katherine give him a chance. You're so used to avoiding commitment. You're so quick to leave."

"Yes, before it's begun. I don't want to hang around for grief and this one has already annoyed me more than I would normally allow."

"Yes, but he sounds like he is genuinely interested. Maybe he is being respectful. Isn't that what he said to you? That he doesn't want to just show up on your door, after he has let you down. And he has had valid reasons. Sometimes things happen.You told me he sounded so sincere and apologetic about the pressure on him with both his boys being a bit out of control, and his businesses. Perhaps cut him some slack. You have nothing to lose and you have only sacrificed a few weeks. Where's the harm?
You should be happy he has his shit together. You know. He isn't living with his mum. He has a job. Property. Respect in his industry. Even his ex wife still sees him. Now that's a keeper right there. He has shown he can commit by being married before. He is obviously better than most of the guys out there. So at least give him a chance. Come on." She stared at me. "Didn't you just tell me that he has already asked if you would be interested in going out this Saturday and meeting some of his friends? That's wonderful. He is really trying to do the right thing."

"Yes, yes, I know Jaq. Even my friends are saying that this is what an adult relationship can look like at the start, because age appropriate men have other responsibilities. I get it. That's why I'm hanging in, but just remember it's against my better judgement. Do you know how many rules I've already broken??"

She gently slapped my knee.

"OH MY GOD. You are so into him. You've cleared your roster haven't you? When was the last time you saw Phil? Have you even been on a date with any on else since you met him."

"Noooo." I moaned. "I don't know what has happened to me. I feel like I have moved out of my own body. It's like I'm possessed." We laughed.

I seriously don't do relationships. I avoid them like the plague. I like my friends. Like my single life. Like being me most of the time. "What the hell is happening?"

"Katherine likes a boy. Katherine likes a boy." Jaquie laughed and teased.

Everyone was on his side. He sounds wonderful. It was just me, ever the sceptic, that demanded the go slow reality check.

Suddenly a text pinged in, and we both looked at each other. Oh god, how late is it?

"I'm early. Be there in ten."

We look at each other. Panicked. I was still in work gear. Nice, but not nice enough.

Jaquie grabbed the glasses and bottle and threw them in the kitchen. I switched the hair straightener on and literally stripped my clothes and grabbed an evening dress that does all the work form me. It's a head turner. Elegant, with literally meters of soft pink, chiffon pleated skirt, I heaved it over my head and it draped immediately into place. Jaquie zipped me as I rolled deodorant on. God, I love girls. No questions asked. Just doing it. She was running out the door, wishing me good luck, as I brushed my hair and simultaneously curled just the front on either side of my face.
"Have a great Easter Jaquie." I shouted after her as I swiped a touch of pink lipstick. Shoes. Done.

He was there. Opening the door as I sprayed some Crystal Noir to my neck.

I admitted my surprise at him turning up, but beyond that was composed.

"Can't believe the effort you have gone to. Thank you Katherine."

He told me I looked stunning and led me to the car. As he opened the car door for me, I noted, it wasn't the white ute.

I sat myself down and while we gathered my skirt inside the car with me, he leant in, with an enormous smile. "Well, at least I've got you in the Maserati without a fuss. Stage one complete."

He gently closed my door and was still laughing as he got in to the drivers side and started the car.

I glanced at the steering wheel. A devils pitch fork thing as the emblem. I didn't know if that was the Maserati symbol but since I'd never seen it before, I chose to believe him. 'Well, that answers whether he is completely full of shit. Apparently not.'

I smiled. "This is just like a silver daddy car. I pictured a Maserati being more flash and ostentatious."

"Well, it's not, and it's actually champagne. Now let's go drink some.

Katherine, I know my behavior over the last few weeks could be misconstrued as unreliable. Please don't. I take pride on keeping my word. Everything has been crazy lately. I'm not used to it being like this at all. Be assured, I have sorted everything, and looking at how beautiful you are right now, you have reminded me that I should be focusing on you. This is why I work. So I can find a lady, like you, with the whole package and here you are. I'm truly sorry for making you wait for me. Let's go have an awesome night and I promise to make it up to you."

He told me how he had chosen one of Melbourne's finest restaurants and that he hoped I was going to feel comfortable in that environment. "It's important you do, Katherine, I live a fairly decadent lifestyle."

I wondered where we were going that I would feel so insecure?

We parked at the back of Crown Casino and strolled towards the Yarra River. It was a rare mild April night. Perfect, as if he had ordered it. The old fashioned street lights reflected in the ripples of the waters edge. Couples were strolling romantically arm in arm, on their way to dinners and clubs and a stoic busker was strumming in the distance. I could just see my old apartment building across the water. As we strolled, I realized he was taking me to one of Ollie's and my favorite restaurants; Pure South. Wonderful. As we walked in, I greeted the maitre de by name.

"Hello Michael. Long time." We gave each other a warm hug and he led us to a spot in front of the fireplace."

"Our best table for my favorite guest."

As we sat, I told Paul, that I took my son to some beautiful restaurants so he knew how to behave and would feel comfortable in different surroundings. Hopefully, later in life, he would be able to treat a lady in the manner she deserved. Paul was impressed that I would do that with him.

We had a lovely meal with a ridiculously expensive bottle of wine and exceptionally attentive service. A perfectly executed night. Some ladies at the next table complimented my dress, and Paul joked that he would have to remember to pay them later. We touched on more intimate details.

He wanted to know about the shop and how the acquisition process was affecting me. He had an in depth understanding of the painful process, as his father had bought tracts of land along the western corridor of Melbourne before the Western Ring Road project was announced. "For all the pain, Katherine, it is always a profitable process. Like winning the jackpot really, which is how I feel about meeting you, to be honest." He reached out and gently put his hand on top of mine as he said it. Seeing me flinch slightly at the overt keenness, he removed his hand and shook his head with a smile. "God, Katherine, I can see you are going to be a hard one to catch. You need to trust me and yourself. Let your heart feel. Life is for loving!"

He changed tack, which was a relief as I didn't want to be dealing with emotional relationship words or conversations with someone I had just met. It always made me extremely uncomfortable when a man leapt into "love" scenarios before they got to know you. Thank god he backed off and switched the dial.

I was aware of how much of a pain in the arse I was. The negative record was spinning quietly in the background of my head. 'I'm such high maintenance. What a pain, I am. I don't let him touch my hand, or to talk about the shop either.'

I don't wish to dwell on it's impending acquisition, because, it's horrible to watch what I had worked so hard to build, now being destroyed. Even though there was supposedly going to be a nice payout at the end. I felt uncomfortable living in perpetual hope that things would work out. It was exhausting, and I hated pretending it was ok. It wasn't ok. It was gutting. It was as if I was selling my business. I just didn't want to. Internally I felt the universe had perversely punished me again. I knew it wasn't a rational thought, to think that there was some omnipresent force that had it in for me, but it was how I felt, and I was sick of my happiness, safety and achievements being derailed. I was sick of having to step up and over disasters and reinvent myself. I didn't want him to talk about the shop, because I didn't want him, or any of my friends, to see how fucked up and disempowered, I truly felt about everything.

I know I'm precious and difficult.

So he tried again, and asked about my son and his recent exploits. "He realized they had affected me."

Regardless of the change of topic, unfortunately it had the same theme. The universe has a bit of an obsession with my son and I. Random good. Random bad. Both extreme with reassuring calm patches in between. This was another topic that was going to be hard for me to navigate, so I rehashed the familiar story, keeping it vague. This was only our second date. I tried to summaries that a few years earlier, Ollie was complaining that I should take him to singing auditions and I wasn't sure where to begin. Suddenly, within the week of this latest teen desire, a show, dropped it's age limit and was advertising for everyone to audition.

Ollie literally had his birthday the week before and I dutifully drove him to the auditions. I went to the wrong place initially, but eventually joined the masses of hopefuls in the queue. Ollie hadn't even learnt the words to his song properly and at the last second was outside singing under the stands.

He went in, forgot his words, and they gave him an unprecedented, second chance. Basically, we went there for an adventure. Something to do on a weekend, and he got through. What were the chances? I know he can sing. He has a beautiful voice. Anyway, that pretty much took up the rest of the year.

"So would I know him?" He had asked somewhat excitedly.

"I don't know. It's a reality TV show. Do you watch that stuff?"

"What did he look like?"

"He is tall with -"

"Here." He had got out his phone and googled. "Yes, I know him! Awesome. Must have seen the ads or something. Why hadn't I realized before. This is him right?" He showed me the page on his phone with my son's pictures.

"Yes, that's him. He is beautiful. Seriously unbiased. My son is beautiful."

"Like his mother. Well, well, well. Oliver De Bois' mum."

"Enough of that. I was here first. He is actually Katherine De Bois' son."

He laughed. "Whatever. You should be so proud."

I pointed to one of the Utube clips. "This one. If you're going to listen to any song. I love that song, 'Paranoid.'"

We listened in silence, watching the small screen. The restaurant staff joined in. He is an angelic looking boy. Charismatic, talented, smart and wise. I love him. He is totally his own person. He is more my world, than he will ever know.

When the song finished, Paul looked up. "He has an amazing voice. So then what happened?"

"Well, obviously he can sing. That's why he made it so far in the competition. I am immensely proud of him. Not just that he can sing, but more so in the way he handled himself as a generous, good sport on the show. He grew up so much that year. He learnt about the hug. I learnt about Autism. He stood strong and solid during the eviction nights. He was genuinely happy for everyone. He thought he might get to the halfway mark, anything after that was a bonus. He did really well.

I let him go through it, because I had naively thought it would put a smile on his face. It looked like it would be fun, but it's not so much. It's hard work, long hours, no control and he needs an inordinate amount of down time away from so much stimulation and other humans. So do I. It was a bit ghastly to be honest.

Would I do it again? Probably not, but then again, I think it was good for Ollie, in the long run, as a man. Honestly he showed such wisdom, and dignity throughout that show. I was then, and still am, in total, constant awe of him. I think it was the right thing to have done for him. Eventually it will work out, but for now it has put a very large wedge between us. I wish everything was back like it was before."

"And your business? How did it cope without you?"

"Not great. It took me away for the majority of 9 months and when we came back at the end of November, my business was struggling. I had left it with staff. My accountant and I both knew there would be collateral damage. I also had a stunning 3 story house in the middle of Albert Park. As you can imagine, in that location, it wasn't a cheap house to run."

"That's pretty impressive that as a single mum you could afford to own there, Katherine."

"I've worked pretty hard, Paul. Anyway I returned to a lot of pressure and I immediately closed the two outlets and brought them into my house which thankfully was a commercial building. I loved, LOVED that house.
And here's the kicker.

Ollie's father's family suddenly remembered they had a missing relative. I told you how, his dad had changed his mind about being a father, while I was pregnant. His whole family never contacted us again until they saw him on TV.

14 years of silence. Not a word from them and suddenly they had my son under their roof. Promised to bank roll a record for him. He believed them. It had me fighting to get my son back. I spent the majority of 2012 in court. I had an unfillable hole in my heart. I was so lost. Worse, I knew he was too.

He came back at the start of 2013. They threw him out in a maxi taxi with his clothes in black garbage bags. Perhaps they didn't get what they wanted from him.

"What did they want? To make money?" Paul had been attentive throughout.

"No. They are filthy rich already. I think they pathetically wanted something that their money hadn't bought them yet. A celebrity from a reality show. A public image pet. Pathetic really. I bet my life, that they would never, ever have contacted him except they saw him on TV. Unfortunately they didn't realise how fleeting that fame was going to be. Tragic. They have done so much damage based purely on self absorbed, misguided decisions, fueled with money.

Anyway, he promptly moved out with his girlfriend. Trust me that stuff wouldn't have been happening on my watch. That family's behavior has disempowered all of us. He stopped going to school and had a lip piercing. All of the sudden, nothing was ideal again. I've been trying to resurrect some sort of relationship with him for the past year but, as you know, teenage boys can be difficult. Although, I'm the first to admit that mine is one of the good ones. I honestly think he is a truly amazing person, and I have to give credit where it is due. He and Sarah are still together living like a happy, old, married couple."

"And the shop?"

"Well the business had been going since 2009, and I opened the new outlet on first of March, 2013, so around the same time I was having to sell my house, I was simultaneously opening the new shop for the salon, and Oliver was moving out with his girlfriend." I laughed at the enormity of the events.

"I told you the universe has a perverse obsession with me though, so with huge humour it hadn't finished playing. Two weeks after the grand opening, the government sent it's first notice that the East-West tunnel project was going through my new shop and there would be a compulsory acquisition. Blah. The process is still going on, as you know. Lets face it, everyone in Melbourne knows it. It's a government thing. I stay out of it. Nothing I can do, that's for sure.
I've certainly had easier times. Life. What can you do? It is what it is, and I've learnt that no matter how bad things are, you keep waking up breathing, so you might as well just get on with things.
Sorry you asked?" I had touched on just the hi and lo lights of the story. Like a summary. I was still dealing with all the changes and impacts, on a

daily basis. I still felt shell shocked and now the shop issue was a weekly beating. I needed a holiday.

"No, everyone has their story. Their past. It's a lot Katherine. You seem to have an amazing attitude about it all. God, I wish I had met you sooner. I could have helped you avoid a lot of that angst. I'm really sorry."

"Well, I don't want a pity party. It could be a lot worse. I'm saddest about the distance between Oliver and myself to be honest. The house is just a house, although it was seriously stunning and it was my home."

"You know. What goes down has to come up. Your luck is about to turn. You have met me, so it already has, and the compulsory acquisition is a guaranteed payout, so that's really a positive. You just have to hang in there. I promise, with me by your side, I know everything is going to work out perfectly for both of us." He smiled. He was genuine. This is what he really felt.

We spent the rest of the night focused on him which was a lot more pleasant than regaling my miserable past few years.

He identified with the celebrity fans. "I used to be a model when I was younger."

'Of course you did,' I thought to myself. Does not surprise me with those eyes, that smile and strong jawline. Some people are just blessed. I know a few. Their looks seriously makes their life easier.

He continued. "When one particular Calvin Klein campaign came out, so did a million girls and their equivalent in male haters. Except the gay guys, they 'lurved' me. It was a tough gig. I couldn't go outside without being hit on in all directions. It was overwhelming, and I was a lot older than your son, so I'm impressed with how he handled it.
It taught me to seek out the company of genuine people though. All good and well to ogle a pair of double D's on legs but if there isn't a brain under the make up, then it's just a waste of time. Don't get me wrong. I made the most of what was out in front of me at the time, but it was quantity not quality. Wild times. Over the years, as my life became more successful, I've culled many so called friends. They were just there for the ride. When I was younger, it was fine, as long as I could provide a party and all the accoutrements." He smiled indicating that it may have been more than just alcohol and music. "Slowly as I got older and wiser, I realized they were mostly hangers on. They were there for what my money could get them. I want to find someone who wants me for me. Nearly having it, thinking I

found it, only to have it taken away so cruelly, makes me want it even more."

He took a heartfelt breath and looked deep into my eyes. "You know, after everything I have done for them. No one from my side even came to her funeral. I understand that none of them particularly liked her. I've always acknowledged that she was fairly anti social. She was often abrasive and self absorbed to a fault, but she was my partner, so that's not really the point is it? They should have been there to support me. That funeral was a huge turning point in so many ways. I always thought everyone would understand that leaving her in Boston would be life changing for me. Instead, it's like she never existed. Never died. No one ever asks how I am. It made me realise no one really cares."

He had lost himself in his own thoughts and suddenly realized. "Sorry. I usually prefer not to talk about it much, but I'm so comfortable with you. My past relationships are not relevant to moving forward, but some stories in my past include them. You understand don't you? Like mentioning Maggie because I have the boys with her."

I nodded. "I totally understand that. Everyone has a past, and at our age most of us have had one if not more relationships." Internally, I reminded myself that there's many topics that I don't want to talk about. I just have a lot of horrible, horrible memories, and they are best left unacknowledged.

He continued chatting. "I tried to do the right thing again only a few years ago. I went to support Julie, a friend, who was trying for Millionaire Hot Seat. You know that show? Anyway, at the last second she chickened out and I ended up doing the interview process with her, and I got chosen for the show. I was the second one in the chair. I tried to play strategically and passed. When my turn came up next it was because the woman before me had got the second last question wrong. I couldn't believe it. I took my seat and expected some crazy impossible question and instead, it was about James Bond. I know everything about those movies. I own them all. My dad gave them to me for Christmas years ago.

"I remember, 'What pistol did James Bond use before the Dr No movie?'

'Beretta.' of course!
One million dollars. Thank you. All that publicity. It's only for a few weeks, but boy, your "homies" suddenly remember you. I got Facebook requests from people I hadn't seen in 20 years.

A couple of weeks after the show aired, I took 8 of my inner circle and their partners, including Julie, out to Shelly's Pavilion in Williamstown for lunch. I've had some awesome events there. You understand, Katherine, I personally didn't need that million so I had an envelope on each plate. They sat down and inside was a cheque for $100,000. It was awesome giving it away. Most of my friends are average people struggling to get their kids through school and pay their mortgage. That day made an enormous difference to them. I took a bit as a holiday and gave some money to the boys, which they stupidly blew. Hopefully everyone else used it wisely. Such a great day. We all got hammered. I'd love to take you there for lunch. It was an endorphin rush seeing their happiness. I give pretty generously now to charities as a result. It's the most wonderful feeling to give back."

I sat there taking it all in. I was impressed by him. He was polite, kind and generous. Exceptionally generous.

Now as I sit, rocking, curled on the office chair, my chin leaning on my knees, wrapped tightly in a wad of blankets, I wonder where this man has gone. A few days ago, I was marrying the most loving, moral, generous and caring man I knew, and now he was gone. In a millisecond he vanished. Replaced with thugs and threats.

Do I know something, that I don't know, that I know? Do they think I know something? What is it about me that is such a threat? I have to think back. Just work through it all slowly. I know to my core, it will begin to unravel. Knowledge and self awareness will protect me. And what's happened to Paul? I don't understand how any of this is happening.

I pulled the blankets tighter, and squashed my aching eyes into my knee caps. I took myself back to the date.


Over dessert, he told me about his scuba diving around the world as he showed me some Facebook photos of him swimming with sharks. He went on; comparing the different quality of the reefs and me quietly adding that seaweed terrifies me. His piloting small planes, flying up to the Whitsundays for a weekend. He wanted to try for a helicopters license. Why not? It looked like fun.

"I'm a bit of an adrenaline junkie, Katherine. I went sky diving last year. What a rush. Clears your head. You should do it. You literally can't think of anything else apart from living in the moment when you are zooming towards earth at a hundred miles an hour."

Again I was a party pooper. I get motion sick on merry go round rides, and I don't like any flying, zooming, spinning or bumping as a result. My body is over sensitive to any external force moving me, even pontoons make me heave. Many of my friends over the years have led similar lives to his and I exclude myself from their activities. They hold no interest because no one voluntarily does stuff that will make them throw up.

He continued the list. "I've always owned sports cars. My brother, David and I used to race them. Well, I suppose we still do, it's just I have been a bit busy and he has a new wife, so I'm sure it's only a matter of time."

"Uh huh, and we both know what I think and know about cars, although I can sit through Top Gear. Those guys are funny and some of the cars are sexy."

"I really like that about you. You are seriously unimpressed with the Maserati aren't you? I've had girls suddenly become so interested when they see the signs of my wealth. You are the opposite. The more I try to impress you with it, the less interested you are."

"What can I say? It gets you around from A to B."

In all honesty it just looked like a slick daddy car or something. I don't know. Clearly just not a car girl. I certainly didn't share my thoughts. No need to be hurtful. I once confused a friend's jag with a holden. They both have tiger/lions in the emblem. Same same.

He flashed his enormous smile at me and the corners of his eyes crinkled. "Well, it's not all about cars. What I'm focused on at present is just getting all my ducks in a row so I can retire and travel. Lie on a deck chair on every beautiful beach in the world. Bora Bora. Simply stunning. I've stayed a few times in those thatched cabins above the water. It's exactly like the promo pictures. Stunning. Gee Jam in Jamaica. Last time I was there with my mates, we tore the place up. Bumped into Matthew McConaughey. Now, he is an awesome dude. I have made some sweet friends through travel. In my younger days, I may not remember most of what I got up to, but I've been told about it. Apparently I once destroyed the Hamilton Island airstrip with a golf cart. I was maybe 22. There was literally two dozen of us. We caused mayhem.

God Katherine, The Riveria Maya, near Cancun. You would love it. That would be a goal wouldn't it. You'd join me for that?" He was quick to laugh and his eyes sparkled constantly.

"Sure Paul, who wouldn't?" I laughed.

He was so enthusiastic about life. He knew about everything, everyone. Had been everywhere. He was the most fascinating man. Like an ever ready bunny: Full of energy and always on. He had been privileged enough to lead the life most of us dream about, leaping at every opportunity to try something new and adventurous. He was fearless. Whereas I am scared of my shadow. Terrified of strangers, new situations, the outside, of change. It's an enormous challenge to talk to people I don't know. My hands sweat, and sometimes when it's bad, my knees shake. My friends would generally meet me outside of a bar so I didn't have to walk through it alone. I've even had taxi drivers escort me in to help find my friends. Often this fear of, I don't know what I'm scared of, is literally so overwhelming that it is physically impossible for me to go out the front door. I can bunker down for weeks, before necessity forces me out.

For as much as we had in common, there were vast differences. His strengths were my weaknesses. My few strengths were also his strengths. He appeared to lack nothing.

We had a wonderful night and were last to leave. He decided to take a selfie of us together on our first official date. He put it on his Facebook which surprised me. He looked good. I looked squashed in a choke hold of his enthusiasm. My hair still destroyed straw.

"Katherine, this is the beginning of something wonderful. You'll see. I'm never wrong. There is something here." Regardless that his declaration was premature, we had indeed shared a genuinely lovely night.

The evening finished again with a polite peck on his cheek, which this time slid into a mutually, long, slow sensual kiss. He gently bit my lip as his hand grazed upward from my thigh, up to my waist and swept powerfully around to my back. His fingers were spread and he encompassed as much of my small body as he could. Pulling me in towards himself. It was hot. We both wanted so much more, but he understood. I believe good things come to those that wait. I wanted to know he wanted me as more than a conquest.

# Chapter 10

I pull myself from my day dreams. The room is cold and my body is stiff and heavy. I drag myself, encompassed in the blanket via the kitchen for tablets and then to the mattress in the small room of the shop. I'm shocked I'm so sick. Sicker than I have ever been. Curling in a ball, I pull the blankets and pillows around my body. I can't get warm. I shiver constantly. I want to remove myself from the present and think back to when I was falling in love with Paul. I can't face anything else yet. It's been two days. But I'm so miserable I can only drag up a pathetic sad memory. It has little to do with Paul.

That's right.
I remember that beautiful evening, the turning point date with Paul, had been a Thursday. I only know, because the next day was Easter. Good Friday.

I don't want to think about it, but the memory floods into my clouded head.

I had spent the whole day with my closest friends and all they did was give me grief. It was an awful, ugly day. They picked on me over everything. I apparently needed to date older men. I needed to just make the government pay the shop out immediately. I didn't understand how they thought that was possible. I certainly couldn't speed the government system up. I was criticized when I asked why, as Catholics, they ate seafood on that day. I had just wanted someone to give me the significance. I had so regretted asking that question. I was hammered. My defense that Easter is a pagan ritual didn't help. They criticized my knowledge on property. All in all, one of the most excruciating meals I have ever sat through. It was a horrid day. They even decided that someone as wonderful as Paul couldn't exist. I was called stupid twice. To my face.

"No one would give you, of all people, their Maserati to drive. Kathy are you stupid?" Di was talking as she plated food in the kitchen.

"I agree. I'm just telling you what he said. I think it's crazy too."

John interjected. "It's probably not even a Maserati. You don't know anything about cars."

"I know, you're right, I don't care about cars. I was just answering your questions about the new guy I had met. Does it really matter?"

Then Di came in serving some more food.

"So you went on Tinder and pulled up an age appropriate millionaire first shot. Can't believe you are so gullible and worse, that you are on those sites."

"OMG chill! Haven't all of you sitting at this table, been on those sites? John and Vikki, didn't you meet each other on RSVP? Dee, you are on them obsessively, all the time. Oscar you are literally flitting between Plenty of Fish and Tinder right now, while we are eating. Seriously! What's with the attitude? You wanted me to meet someone. I did. He seems to have his act together. He seems nice."

They didn't let up.

"And he offered you a job on your first date?" The scorn dripped as Di asked. "Seriously Kathy, you are an idiot."

"I'm just telling you what's been happening. You're free to make your own judgements. Yes, he has offered me a job several times now, over the phone, over cocktails, over dinner. So what if he is just trying to impress me. Why aren't you all being happy? You wanted me to date older. I've met someone older."

I wanted to cry with frustration and hurt, but I never do. This was just an exceptionally blah day.

"So you're going to stop dating the younger guys. That was just wasting your time. It was embarrassing." Di, apparently was on a roll.

"I don't date them. I'm not looking for marriage. I see them because, in general, they are nicer. I see them because I can. They are not in a position to hurt me. I see them because they are attractive, funny, full of life, educated, articulate, stimulating. I see them because we get along. But, most importantly I try to hang out with people that are nice and if I had ever met someone older that fitted that, then I would have dated him. As you well know John. But most importantly it's just "seeing" because I haven't wanted anything more. You know me. I don't seem to do relationships well."

I looked at John. We had turned a business relationship into a long friendship and then we tried to date and it hadn't worked out. He was ten years older than me. What was everyone's problem today? Seriously!!

I felt so disrespected. It suddenly seemed that I was in the wrong, in their eyes, regardless of whether I had been dating younger, poorer, richer, nicer, meaner or this new guy. Add to that, the criticism of the shop situation. It just went on and on. I left them to it and went home. It hurt deeply that they thought any of that about me.

Paul had phoned that night, and I had told him about my day. He seemed genuinely distressed when I told him about how unpleasant my Easter lunch with my friends had been. I had avoided sharing certain topics, but told him how they questioned my knowledge of building codes and property sales protocol. I even told him how they said a guy like him didn't exist.

"What do you mean? They think you made me up?"

"Something like that, yes."

"I don't understand. What is it that they found so hard to believe?"

"Simply, that I met a successful guy who genuinely wants to find someone, regardless of whether that's me or not. That's all."

"I don't just want to just find someone, Katherine. I want to love, and be loved like no other and I do exist. I'm already surprisingly quite fond of you. To be honest I think you're amazing. If I was them, I certainly wouldn't be questioning your knowledge of the property sector, either. It's beyond solid, and evidenced by your past properties, which is why I genuinely offered you that job, which you should take, by the way. I'm a bit shocked though, I thought they were your close friends. Maybe you should re think your circle."

"They *are* my close friends and maybe that's why they thought they could say all this to me. You know how family can be mean sometimes. I'm just so hurt if that's what they really think of me. I am going to talk to them about it."

"I'd love to meet them and tell them what I see."

"Ha, Well, Paul, I could have done with that back up, earlier today."

"Next time it's a date. If I turned up, then they would feel like idiots wouldn't they? Age appropriate with my act together. I'd like you to think I have your back, Katherine, and I'd like to hope we are going to get to a place where you know that."

The next day, I remember phoning those friends, individually, all 7 of them, and at least having the courage to say that the bullying was ridiculous. I was saddened to think they saw so little in me. Di told me to grow up. 'I was being delusional' that such a wonderful person could exist. I agreed, except I'd met him.

John apologized and was sorry that I had felt ostracized. To soothe troubled waters, he organised a dinner for all of us on the following Friday. I accepted and said Paul would be coming. I knew they wanted proof he existed……....

# Chapter 11

It was the week after Easter and the first time my friends met Paul.

I was nervous as I waited for him to pick me up. After the character assassination from my supposed closest and dearest, I wanted them to like him. I didn't want a rehash of all the negativity from the previous week. I still couldn't understand where all that hostility had come from. I had internalized their solid message. "I'm a loser. I'm ugly. I'm worthless and stupid. And dumb and ridiculous. Worse still I *am* alone. It was rhetoric added to an already existing record that played continuously in my head.

When Paul arrived, he had laughed at my state. "Katherine, trust me, they won't be saying anything mean. It's going to be an awesome night. Come on."

We were walking out of the shop and I was locking the door. I glanced over my shoulder at him.

"Paul, you know how you said you were going to buy that other car?"

He smirked. "Yes."

"Can you tell me when you do?"

We were now walking up the road.

"So I can act as if I had noticed and be enthusiastic and happy for you, because you boys like your cars and I don't want to seem rude. I'd like to share your excitement. Ok?"

We were standing beside his car, and he was opening the door for me.

I got in. He was still smirking at me.

"Ok."

He was doing his seat belt up, when he looked at me. "Katherine, this *is* the new car."

"Really?" I was surprised. "I felt like I had just failed. See. STUPID!

"Yep. New, new new."

"I'm sorry it looks the same as the other one. Are you teasing me?" I was hoping he was joking.

His face was a bit crestfallen. "Katherine, they aren't even the same color."

"Yes they are. Silver."

"You're right Katherine. This *is* silver. The Maserati, however, is *still* champagne and nothing like this at all. This is the car James Bond drives."

I looked at him intently, still drawing a blank.

"Oh God, Katherine. This is an Aston."

Yep, clearly the biggest fail.

He was pulling out into the traffic as he said. "You may not be impressed, but wait till your friends see us pull up in this, then you will understand. The guys will cream themselves."

Really? It's still just a silver daddy car. I did not share this thought.

As we drove, he turned to me, reaching for my hand, he gently raised it to his lips and kissed it.

"Katherine, I won't tolerate any disrespect from your friends towards you. I hope you know this. I already adore you. I think you are my reward. I know you are my future happiness. I think life has served some fairly shitty things your way and mine, but I'd like to think that me randomly finding you, is the universe's way of changing that.
And, just so you know, I am an exceptionally demonstrative man. I like to touch and hug, so I'm hoping you don't have any issue with public displays of affection, because I don't want to have to reign in my natural desire to touch you. Is that all right?

"I'm fine with that Paul, as long as things are respectful, I don't mind that at all."

We walked in through John's back door to find three of my friends already around the kitchen bench, pouring wine.

I had already primed Paul. I have several different groups of friends. They are all very real people. Down to earth.

John; a school principal and maths teacher. Very conservative. Football, -Tigers fanatic. Runner. A remorseless conquest hunter. Doesn't realise how OCD he is. Known him for at least nine years.

Dianne, an accountant. More conservative than she thinks. Single mum raising two boys in their early 20's, who had both currently lost their way. Essendon all the way. Known her through John, for perhaps 5 years. We have only been close in the last few years.

Vikki. John's new girlfriend. New job in pharmacy chain, window dressing or something. Relatively nice. Don't worry too much about her. He is like a dating revolving door, and generally only introduces us to his girls when he is already onto the next one.

Oscar. Loyal, placid, Oscar. He has his own truck business, working in road construction. Lovely. Genuine. Italian. Traditional. Quiet.

Thus armed, Paul separated from me, and smile flashing, warmly greeted each of them, before walking straight up to Di and saying.

"Hi I'm Paul. You must be Dianne. I hear I don't exist."

She looked taken aback at the friendly, confident self introduction. It was immediately clear Paul knew about the Easter lunch, bullying session.

Oh, tonight is going to be a balls up, after all.

But, after a second of hesitation, everyone just laughed, and made jokes that he did sound a bit made up.

"Well, Paul." Di said, with her hand flirtatiously resting on his arm. "We know her better than you do, and if you had seen who she's been dating lately you would understand our disbelief as to your actual existence. We have had to meet some doozies. Katherine's been making some grandiose statements about how wonderful you are. We will see how close to the mark she is."

I was fuming. OMG it's started again. Who are they basing this on? I don't remember the last time I even had a relationship. Let alone brought someone to dinner. Oh, except Oscar, and that was more than a year ago and he had become such a firm friend that he was having dinner with us tonight. Yes, I must have bad taste in the guys I date. Oscar and I didn't work, but we all like him enough to maintain a friendship. What is this? As for talking Paul up. You can't. He is bigger than anything I could make up.

Paul allowed the banter at my expense to continue for a few minutes before saying.

"Well, I hope that's all in the past now and I'd like to think I'll be lucky enough to hang around and rectify the situation. I think she deserves more. Don't you?"

Just then Oscar came bounding through the back door.

"Whose is that in the driveway?"

Paul just looked at me, knowingly.

They all went outside and stood there staring at the new car. Apparently Paul was right. They were beyond impressed. I was just bewildered. It's a car. A silver car.

"Glad you like it Oscar. Now we just have to convince Katherine to drive my old one."

The whole conversation about cars fascinated me. Why do people even care? Regardless of my lack of interest, the consensus was that it was hysterical to imagine me driving a Maserati. I'd have no appreciation of it. Oscar volunteered to look after it for him.

He spent the rest of the night talking me up. Telling them he was into me, and being very tactile just as he said he would be. He made us laugh. He spoke business. Finance, cars, football. He knew the suburbs they grew up in and some of the same people. It was like he had always been there.

My friends approved. They liked him. They liked him enough to tell him, that they liked him.

It was nice having my friends and my apparently "instant" boyfriend, getting along. There was no pressure or awkwardness. I wasn't baby-sitting and neither was he. It was comfortable and natural. We worked.

He reciprocated by telling them how much he liked me. He thought this could be something special.

"Sometimes you just know. And when you know, then you shouldn't let the opportunity slip by. It's that belief that has got my businesses to where they are now, and my personal life to here, today."

John, a professional commitment phob, looked puzzled.

"I've been through my share of heart ache. When you think you have something and it's suddenly torn away from you, well you learn to appreciate what you have, while you still have it."

It was obvious, he was going to have to expand on that and he did.

He touched their hearts as he shared how his last relationship had ended so unexpectedly.

Money doesn't guarantee happiness. Paul and his last girlfriend had travelled the world together. Stayed in some of the most exotic destinations. Sailed, Scuba dived. Adventurously parachuted in the Bahamas. It had been a wonderful time, just as he was coming into serious wealth and leisure time.

She was a very quiet, anti social sort of girl. She didn't have friends but that had complimented his outgoing personality. Ying and yang. She was analytical and distant, and he feels with his heart.

She was studying to become a lawyer when they first met. But after a year she started to get sick. They tried everything. From initially thinking it was just the flu, she just got worse, so fast. They had been on his boat in the Whitsundays when he realized it was something more serious and within 4 months it turned out to be leukemia. She was American, so he flew her back to the USA, to be with her family in Boston. He took 6 months off to be by her side, and at the end asked her to marry him while she was in hospital. He even had a ring. She turned him down because she didn't want to leave him as a widower. He had stayed by her side while she had wasted away, becoming skeletal. The hollow cheek bones and bulging eyes with that deathly, glassy, stare.

"It is just the most horrible death. Her eyes would roll into the back of her head and towards the end she smelled so bad. The smell of death, of rotting flesh from the inside, like decaying steak, and when she tried to speak, her breath: It made you gag. I sat beside her in that hospital bed while she slept. I fed her and wiped away her drool. Listened to her rasping, labored breathing.

I can promise, I never once thought of leaving her, even when both my family and hers were urging me to leave and get on with my life and be happy. I loved her and when I love, I love like no other. I am completely faithful. I willed her to get better but she died. She died knowing she was loved and that's important.
He had kissed her as she took her final gasp and said.

"I love you Baby."

He learnt he was a stayer and loyal.

"I could have walked out and left her in America, but I stayed right to the end, even when it was obvious, the end was inevitably going to be her death. For me to watch her die, was apparently written in my life plan, before I even met her. She literally had to die for me to move forward into a better future. I couldn't see that at the start, but I can now.

Then I had to speak the eulogy at her funeral. It was the loneliest thing I have ever done. I was outside surrounded by fresh spring greenery, in front of a few hundred people and I remember saying. 'I have never felt so alone.' And I meant it."

I noticed Di, wipe a leaking eye. It was sad. It was very, very sad to hear of the pain he had gone through, and the awful suffering she had endured. But deep inside, I didn't want to keep hearing this story. I'm a bit cold hearted sometimes.

"With her gone, I was surrounded by strangers in a country where no one knew me. Her parents had told me to just leave.They genuinely wanted me gone. That they would look after her, and encouraged me to move on. I tried to explain that I was better off being with her to the end., but they saw no reason for me to stay. They felt that my presence just made things worse. They wanted me to move on, and get on with my life. Start afresh as if my relationship had never existed. I realised they didn't want to even look at me."

I flew home the next day. There was nothing for me in Boston.

Hardest part is thinking you may love like that again, only to lose it. It's my biggest fear. Going through that pain again. I know it sounds selfish but it's true. By the time she died, she was better off. Finished in her prime, but I was left with plans for my life, and I just haven't seemed to have been able to find any one special enough to make me feel that way again."

He looked at me and put his hand across mine, gently squeezing it. He turned it over and in front of everyone kissed my palm.

"Until, maybe now."

Huge statement. My friends were sold. When he went to the bathroom, John said,

"Don't stuff this up Katherine. He seems really nice and clearly adores you. He is a man. This is what you should have been looking for."

In less than a week from Good Friday, my friends had gone from disbelief that a man like Paul could exist, to becoming the cheer squad. Clearly, Paul not only existed, but was pretty awesome in everyone's eyes.

Di, Paul and Oscar went outside for a cigarette break before dessert, and I skipped off to the loo. When I went out to join them, the boys were standing on the lawn and Di was sitting on a deck chair under the verandah. She said,

"That would be awesome, honestly. If you could just give them a chance. They are great boys. Ash and Sam would be so grateful to be given a break."

They exchanged business cards.

I looked at her confused. What did I just miss? Had she just hit Paul up for jobs for her unemployed sons? She was meant to be playing wing woman, not looking out for herself. Seriously? This is technically my second serious date with the guy. Talk about loyalty.

She followed it up with. "I suppose you two will be heading off home soon for some down and out, dirty, hanky panky."

Good lord. Where did that come from? We haven't even finished dinner yet. I leant into her and whispered that I hadn't gone there.

She looked up at Paul. "Wow, she must really like you if she hasn't slept with you yet."

What the actual hell?? I remember looking at her, and thinking, you really don't like me, do you. These were meant to be my friends. I had been playing it cool with Paul, and you go and say that. Why. Seriously Why? What is wrong with people?

One second you are happy that I have found an awesome man, the next you are sabotaging it.

Why, just why?

Once dinner was finished and we had left with much fan fair about the car, I felt that Di had forced the issue and sealed the deal that tonight, most likely now, would be the night. I had planned on dragging it out longer.

As we drove away, Paul took no time in quizzing me about her snide jab and I could only say.

"Yes, I suppose it's true. I haven't slept with you yet because I am interested. I'd prefer to get to know you on a deeper level. I think sex messes peoples' views of each other."

"So would you have slept with me if you hadn't been interested in me in a more meaningful, longer term thing?"

Entering murky waters, for anyone in todays dating society. I looked at him as he drove and answered honestly.

"No Paul, I wouldn't have slept with you casually. You don't fall into that category." There's a truth.

"Because you know it's not my sort of thing. I don't sleep around Katherine and if you do, we have a problem. A big problem before we even begin."

"No, Paul, because there's more to you, and I had wanted to see some of your layers. If you had been lesser of a man, I wouldn't be contemplating it at all. I'm pretty fussy." Another truth.

A huge thank you to Di. Thank you. Thaaaaannnnk yoooou!. For opening such a can of worms. Putting doubt and disrespect into Paul's head. Well done. Thank you. I was furious and fuming silently in my head.

What I didn't say, was to fall into the steamy, casual encounter brigade, the guy needed to be an open flame. Paul was a smolder. I wanted to wait.

# Chapter 12

But that was before the universe punished me and took him away.

Now I am stuck, lying on the floor wrapped in the shop's spa blankets, holding my head under them, desperately keeping my eyes away from the harsh reality that the bright light of day brings; a spearing pain, physically, and an honest reminder that time is still marching forward. I have things to face.

Remembering how wonderful he was, makes me feel painfully better. Thinking back and seeing my friends happy and laughing with him.

I stare blankly into the dark under the blanket and zone out.

I remembered after only a month of being with him, walking into the shop's kitchen and taking a moment. A small, three second, pause from the merry ground of life. I looked up towards the ceiling and said thank you. Thank you to the power that had allowed Paul into my life. A moment's grace to genuinely say out loud.

"Thank you for giving me Paul. A real gentleman. Thank you."

It felt overwhelming to think I could breathe. That I could finally relax. That I could be loved. Protected. That someone so wonderful wanted to be with me. That I was allowed to adore this man.

And then there had been a flash of anger aimed at the very same omnipresent force that ruled my world. Generous and kind then cruel and vindictive.

"You didn't have to put me through hell for these past few years just to balance it out with someone so wonderful. I would have been happier with a little less shit before, and a little less perfection from Paul. I'm grateful. I'm just exhausted from coping with the major random crap you keep piling my way, and just at the point of cowering completely to a life of struggle and injustice, you throw Paul at me. Like seriously? Have you finished playing?

Can life just be calm now? I'm saying thank you but, please, please let me breathe now."

Paul had once told me that he was the balancing weight on the scale of justice in my life. For all the horrors I had previously endured, for all the sadness and hurt, he was put in my life to right that. His amazingly blessed life was going to beat my curse of left of centre universal cruelties.

"You may feel like you are cursed Katherine, but I am blessed. Everything I touch turns to gold. We will be perfect. I will look after you. No more harm will come your way. You'll see. We are meant to be together. You are going to help complete me, and for that I will be the protector you deserve."

I had desperately wanted to believe him.

I was standing in that tiny room facing the white pantry door, aware that a tear of anger, or gratitude or happiness was trying to escape from the bottom rim of my right eye. It was relief. It was exhaustion. It was the release of all the pent up anxiety from years of struggling, from passing through fear. From thinking that now I could breathe. But, I just couldn't let it fall. I still couldn't trust yet. Not completely. I was grateful, but scared it would be taken away.

So much to be grateful for.

# Chapter 13

Grateful for the first night he took me to his house.

Even after Dianne's comment which had set a tone of awkwardness and strangely a silent unified closeness. He had driven past my shop and continued on through to the more conservative suburbs east of Melbourne. Down Toorak Rd. At one point, he indicated towards a fenced block of land with building construction in progress.

"That's where the penthouse will be, if they ever finish it."

If it was meant to impress me, it didn't. I dislike the suburbs. Too much went down for me as a child out there and I want nothing to do with anything further than walking distance from the city centre.

We eventually ended up in Box Hill. He had made the decision for us. He hadn't asked.

We parked at the front of a house with a tall portico, and walked in through a small foyer. A huge abstract oil painting was leaning against the wall opposite the door. It took up the whole wall. Purples and yellows. Very modern.

As he led me through the house, we went past his office. Another statement piece. This time a mirror, again sitting on the floor, just propped against the wall. It looked temporary.
The desk had organised piles of papers and files and a black Asian inspired bookshelf full of folders. There was an entire red leather lounge suite in there, and a kimono draped across the back of the couch. It had a pole through the sleeves and was clearly waiting to be hung. The floor had several blue prints and architectural draft papers strewn carefully in a line, along the floor.
To the side of us was a living room. It seemed to have mismatching furniture. Brown tables, grey modular lounge, black shelves. I'm very visual. It seemed odd.

He was in front, holding my hand, carefully leading me up a small flight of three stairs. As we reached the landing, as if he could read my thoughts, he said casually.

"Most of this furniture came with the house. My stuff is still in storage waiting for the penthouse in Camberwell to be finished. It's meant to be complete and I'm sick of being here. This is a short term rental that I took when we rushed back from the Whitsundays, and then with all the illness and going back to Massachusetts, well I just never focused on moving forward. My life has been in a holding pattern for so long.
My stuff is the modern bits. I brought those paintings, with me, thinking that I would hang them, but they are way too big for here. My last place, in Malvern was somewhat larger. Nothing fits or suits this place. It's ok. It's just a transition, like everything unpleasant, it will pass. I'll return them to the storage unit one day."

That explained that, then.

I acted as if I hadn't noticed anything except to say.

"Yes I think those book shelves are Ikea. Oliver had a white one in his room."

"Maybe? Pretty much everything down to the crockery and cookware came with the house."

He turned me to face him and slid his hand under my hair, cupping the nape of my neck, pulling me into his body. His other hand purposefully and forcefully slid across my waist and back, finishing across my bottom, grinding me into him. He stroked my jaw, with his thumb, as his tongue gently explored my mouth. He caressed my lips with slow sensual licks.
He literally picked me up and carried me up the stairs, across another landing and into the bedroom.

He lowered me carefully on to the bed and with passionate kisses, began to undress me. Literally worshipping my body as each inch was uncovered. He was a big man and as I undid his buttons and slid his shirt off, was surprised to see a full sleeve tattoo on one arm and a half sleeve on the other. His biceps were huge, nearly as big as my thigh.

With his fingers twisted gently in my hair. We slowly made love. It was gentle, caring, loving. He was tender, and considerate. At just over 6 feet, he had enough strength and height to lift me where he wanted, and he did. He was powerful and totally in control. He flipped me into positions and as much as he was forceful and demanding, his hands were incredibly gentle yet firm. He knew what he was doing. This wasn't average sex. It was years of experience. He took his time. My inner calf, the curve of my back, the top of my thigh, the nape of my neck. Kissing, licking, touching everywhere. I was equally curious and reciprocated in kind. He ensured I finished and then he climaxed and rolled onto his back pulling me into towards his chest.

He blissfully groaned as he enveloped me with his muscular arms, maneuvering me into his body and wrapping my leg across his. I nuzzled my head onto his chest, across his large shoulder, smelling the sweat on his neck.

"You fit perfectly Princess, I knew you would." He took a deep, satisfied breath and kissed me on my forehead, and fell asleep.

# Chapter 14

I woke in the morning to an empty bed and lay there feeling awkward. Do I get up? Where is he? How long should I wait?

I could hear noises downstairs. He was talking. I waited till it was silent again, got up, put my clothes on, and tentatively made my way down to the kitchen. He was in front of the sink, washing a dish. I could smell toast and eggs. He had eaten without me. Strange.

He asked what I wanted for breakfast and I explained that I only drank coffee. He came around the bench and kissed me good morning and then led me into the kitchen. He then showed me where everything was and stopped at the expresso machine. "And this is how this works." He pressed knobs and showed me where the cups were hidden. "I want you to treat this as your own Katherine. Like this is your home. It will be."

My head freaked. I need my coffee. Sane people don't say stuff like that.

He moved me back to the other side of the kitchen bench and pulled out a stool. I drank my coffee and chatted, while he cooked me a breakfast of bacon and eggs.

"Katherine I am successful because I trust my instincts. You and I are going to work. You will realise. It's not crazy. It's just how it's going to be. I meant it. Treat this house as your own. Go on up and have a shower and we can go spend the day in a park."

He escorted me upstairs, and showed me through the walk in wardrobe into the ensuite.

"If you need anything; deodorant, hair ties, just go through these drawers. Use what you want."

He opened two drawers and they were full of expensive girl products. Creams, perfumes.

Red flag. Aw crap. I felt the let down. Had to be something wrong.

"I've been single a long time Katherine. Sometimes shit gets left behind. Some of it's from the boy's girlfriends. It's nothing. If there's something you like, then please use it or just take it home. Anything you want.

I didn't say anything. I was stunned. Then I felt my nose scrunch and in my typical, 'no filter response,' I blurted. "Yeah I'm not sure I feel comfortable about that. I think it's not quite right." I was aware I needed a shower and would require something to keep my hair dry.

"If it bothers you, I'll get rid of it. I want you to be happy with me, Katherine. Meantime it's there and you don't have anything with you because last night sort of, just happened, unplanned."

He left me with a fresh towel. I showered, looking like I was practicing yoga. Leaning forward, and then leaning back, to avoid getting my hair wet. I stepped out to to dry myself and casually glanced into the bedroom.
Ooh, that doesn't feel right.
He had changed the sheets and the doona was folded, airing, at the end of the bed. I could feel the red flags. I could visualize signaling a time out to myself.

I was literally just pulling on my skirt from last night when he walked in, kissed me and picked up my towel. He was talking as he turned towards the door.

"It's a beautiful day, Princess, which park?"

I followed him down the stairs. "I think Fitzroy Gardens would be nice, but really anywhere with a newspaper and coffee will be perfect."

We were heading to the back door, but he stopped off as he passed the laundry, threw my towel in the washing machine with his and flicked it on. The kitchen was spotless. Ok, he's a neat freak.

Not such a bad thing. My old place was immaculate. I understand that. I am a minimalist and everything has it's place. I started telling myself off, for being so quick to always look for an excuse to be out before anything begins.

Turn off the freak flag. He is more a unicorn by the hour.

We had spent the entire day together, lying in the sun on a picnic rug, just reading and chatting and enjoying a perfect Fitzroy coffee. We went to my place and grabbed some more clothes.

"Princess, bring enough to see you through till Monday."

Apparently I was staying over. I grabbed hair ties, deodorant toothbrush and clothes. We went out for local Italian. Thank god, I have a beautiful wardrobe. I had something appropriate to wear, scrunched in the corner of the over night bag. That little black dress gives me a cleavage I do not own, with an elegant maxi dress flowing from under the bust line. It's simple and elegant, and crush proof. I've had it 20 years.

The next day the stuff in the bathroom drawer was gone. - Good!

That second night was like we had been together for years. He had kissed me on my forehead, down the side of my face and along my jaw line. We were standing at the foot of the bed and he slowly turned me around, lifting the dress over my head. He gently pushed me on to the bed and lay on top of me, his trousers already undone.

He was focused on his task several times. Wow. It was everything.
Hot, passionate, seductive, powerful, gentle rough, hard, slow, fast pounding, grinding but at all times loving. I was happy and impressed I got to cum while he was on top of me, but I was shocked that over the course of two hours, he had just managed to achieve back to back sex and cum three times. This age appropriate thing may not be so bad. He lay sprawled on the bed beside me, panting. His body glistening with sweat.

"OMG. OMG. I have never done that. Never fucked, cum and stayed hard, fucked again and cum again. What was that? OMG perfect. Even when I was younger I've never done that."

He was out of breath and pulled me closer. He kissed my forehead. In my head I was impressed. That was good sex. We work well together.

"Have you ever experienced anything like that? The world is still moving. Oh, Princess. Ooh my GOD."

I didn't answer, it wasn't in my interest. He fell asleep wrapping me around him.

# Chapter 15

We became instantly inseparable. Socializing with friends, cozying on the couch, going out for romantic dinners and making time for steamy sex. His desire was insatiable. Constant and animalistic. The more he got of me, the more he needed. His desire was extreme.

"Katherine, you are like a drug to me. I literally can't get enough of you. I have never felt this way before. What have you done to me? I have never been able to cum this much before. You are like heroin. You are my heroin. I am so addicted to you. Have you heard the band, Goldfrapp? Their song, 'Number one.' He sang. "You're my favorite moment. That's how you make me feel."

Dating Paul brought a passion and zest for life that I don't think I had ever seen in another man before. It was an instant buzz of activity. Never still. He took to leaving work early, and ensuring he made the most of any free time I had. He wanted to pamper me and in return, be pampered back. He sucked in every nuance of attention. It was a fresh romance and everything was how it should be. Perfect, attentive, happy and loving.

Because he wanted to be with me as much as possible, we spent all our time at his house. His office was there, it was easier for him, and as he was the busier of the two, with so much more responsibility, it seemed sensible and convenient. He drove me to and from work every day and kept offering the use of the Maserati, which I continued to refuse.

"You'll have to drive it at some point if we keep seeing each other. I have some very busy weeks coming up and you need to be able to get from my place to work. Katherine, it's just a car. A meaningless piece of metal unless you use it. I was meant to have sold it, but I am keeping it, because I know you will change your mind."

It hadn't caused an issue, but it meant that within the first week of seeing him, he had gone off to work and left me in his house alone. He came home and was so excited to find me cooking dinner.

He came around the kitchen bench and hugged me tightly. He had tears in his eyes.

"Thank you Princess. I don't remember the last time, someone cared enough about me to cook dinner."

I was shocked at how moved he was over a meal. We had to eat something.

"Baby, why is the house so cold? Didn't you put the heater on?" He had pulled back from me, taking on board that I was draped in one of his jumpers, which engulfed me.

I had been cold to my bones, earlier in the day, but cooking had started to thaw me.

"I didn't know where the control was and I didn't want to go snooping. So I just grabbed this off the airer because I could see it." I pointed to the end of the kitchen bench near the couch.

"Oh baby, I know you haven't gone through anything. You're not that sort of girl. I trust you ,or I wouldn't leave you in my house. I know the risk I take if you wanted to rifle through my things. There's a lot of confidential papers I store here, but I know to my core, that you haven't.

However, the heater is different. You should make yourself at home. Please treat this as yours. The laundry, lounge, kitchen, cars, it all for you to use. I want you to be in this house with me, so you need to be comfortable, ok? As for the heater, the control is here." He walked over and showed me how to use it and then showed me where the DVDs were and how to use his Foxtel. Finishing his tour with the overstocked chest freezer in the garage. "I cook in bulk and freeze it, for when I'm eating alone, bachelor style, infront of the TV. Feel free to eat what you want from it."

I noted the neat hand written labels. He is a hard act to follow. A better house wife than most.

He immediately took to waiting for me in the reception area of the shop, every day, so he could take me back to his house. I was happy to let him go do his own thing, but all he wanted to do, was me. So he dropped me off in the morning and picked me up in the evening. I'd suggest he go catch up with his friends and he would look hurt.

"Katherine, let's enjoy this now. My friends will be there later. Being with you, is no inconvenience. I want to see you. I want to make you happy.

Seeing you smile makes my day. Let me do this for you. Surely staying at my house is nicer than yours. Don't you want to be with me?"

I had no come back. Why wouldn't I want to be with him? He was easy to be around. He made me melt.

He met a fair few of my clients and girlfriends this way by sitting in the foyer.

They love, love, loved him. He was forming his own little fan club.

It was one of these afternoons, that he met Louise, a client, come girlfriend, of 5 years. I was finishing in the back room, and I could hear them introduce each other and start to chat. She was telling him about how she was an accounting business analyst, but she was more interested in the fact Paul had a building company. Louise had sold her home and settlement was imminent. She was looking at purchasing an old house and knocking it down. He was recommending designers.

The next day, she texted me.

"I was pretty impressed with Paul. He seems like a genuine business man. I loved his ideas. Would you recommend him for our building project and would you mind if we used him."

I texted back.

"I believe he is well respected within the industry and I'd be happy for you to use him."

She and her lovely husband, Darren, were excited and met with him the following week. She told me later, that the way Paul spoke about me, had them both in tears.

"Katherine, that man loves you so much. He aches for you. He wishes you would hurry up and believe him. I get that it is quick, but he has fallen head over heels with you. Sometimes people just know, and he knows. I mean, to make Darren well up, over Paul waxing lyrical about you. That's a feat. He went on and on about how much he adores you. It was beautiful."

Oh, and we are going with him for the build. He made us an awfully good deal. I think because he loves you so much. We are getting top of the range options at the base rate, so thank you for facilitating us getting together. We had such a lovely afternoon with him.

Not that we had any reservations, but he even told us about his previous girlfriend, and how she died of leukemia. It was hard to listen to, but it was good to talk to someone who has gone through what we are dealing with right now with Charlotte. Hearing him be so open and honest with us about how he coped, and the journey, and then finding you, well it cinched the deal."

My heart bled a little as she spoke about it. The pain of watching your own child slowly die of cancer would be heart breaking. Permanently.

I admired her strength, and her amazing ray of sunshine attitude to life. I was glad Paul had been able to give a bit of comfort. Apparently he had described the painful, slow process of her death, but then focused on the healing.

He'd told them. "You can get through it, by focusing on her whilst she is alive. Celebrate not mourn. Then you have to honor their memory by taking what you can from their life, and use it to help move forward."

I was grateful that he had met Louise and Darren. He was entrenching himself in my friend circle, and looking after them. Doing this was showing everyone, not just me, what calibre of man he was.

# Chapter 16

Things were happening so fast. It had taken months to finally get together, and suddenly I was on this speeding train. The universe was determined to embed him in my life. Within a fortnight of dating, he accidentally met Oiver. Something I wasn't happy about, at all.

There they were in the reception area of my shop and Ollie was openly talking to this man about the challenges of being so young and trying to live independently out of home. Obviously they had introduced themselves in such a manner, that Oliver decided he was acceptable, and Paul knew he was my son.
They were chatting like friends. I was caught up in the back room of the shop, but from the sounds, I could tell Ollie had taken possession of the receptionist's chair and Paul was comfortably ensconced on the couch. I was with a client and try as I did to finish as quickly as possible, by the time I got out there, they had organised a date, to go looking at motor bikes together, with Paul offering to buy him one, if they found a suitable replacement for Ollie's current bike.

I was horrified.

When I came out to the reception area, Paul excused us and we walked outside. He explained. "Katherine, do you realise Oliver is currently driving a death trap?" He went on to explain how many things were wrong with Ollie's current motorbike and that he couldn't live with himself if he died on the road.

I would now look like the meanest mother in the whole world if I took this offer off the table, and had to acquiesce. I went back inside, while Paul finished his cigarette.

"Ollie, don't abuse this man's generosity ok? I haven't even started to date him. There's a lot of water to get under the bridge yet."

Ollie looked at me wisely. "Mum, as if he is actually going to buy me a bike. I just figure, I'll get a day out looking at dream machines with someone who used to have a bike shop."

"Really? I didn't know that." So much to this man. He has literally done everything.

But when they returned from the trip a couple of weeks later, my son had a new bike, and Paul had arranged to pay his rent for 6 months. Again, I was aghast.

"Paul, you just can't go doing that sort of stuff. You have to talk to me first. I'm not in a position to undo what you have offered and now done, because I'm not letting you make me look like a cow. But, no more."

"Katherine. He needs some help. He needs to be able to breathe and settle into all the pressures of being an adult. Let me give him the chance to save some money and get a step ahead of the game. He has gone through so much. I won't notice it. It's all good. Even if it doesn't work out between you and I, it's something I'd like to do. He's a really good kid. He is a great young man, who is trying to be a good adult. Let me help. You should be proud."

Later Oliver and Sarah popped into the shop discussing the pros and cons of renting a new apartment from Paul when he finished a multi home development in Fawkner, around the corner from where they currently lived. Paul had offered a substantially subsidized rent for the three bedroom apartment at the back. They were not leaping at the offer, but taking their time and seriously weighing it all up. They didn't want to get involved in a complicated situation, if he and I broke up. I totally understood. My mind was still reeling over the fact Paul had offered a solution to them, again without talking it through with me first.

Paul just wanted everyone happy and if he could fix something he would, with or without my permission or knowledge. As I was learning, this often involved him spending money, which made me extremely uncomfortable.

"Princess, it makes me happy to see you happy. It's my job to make you happy. When Oliver is happy, you are happy. So let it be. Let me help Oliver. My actions have made all of us happy."

# Chapter 17

Dating this man was exhausting.

There was no 'stop' button. He was go, go, go all the time. Up for his early morning run. Then showered, dressed, meetings, dinners, socializing, clubs, drinking, dancing, Sex, sex and more sex. Laughter, friends, business calls, more business calls, jokes, more work. More sex, bed. Four hours sleep and it's on again. I prefer my ten hours deep comatose rest.
He stopped for no one. He controlled everything around him, except me.

"Commit to me, Katherine. Be mine. Princess, when are you going to realise how good I am for you? I'm falling in love with you, when are you going to catch up?"

In all honesty he could be like a girl. Constantly needing reassurance.
Bloody high maintenance, hard work. I called him a Vagina. I called him that to his face. He was a pussy.

"One of us has to be Katherine. It's not good to be made of concrete."

From the moment I met him, he was determined to make me his. He wanted to crack through my walls and see my marshmallow. I awarded him an elephant stamp and an A+ for effort. It was constant. Drip, drip drip. He never let it go.

I tried to explain using an analogy.

"Paul, we are like a book. So far we are in the same novel, but at present, even though we know each other, we are still in different chapters. Just wait. Before the end of the story we should be on the same page. The same paragraph. Let the story unfold. I promise if you can be patient our names will be together, forever, in the last sentence."

But there was no holding his enthusiasm and optimism at bay. I had been seeing him three weeks and we had been at home around the dining table eating dinner, casually chatting about our day, when he suddenly put his hand on top of mine.

"I would like to get married on a beach."

My head jerked up. "What? Well, good luck with that."

Unfazed he continued. "Here."

He showed me pictures of paradise on his phone. Idyllic huts over crystal, clear water. Several of him scuba diving with sharks. He flicked past some pictures of three hot, topless, young girls on a boat, another thin young busty thing, luxuriously sprawled across the seats at the back and a silhouette of a girl cart wheeling as the sun set on a beach. I felt the irrational ping of unfounded jealousy and as quickly dismissed it. I wasn't jealous of him being with them. I was jealous of their perfect bodies. I presumed the honey haired one, was his last girlfriend. Erk! Now I have an image. He stopped to show me another perfect beach shot of pristine sand and coconut trees swaying down to greet the lapping water.

"Bora Bora, you know I have been there before. It is beautiful. Can't you imagine marrying on the crystal white sand and then walking off to your honeymoon at the end of that board walk? Just a small group of friends. I could fly them up. We could all stay together, and then they can leave and we would stay. From there we could travel for a while. I'd think it would maybe cost just shy of $500,000.

I looked at him."Well, no actually. I need to marry in a church and it's beyond crazy talking about it. It's way too soon, even for jokes. It's bordering on offensive and demeaning the importance, and wow, you have given this way too much thought."

"Yes, but if we were to talk about it? It's something I want, Katherine. To be married again. It's important to me. I thought that's what you were looking for."

"Yes, I suppose in the grand scheme, I am, but my answer would still be, No. Not a beach. And it's not an appropriate discussion of now."

"Ok I can compromise. How about we get married on the beach and then in the church?"

"Again Paul, no. You only get married once."

I looked at him.

"You know what I mean. You can only be married once, at a time.

So no. I'm not getting married on a beach first. Then it would be just a blessing in the church. Sorry, if I ever get married again, I'd ideally want it to be in my church at St Michael's. Then you can have a blessing on the beach at Bora Bora with all your friends. However, since you brought it up, if that place holds some significance with another woman, then it would obviously be out as a wedding destination."

He looked down and then back at me. There was a hesitation in his eyes.

I looked back down at my food, so he couldn't read my thought. Who ever she was and whenever it was, that works out for me. I don't want a beach wedding anyhow. I couldn't imagine getting married without wearing gorgeous heels. Oh my god, I just got caught up in his crazy fantasies.

"So, we can finish dinner in the real world now?" I laughed at him and told him he lived in his own crazy Paul, alternate, parallel universe.

"Katherine I know things. At some point you will understand what we have here is special. It's unique, and awesome, and I need you in my life. You are part of my life plan. Our mutual destinies need each other, and if you don't believe that, then I'm prepared to swear on the lives of my children. The future destiny of my life, depends on you being in it."

"At some point, you will realise you are just talking crazy. Let's just settle and take our time. No rush. There is no reason to be on speed dial all the time. Enjoy the journey. Please."

We had finished dinner and he chose a chick flick. "Runaway bride." God, he never gives up. Hahaha, yes, yes, very funny.

# Chapter 18

My head pounds me back to reality as something heavy smacks into the back window of the shop. It scares me and my heart races. Whatever it was hasn't broken the glass, but it was big, and it's unlikely to be accidental. I literally don't have the strength to investigate further. My mind is trying to be alert and focus, but all I managed was to be sick again. At least I forgot about the window, to sick to care, I curled up inside of my black sanctuary. I reluctantly stretch my arm out, holding the edge of the blanket so I don't feel the cold as I search the floor for more tablets. I bring them and the glass, which was sitting beside me, in under the safety of the blanket. Darkness is my home. I do not want to leave it.

He was always so passionate, driven and demanding with everything he did, regardless of whether it was contracts, clients, sex, friends, dinners, reservations, contractors, his opinions. He made decisions decisively and quickly. He wanted more of everything.

"Katherine I got to where I am, by trusting my instincts. They are never wrong."

He had "known instantly" that I was the one, and my slower more hesitant nature frustrated him.

"I am just aware of more things than you, Katherine. I know you are more than perfect for me. My plans include you and if you would just love me back, you'll find that I'm more than perfect for you. I know that you can make all my dreams come true.
But, I feel like you are making me hunt you. When the time is right, I want you to be able to look back on this, and know you chose me out of your own volition. That I was your choice. I don't want to drag you into this. Eventually, you will see, we were destined to meet. It's as if I knew you, before I even met you. We will have wonderful lives. You just need to feel it. I can't wait forever though. Souls know each other Katherine. Ours know each other. Why are you not understanding? What has happened in your past that you trust your inner self so little?"

That struck a chord and I felt guilty, for it wasn't the first time I had been accused of not wanting to commit and I definitely had ghosts haunting the back of my mind. Doesn't everyone?

It was hard to argue with him. Those pale blue eyes, his endearing smile, the genuine warmth and charismatic manner that ensured everyone acquiesced. He was used to getting his way and I was never sure if it was purely because he had always been so ridiculously good looking or whether it was because he was so powerful in his own world.

Regarding affairs of the heart, I am by nature, reticent and whenever I tried to press the go slow pedals of his control, he would literally burst with frustration. Even though it was clear I hurt him, I couldn't stop my need to objectify our relationship and rationalize his over the top emotional intensity as crazy infatuation. It was all too much, too soon. It defied my logic. I just didn't want to feel that exposed and reliant on another person for my own happiness. I was not going to leap in.

"Paul, passion is great, it's just not reliable. You know that love is technically a chemical inbalance in our brain. It's why, when we break up it feels like we are withdrawing from an addiction. So just chill. I do not feel like going through that painful process when you suddenly leave me bereft and confused after you lose this intense interest in me. It's not sustainable."

"God, you're so annoying, Katherine." Feel here, he would say holding his chest, not here. Thumping his head.

"Paul, just slow down. There's no hurry. It's a journey. Enjoy our "now." Please stop rushing towards an imagined tomorrow. Get to know each other's everything in the present."

"I am the one living in the present Katherine. You can't see the forest for the trees. I am waiting here, in front of you, so we can have a future together. The sooner you realise and jump on board, the sooner our life can begin."

The frustration over such a stupid issue, way too soon. Neither wanted to see the other's point of view.

"It takes time, Paul. I think love is complicated if it's to last. The perfect combination of meshing individuals together. It's the blending of practicalities, habits, histories and chemistry which given time form a balancing act, creating long term happiness and contentment.
To know love, you need to see the full cycle of each other. You need to know each other's truth. Rose tinted glasses get scratched. Falling in love in

an instant, only happens when someone has a deep void they are trying to fill with someone else's being. Because they feel too little for themselves that they can't fill the void on their own. It's irrational hope and emotional desperation poured into a stranger. What burns fast, dies quick.'

He hated it. He just wanted to feel the passion and rush to the finish line, logic out the window.

Regardless, his enthusiasm for life and for me, was hard to fight. I felt like I denied it for ages and it surprises me, looking back now, at how quickly I actually succumbed to his love. So much seemed to happen in such a short space of time. It was dizzying. Even my friends were telling me to get on the Paul wagon, and I would tell them to all slow down. Everyone was on his side.

He was so full on about being in love: that I was the one. He was so vocal to everyone. He'd tell me that he was successful from identifying the right products, the right deals, the right markets and trusting his gut.

"Katherine, your instinct, that first reaction, is the correct one. So stop stalling. Stop fighting us. It's wasting our time. I'm awesome, We are awesome. When are you going to realise, so we can get on with things, rather than pondering the long term implications of what will happen if it doesn't work out.
It's working now. In the present. Stop living in the past and future. Live for now. Feel for now. It's all we have. Live in the now so we can have the future we deserve."

Sometimes being with him was like attending a personal growth seminar.

And he wanted to help me with the situation with the shop. He begged.

"You're my little Katastrophe sent for me to look after. Talk to me. Sometimes problems are just disguised opportunities, like giving both of Di's boys jobs. Some things are just easy to address and often it's mutually beneficial to let someone help.
Princess, you have the government payout coming which will be based on your turnover amongst other things, so ideally you should be ramping the business up, not allowing the slow process to bully and beat your business down. Get some staff back, run a spectacular special and re book those clients."

I must have looked horrified. It was the last thing I wanted to do. I just wanted to plod along as it was. It had been a long few years and I was tired.

Internally exhausted and running on air. If Paul hadn't been in my life, I would be taking it easy until the shop was closed. I had no more fight. Having Paul in my life didn't and shouldn't change that.

"Seriously, Katherine you know you will definitely get $250,000. Surely for another 100, you would do anything. A couple more months of hard work. Aren't they meant to finalise their offer based on your figures provided in August? So if it's end of April now, that isn't a very big commitment is it? You're being silly and lazy. $350,000 is life changing. That's how much you could get. Don't look a gift horse in the mouth."

God. I remembered, I had literally just sold equipment because many of the staff had left under the pressure of uncertainty which the impending tunnel project had put on the business and their job security. My plan was to just plod along as best I could until the bulldozers arrived with a small bag of money.

He read my mind.

'I know how you feel and appreciate that you were down sizing, but you aren't seeing the bigger picture. You let the events of the past exhaust you instead of continuing to soldier through.
Look, here's what I'll do, because I want to see this money in the bank. I'll be disappointed if you don't get a payout of at least a quarter of a million. Imagine what you can do with it. So, I will buy everything you need to repurchase stock etc. Just give me the list. I'll even pay for the extra staff member, because at the end of the day, I have to admit to an ulterior motive. If you have staff again, then you can go away with me. As you have seen, I need to travel, and I want to go away for weekends and mini breaks and at present we can't. So stop being difficult. You're still trying to road block our relationship and your own success. Ok? The problem is easily solved, and I want to take you on a small holiday soon."

He always needed to fix things. He couldn't help it.

"What about my furniture? It's stored in the back room here. It's just too much to re-organise. Let it slide. Money isn't everything."

"Princess, there is a storage company literally across the road. You can see it through the window from your shop."

"Yes." I had replied somewhat sulkily.

"Ok, it's settled. On the weekend I will get the boys from the Byron St project to come over here and load your stuff and move it all into a storage unit."

God another expense. No. I didn't want this.

"Stop fighting logic. I'm trying to make life better. I'm offering to pay your new staff member, and the storage fee, and I'll purchase everything you need to ensure you get the biggest payout that you can be entitled to. OK? Let me help you. I know you want to do everything your way and on your own and you will. I won't be in here working with you. I'm paying a little bit out now for the better good. Once you get the payout, you can do what you want. It would be yours to use and that would make you feel in control and not reliant on my money. I won't ask you to do anything else. But money is money and this is a life changing sum."

"What can I say? You seem to have thought it all out, but I need a break so badly Paul. Honestly I can't keep pushing myself. You don't understand you weren't here for what I have gone through. I'm bouncing from Ollie being on the show, and the house being sold, me moving twice, the shop opening, the shop being bulldozed, and then dating you. I just don't have the energy to face it. I need to recharge and breathe for a second."

"I know, Princess, but I'm here now. I want to take care of you. Why don't you make an appointment with the solicitors and I'll come. If I take all that pressure off you, then you don't need to be worrying about the payout or making ends meet. I have your back and I'll make sure those lazy lawyers of yours get off their arses and look after you. Alright? What if I take over the negotiation? I can answer all their frustrating questions and keep control of them so they stop upsetting you. Use me as a buffer between you and them. Would that help?"

"Yes, Thank you." In truth I wanted to burst into tears.

He leant back on the couch, pulling out a slip of paper from his suit pocket. He handed it to me.

Two confirmation E tickets to Fiji. Flying out June 17th. In just over four weeks.

I looked at him. "You were pretty confident this would go your way, weren't you."

"Of course, my precious Katastrophe, I alway know the outcome before I begin."

Bizarrely as Paul had said would happen, the universe provided the solution. A girl walked in, and offered her services early the next week. She had met me a few weeks earlier, when she did my lashes at a competitor's salon, and now she was asking for a job. Fate.

Paul negotiated a contract with her and the next week, Joy began working as a self employed contractor. I immediately started running new specials and bringing fresh business in the door again. I was suddenly working 10 hour days, six days a week and taking paper work home. Paul was proud. I only needed to buy one massage table. I managed to make do with everything else that I still had.

The boys and Oliver moved my personal belongings into the storage unit, literally across the road. It all worked out smoothly, just as Paul had said.

# Chapter 19

Lying, curled under the blankets aware of the acrid smell of vomit, I can't make my brain make sense of how I got to be in this situation. Paul and I had such a wonderful future. We were insanely happy. How can the universe have turned it into such a nightmare? Why does someone want to kill me? I'm grieving and confused and so sick, I have to shut my eyes and roll over. I'm still nauseous and the memories flicker in my head like a damaged film roll, flashing before my eyes, bright and garish; psychedelic, then soft and smooth. I want everything to be still. I try to force sleep by re living our life together.

There was the night of the BBQ at his house, in May. Before we were perfect. While I was being difficult and not leaping blindly into love.

He wanted me to meet his friends and family, and for my friends to meet him. We invited so many people, I couldn't imagine where they were going to stand, but it had become a mute point, as he had broken up with me two nights before because I wouldn't rush into a relationship, and therefore he could see it was a waste of everyone's time to meet. Apparently I had commitment issues, and the rest, I heard through a filter of blah, blah. I always stop listening after the initial, 'I think we should stop seeing each other' part. The rest is just noise.

I'm angry remembering this night. The breakup. It started because I served him a cup of coffee in the morning, in a "yummy mummy" mug, that I found in his kitchen cupboard. I was aware, that I was experiencing the emotion of jealousy and I didn't like it. I'd been in a relationship before, where I was in that green eyed state constantly. It took years for me to learn, that I just needed to leave to be happy. I suppose I did think the cup was odd, and ugly, so maybe I had wanted him to explain why it was in there. I could have chosen the other more offensive pink one that said. 'Princess' in a heart. I was trying to be subtle. I got the reaction I sought. He had scrunched his nose and reminded me, that everything in the house was part of the fully furnished deal and if I didn't like it, just throw it out. "Look around, do you think any of this is mine. The guy who owns the house must have a partner who is a 'yummy mummy.' I don't know, I've never met them." He had scoffed and laughed, looking disparagingly across the living room. "I've told you, my stuff is in storage. I'm going to the unit this week, if you want to join me, and then, if you see something you want there, we can bring it back." Then he followed it with a reminder not to go sabotaging relationships by looking for trouble. "Katherine, what we have is pretty perfect, don't go looking for ways to wreck it. Just throw it out. Seriously." He had scowled at me, and I felt the scold.

We then spent the day wandering down Chapel Street and we popped into see his lawyer friend, Randy, in Queen Street, for a quick meeting. I sat in the foyer and could hear Paul talking through the wall. We had then gone for a leisurely lunch down at Southbank, but he had got increasingly agitated throughout the day, cumulating in driving me home, to his house from a restaurant near mine, and having him escalate the situation of my mere curiosity over a mug, to huge international scandalous proportions. I was confused.

He raised his voice at me, That I was looking for an out. "If you want to go, just leave." "I can't keep trying to convince you that I'm awesome. I am." I can't believe you treat me with such disdain. Everyday, I show you how much I adore you. It's exhausting being with someone with only a toe in the relationship." "If you don't want to be with me, because you want to be fucking half of Melbourne, then go. It's not my thing." "I'm looking for commitment and undying love and devotion. Katherine, I want to be happy." "Of course, there are odd things in the house. The only stuff in the house that is mine is in the office and my wardrobe, and yes if you go snooping, there maybe still things lurking in the back of a cupboard, long forgotten. Stuff that I haven't even thought of in years. Kids' stuff, and girlfriend stuff. Katherine, there is nothing that has any significance. I didn't know I was going to meet you, and I didn't know that when I did, that you'd want me to remove all evidence that I had had a life before you, but don't compound that innocent laziness to clear everything out, with junk that isn't even mine. I get the ridiculous insinuation with the coffee mug this morning. It was crazy. You were looking for drama. There's only one mother to my children, and thats Maggie, and clearly we haven't been together for half a lifetime. Katherine, if you find something you don't like, just shove it in a cupboard."

I sat there at the kitchen bench, looking at my feet. His words were washing over me. Apparently this morning was now being intermixed back to the bathroom cosmetics in the drawer, from the first night I stayed over. Glad I'd never mentioned the shabby chic decor items, with the words, "Love you Princess" carved in them. Not my style, and not my Princess. These were the remnants of an old relationship. Either his or the owners. I wasn't sure, and apparently I shouldn't care. Yes, finding them around the house irked me, but I had actually never commented. And now being reminded that they were not even his, I was glad, I'd kept my mouth shut.

It made me uncomfortable, but at the end of the day, I have some less personal decor items from boyfriends, that I still keep, and I knew there was no sentiment attached, I just liked the pieces. But in his house, I felt like I was a shadow. It wasn't my home. There were a lot of furniture and decorative things throughout the house, that weren't my style, but it wasn't my place, so it wasn't my concern.

He didn't leave me much room to answer back, and I was too baffled to enter the fight over something that should have been dropped after this mornings conversation. I couldn't see how he had converted it to this ugly fight. He told me to leave, and made me pack everything of mine into bags. I had to call a taxi and then spent the night in the back of the shop, confused and embarrassed, that I had to un-invite my friends from the party.

The morning of the BBQ, he had messaged and apologized. Apparently 'his head told him one thing, but his heart another.' He was sorry for pushing me away and asked if I could still come. "Katherine, you have to grow up though. Stop trying to find issues. I want to be with the wonderful you. The happy, gregarious, loving you. Please stop trying to rationalise affairs of the heart. I'm putting in such effort, but you are exhausting me. We are good together. End of story. The rest will sort itself out, if you let it."

It was a strange evening. I was walking on egg shells when I first arrived, having to fly up and have a shower, and brush my hair, having left my bathroom things at his house. He greeted me with a passionate make up kiss, just as Ollie walked in the door. There were so many young people there, mostly his workers and their girlfriends, and they spent the majority of the night outside smoking, or on the couch with the music channel blaring. I was introduced to all of them: His sons, Andrew and John, then a collection of youth: Tony, Kara, Aaron, Jordan, Liv, John, Liz, Vicky, the list went on. I knew Ash and Sam, my girlfriend's boys.

His brother, David, and Anna, kept to themselves and were responsible for the food, which quietly upset me, as it should have, and would have, been my responsibility. There was also a somewhat rough looking man; 'Haggard,' would perhaps be a more apt description, whom Paul had grown up with. Paul went on to be a success, and his friend clearly took a more easily walked route through adulthood. His girlfriend had plied on way too much fake everything and scared me. Thankfully, I had forgotten to un-invite a few of my friends, so they were already there, oblivious to the previous nights' debacle. Oscar and my girlfriends, Louise, and Di, with her two boys, who were now working for Paul. It was a motley collection of humanity.

My friends reminded me, that I shouldn't mess it up with Paul. He was clearly besotted with me, and I had a track record of avoiding relationships. Infact, I generally chose the biggest loser to try to make a relationship with. This, obviously all being true, I had no defense. I was in the wrong and needed to grow up and stop playing games. I got it. I promised Oscar, I'd try harder, and told Louise that I would try to be less sensitive. Di pointed out that successful men generally won't tolerate being messed around. At the end of the day, the world is his oyster, and he could literally have anyone he wanted. I should consider myself blessed that he wanted me.

I took it all on board and tried to mingle with the strangers and not be needy.

Ollie and Sarah were there only an hour, before he pulled me aside. "Mum, you don't belong here. This is the antithesis of everything you are. You hate tattoos, beer drinkers and suburbia. Look around mum. It doesn't make sense. It's like a work party for his apprentices. Where are his friends? None, of the few he has here, have a shred of class. That woman's tits are hanging out of her dress. What is she? A retired Saint Kilda St hooker? And his kids. Seriously, they are bogan born and bred. It's like they are from the northern Suburbs. Mum, they are the sort of shits who used to beat the crap out of me. We are going to go. It's freaking us both out. I can't put my finger on what's going on, but something's not kosher. Sorry, but we don't feel comfortable."

I was gutted that Ollie felt that way, even though I knew it to be true. There were more tattooed arms and legs in the room than I had seen in Bali nightclubs.
I didn't want to be judging as a snob, but Paul's friend did look like a drug addict, and his girlfriend did indeed look like a hooker. They knew the same places as Di, having grown up in the area, and thankfully spent the night reminiscing with Paul. Louise stayed, chatting to everyone, even though the smoking was choking her, and Oscar just stood quietly, propping a wall up. Watching.

I remember, bizarrely at one point, Di had brought up the subject of my small breasts. I had said maybe I should get a boob job, and Paul had not defended me, but instead said DD's or E would be perfect. His son, Andrew, leant across the bench and laughing said. "Well, it wouldn't be the first pair you bought, would it, you old cunt."

I literally didn't know what to do with the whole situation. None of it. When Louise and Oscar said good bye, I felt stranded, and was enormously relieved when everyone else finally left.

Paul took me up to bed, leaving Andrew to sleep on the couch downstairs. John drove back to his mum's. Once in bed Paul explained that Andrew had always preferred the couch, even as a child, and that had he wanted, he could have gone to bed in his room upstairs. Then he explained the bizarre friend situation that was apparent to Louise, Oscar, Ollie and myself.

"None of my close friends were here tonight. I wasn't going to let myself be embarrassed. What's the point of having my close friends here to meet you, if we have broken up? Katherine, of course I uninvited my family. That's just a waste of their time. As for the kids, well, who cares. I let them all still come over, eat the food and drink the beer. It's good for the morale at work. You know I take them out all the time. No point putting out the wine. It's all in the garage still. Sorry if you felt a bit uncomfortable. I didn't think you would judge them. I'm a bit surprised to be honest. I like keeping things real. Hanging with people that are salt of the earth, blue collar workers, it's good for your soul. Don't be a snob. I expect more from you. You of all people shouldn't judge, you have been poorer than most."

All I could do was agree. But silently I thought. Being poor doesn't mean you have any less class, than being rich means you have it. I knew today wasn't the day to raise esoteric arguments so I kept quiet. I was going to try harder to be in a relationship with a normal, successful, human being.

Erghhhh. Now I'm reliving the frustrations of us settling into perfect. I had to learn to curb my bad habits, formed from living by myself for so long. I rolled over, dry retching and groping for a hand towel from the drawer beside me, to wipe a pool of sweat that had formed between my breasts and in my belly button. I threw the blankets off, and lay there spread eagle like on the mattress, my legs dangling over the edge. I had to pull my head back and arch my back to get enough oxygen. What the fuck is wrong with me? I should be in hospital.

I woke some time later, freezing and aching. I was shivering. I pulled the blankets over me, using the last of my strength and lay there, now too sick to try to get any tablets. This was now misery in the extreme, and my shut eyes flashed purples and red, with sparks of yellow. I could find no peace in this reality, and quickly took myself back to Paul.

# Chapter 20

I remember, we were in his car, heading out to have dinner with friends and there was an awkwardness in the air between us. Unspoken confusions.

While I was getting ready, I had been looking for a hair drier, and had inadvertently, just found some long, thick, dark brown hair extensions in the bathroom. This was not the owners. And this was way too personal. This was not a cup, or the tacky letters spelling out the word LOVE, that sat on the bookshelf. Now I was torn.

When my furniture was put in storage, Paul had personally moved all of my clothes that he approved of, into his house. We had gone through my wardrobe together deciding what stayed and what went into storage. Up until then, even though I had slept there every night since that first night at Easter, I had still hustled my belongings subtly between the two places. I knew it annoyed him and inconvenienced me, but I was being realistic. You don't rush that sort of commitment. Especially me. He had shown me the empty drawers that I could use and then he hung everything on hangers, himself, whilst I had sat at his feet and put my shoes and lingerie away. He had officially asked me to move in when he had picked me up from work a few days after Joy started working with me. 'It didn't make sense juggling my belongings' and to him it was a natural progression because he knew we were going to work out. To me, he was always in a rush. To him, I was just stalling our happiness of being together.

Now a mere week later, after unpacking and moving me physically in, and we were nearly ready to go out when he said, the weather just turned, and it would be best if I wore my new cream and black coat. He was right. I had a silver, backless dress and strappy stilettos on. Clearly not much warmth. Paul had asked for my hair to be up, to accent the long delicate diamond drop earrings, that he had showered me with, after the BBQ debacle. In search of the coat, I went upstairs and flicked through my clothes, which were now neatly hanging up opposite his. Taking up less than 5 feet of space, but it represented a sense of belonging. This is going to work.

I calmly exhaled. I am safe. I am wanted. My being relaxed and felt soothed. That sense of calm lasted less than a heart beat.

A flicker from the corner of my eye. A glance to the right. A different kind of deep breath. The one where the air doesn't come back out. I shook my head a bit to clear it.
Next to my new clothes... Are you serious?

Seriously?

Another woman's clothes. I felt sick. How had I not noticed, walking through here every day to have a shower? In my defense, why would I have thought to look, but now in front of me, for a foot and a half from the far wall, there was someone else's clothes. Girls clothes. Whose? His? A woman's? Confused, I got my coat and scarf, and looked around me. There was material draped over boxes on the top shelf. I quickly pulled back a sneaky corner and thought I could see the triangle shape of a bikini top with an American flag print. What the hell? Don't make a scene, Katherine.

I didn't want to raise the issue before dinner with my friends. I didn't want them thinking I had failed with Paul, and I knew this was going to be the end. Obviously the man had another woman and I was going to have to break up with him. I was never going to be just an extra in my own life story.

I had just gone into the ensuite and was taking a moment to check my make up in the bathroom. Really, I was stalling, giving myself a pep talk.

Brace yourself, put on a smile and cloak your feelings with a cling film of dignity. Go out with your friends. Do not ask him whose they are. For the moment you do, no matter what the answer, you know you will have to leave.

I was pretending to adjust the lipstick in the corner of my mouth, when on cue, he appeared from beside me, walking through the door.

I began to turn.

He stopped me. "No. Look." He gently guided me to face the mirror again.

I wondered what I was about to watch.

He lifted his hands together, above my head and now lowered them in front of me. He was standing against my body, looking at our reflection. He slowly pulled his hands apart. Between them, hung a stunning diamond necklace.

I gasped, and then needing to make light of his dramatic gesture, and a bit to sting him, for what I had just found.

"Cubic Zirconia?" I queried.

As he put it around my neck, gently doing up the clasp, he leant in and kissed my neck.

"Hardly. You are my everything. My world. Without you I don't breathe. You are worth it. Treasure this as much as I treasure you."

I was overwhelmed. Not a diamond ring. A ring of diamonds.

"Paul, It's too much."

"Don't you like it? I want you to alway sparkle, so when I saw it, I just had to get it. Princess, you are more precious to me than this. I want you to know how much I love you. Please never take it off, then I will always be with you."

I thanked him profusely. I felt so ridiculously spoilt. I was constantly over whelmed by his actions.

It was as if he had known what I had just found and how hurt I was. The necklace felt like a telepathic apology gift. It was inordinately bad timing. I received it with a heavy heart. Did he have a girlfriend, a fiance, a wife, was he separated, going through a break up, a bonk buddy? Was I filling in? Who and where was she? Interstate? Obviously I had been in this house since the first night. 25th of April, the week after Easter and there was literally no opportunity for him to be entertaining another woman. Do I have to contemplate them being his? I didn't get it. Has this relationship got a pre ordained end date?

We were backing down the drive when he started.

"Katherine, we need to talk. Seriously, You are avoiding me. Do you know what it's like for me at present? I want you to show me your marshmallow and stop this concrete facade. I want to see your softness, your weaknesses, your truth and vulnerabilities.

Katherine look at me please. I know you don't like looking at peoples' faces, but look at me. I'm trying to tell you that I'm falling in love with you. I am in love with you and you can't even look at me.

If you can just let yourself go, we will be amazing. We will be awesome. What is wrong with you. I'm awesome. I'm amazing. Why aren't you falling in love with me? Seriously, why can't you see what everyone else sees?"

I remember, I continued to stare across his face and out his side window and I was thinking that I wasn't going to be falling in love because I was seeing something that no one else was seeing. I was extremely uncomfortable. He was genuinely angry. His frustrations with my sensible, non committing attitude had already over flowed.

Is he raising his voice at me in the car, demanding I love him after four weeks?? Seriously??? A month, man, seriously not rational.
And, what? You're in love with me? My mind was a whirlwind of confused thoughts. Flattered, dumbfounded, bewildered. and really pissed off that there was girl stuff in his house. I knew I had to ask the question as to whose.

"You're right, Paul, I am uncomfortable with this conversation. I'm not ready to have it. Can I look away now?"

"Yes."

"Thank you." I turned my head back to stare blindly out the window.

As we drove through stationery traffic slowly towards the restaurant, the tension was mounting and I felt the need to disperse it before reaching our guests and my friends, who had only recently unleashed their disappointment in me. I didn't want to give them ammunition for a failed relationship with the man they had all fallen in love with. Not tonight. Not publicly.

"Paul, Paul? I'm sorry. I'm not used to this."

"What? A man who knows his own mind?"

"Yes, well maybe. I'm just not used to rushing. Sometimes there are roadblocks that need to be worked through and I just like to analyse and see things rationally."

"There is nothing rational about feelings of the heart, Katherine. They aren't even located in the same area of your body.
Brain for thinking.
Heart for feeling.

You should just let yourself feel for a change. You know, you will come to realise you are safe with me. I promise to protect you as long as you are by my side. I will love you like no other. Trust me. You just have to let me."

I sat silent. My inner dialogue churning. 'Yes, well, my heart is feeling, and my brain is not stupid.' I kept silent.

His phone pinged and he glanced at it. "I give up, that's all my side out for the night."

We were meant to be having some of our friends and a few close clients, finally all meet, but apparently it was just my side left.

I had known that George and Bill, both clients of Paul's, and whom I hadn't met yet, were under enormous pressures staying on top of their progress payments to Paul for their constructions, and had tactfully declined the invitation. Paul's brother and new wife were busy, but I had already met them and we were having dinner again later that week. One or two of my friends couldn't make it as well, but that still left a large group to party on into the night with. I was no longer looking forward to the night but had to save face.

He was growling. "Belinda is plain unreliable. I'd already predicted her not turning up. Gerry's kid is sick so they can't make it. Sorry, I was going to tell you, but then you had that meltdown in the car before and I forgot. Now Janine can't make it either. Her message says. 'Sorry can't make it. Another time. Maybe when you're free. Xx' Apparently there's a bit of jealousy. I'm surprised because I didn't think she was like that but, maybe she thought there was a chance. We've never been together: bit too large for my liking. I wouldn't do that to you: invite exes, especially since most of my previous girlfriends were models, and I wouldn't want you to feel insecure."

Cheap shot because he was still hurting over my lack of illogical commitment.

"Interesting. Paul, just so you know. If you are friends with your exes, I expect it's because they are lovely people and therefore they will be nice to me and if they don't want to be nice to me or accepting, then they probably aren't so nice in general and you should probably not be seeing them anyway. However, in regard to feeling insecure. I value my worth by what's on my inside. Not any outer beauty."

"Oh god, Katherine. I've had a shitty day, I'm just disappointed. I had wanted you to start meeting my friends. You can't meet my parents, as much as they want to, because the four of them are still away. The only people you have met is my brother Dave and Anna, and they had hangovers so it hardly counts, and I don't understand why you can't just have faith that I know what we are doing. Just trust me and leap."

"I'm sorry you are disappointed too. I wanted you to have a lovely night with everyone, but it can still be wonderful. You can talk about cars with Oscar, and Di already loves you because you employed her boys. How's it working out with them? Thank you for doing that for my friend. For giving them the opportunity to work. They needed the break, and it has allowed her the opportunity to take a breath. I'm really grateful that you have given her the chance to relax and feel that things might finally work out."

"I did it for you, Princess, not your friend and not for Ash or Sam. I have created job opportunities and it's now up to them to prove their worth to the company. They need to justify their existence in the business to make their wage viable."

Success. I had changed the topic and by the time we got to dinner, he was his normal happy self again. I was going to get through tonight without being humiliated and I would deal with the girl stuff afterwards.

# Chapter 21

After a long night pretend partying, we had returned to his house. He was happy and I was exhausted from light chit chat and enthusiastically dancing whilst my head ran over and over what I had just found in the bedroom.

I sat on the couch, looking at the carpet. "Paul, tonight you said you loved me." He came and sat beside me, instantly attentive. "But there are logical reasons to take your time and get to know someone. For instance as much as you professed your devotion to me earlier, unfortunately I think I am not the only one."

"What are you talking about?"

"Well, there's a wardrobe of girl's clothes, and brown hair extensions stored at the back of the cupboard under the vanity. I have never snooped, so I don't know what else there is, but to be honest, I feel the need to leave."

"Oh my God, Katherine. They're Brooklin's."

"Brooklin?"

"I can't believe you want to get upset about that stuff. I didn't even realise there was anything left."

"Who is Brooklin?"

"What do you mean, who is Brooklin? My girlfriend who died. You knew that. It's her stuff. I'm sorry if it bothers you. Bit heartless. I'll deal with it though, Ok? I hadn't even thought about it. Princess, don't think the wrong things. Sometimes guys are slow. There's only you. Give me a day and I'll sort it."

I was shocked. He had never used her name before and I'd never noticed. "Paul, you have never mentioned her name until just then and I was under the belief it was 8 years ago. Leaving things like that around for such a long time, seems to be a pretty big indicator that you haven't dealt with everything. In fact, quite the opposite."

"Don't be crazy. I admit, it seems ages ago in the sense that I have totally moved on. Obviously because I'm with you now, but in reality, it's only been, a year. She died last April 25th. You know I try not to talk about it with people. It's morose. I don't know where you got your time frame from. I've had a few girls here since then and none of them have had issues with it. I just never needed to deal with it."

I felt a slap in my head and my heart. Only a year? I am in a threesome of sorts. I slept with you the first time, on the first anniversary of her death. I felt creeped out. It didn't seem right. Breaking a rule. I'm sure he said 8 years. What? How can that be? Am I a rebound?

"What, Katherine, what are you having trouble with?" He looked genuinely confused. A reflection of my own befuddlement.

"I'm just surprised that's all. I didn't know this was the situation. I'm not quite sure how to handle it, and now I feel like I am suddenly moving into someone else's territory."

"Katherine, I think it's harsh that you demand I get rid of my past. You have photos of your ex on your side board. You're actually being exceptionally childish and selfish.

"Paul I don't want to fight, but for the record that photo is of Jess with Oliver and he has been in Ollie's life since he was 5. It would be churlish for me to get rid of it. I have no ill will and I'm not asking you to get rid of anything. I think it should have been done before you invited me or any girl that you want a future with, to be with you. This process should be nothing to do with any new girl and it definitely should be done separate to me. I don't want to know about it or have anything to do with the issue of you moving forward. I think it best if I go and let you sort yourself out. If you are ever really free then contact me. Sorry."

"So because I don't have a child with her, I have to remove all traces of the relationship? I can see you aren't coping. Obviously I have to eradicate all evidence of a past life, even though you knew about it and you have pretended to be understanding. Sure, I'll get rid of my past and yet I have to live with the daily battle of yours. When are you going to address your past?"

"I'm not sure what you are talking about Paul? I just don't want to be involved in a relationship with three people. It's a rule."

"She is dead!

"Perhaps, but, really, she is still here and that's just not my thing. Sorry."

"Katherine you are literally doing what everyone says you would do. Sabotaging what is best for you. You're so damaged Katherine. You haven't dealt with your past. The rape. You never went to counseling and that's why you get into relationships with all those young guys like Phil."

"What are you talking about?" His words had stung me.

"Don't deny it Katherine, Here." He was rapidly scrolling through his phone, clearly looking for something. "Here. Read it. It's a text from Di."

He handed me his phone which I took, still in disbelief that he had known of both the incident from my childhood, and separately, Phil's name.

*"She is emotionally stunted. The rape when she was thirteen froze her development. She never got over it. Didn't get help. It's why she dates younger guys like Phil. He is only a bit older than Ash. They offer nothing but physical. She thinks they will marry her. Stupid. Wastes her time. We tell her. She is scared of real relationships and the troubles you have been having with her are typical. She always sabotages anything good."*

I had read the text. Now I was just pretending to still read it, as I gathered my thoughts. 'So Di and he have been messaging about me, behind my back. Why would either of them do that? I helped her boys get jobs.' I'm shocked. She mentions some serious stuff here. 'How dare she. What a total betrayal. Why would she have done that, and why had Paul felt the need to ask her questions in the first place?'

I looked up. I could feel my knee caps twitching, and my fingers were visibly shaking. I folded my hands together and placed them on my knees. One ankle folded in front of the other. I tried to relax. Being tense makes the shakes worse. I didn't want him to notice.

The night had gone in an unanticipated direction, and I was suddenly on the defensive. My heart was pounding behind my sternum. I could feel the pulse in my throat and my fingers were tingling. There was a loud buzz in my right ear. I'm not crazy. This is an acute stress reaction. I live with it. I deal with it. I am not my past. I am not the future. I am the present, the very now of the combination of everything I have ever experienced. I am strong.

"Paul. I am going to need you to really hear me.

Firstly, I'll probably never speak to Di again after that betrayal. It's really not her place to have spoken about any of that.

Secondly, when you both so casually drop the pert sentence, "She was raped" It is just that. To you, it's three little words. You think it conveys something but it's just a highlight sentence, like "he is an arse." It merely labels one facet about someone who could be many other things. He could also be a good father, a dentist, a runner, an old man, an author. You are both using those three little words as an excuse, a hook for blame, an explanation as to an area of my current accused behavior. You want to find a reason for me not leaping into a relationship and freely saying I love you.

But to me, that highlight sentence, opens a pandoras box that I keep locked with the biggest antique bronze padlock in my head. The key is kept separate. That lid is best kept shut. For me, it's the flash reminder of infinite definitive moments, frozen in time. The smells, sensations, it's fear, it's questions, it's actions, it's inactions. It is details of the minutiae. And the incessant spinning record of innocent why? The myriad of questions. Trying to find justice. Realizing there is none. Of trying not to attribute meaning to my life because of the random act of someone else. To fight the memory of one experience which you and Di, now wish to use to define all of me.

Well, fuck that Paul! It is an event. It's the past. It's done.

The details so casually dredged up took seconds for you and Di to invoke and will take days and weeks for me to pack back into that safe chest. It's my personal nightmare, I'd like the prerogative to chose when it's ugly fingers try to drag me back into the filthy black pit of hopelessness. It's no one else's right to ever bring it up, let alone try to use it against me."

"Katherine, don't kid yourself. If you'd dealt with it, then you wouldn't have these issues with commitment and you wouldn't have an imaginary locked chest of memories, in your head."

"For the record, Paul, I have spent a lot of time and money on counseling. I had to because for a long time no one else knew and I had no support. When my mother found out years later, she slapped my face.

Perhaps Di didn't know that. Shame.

You know what, though? I felt better when I wasn't going to psychologists. I moved forward when I decided to think about helping other people and stop thinking about my past. I do not deny I sometimes have random flash backs. I do physically recoil from a memory in my head, and I see my own hand physically raise in real life to defend myself. I get it. They are my personal nightmares in the day time. It is what it is.
I choose to ignore it. It goes away. Don't feed the dog and all that.

I have a lot of theories and one is - it isn't true unless you speak it out loud. That kept me safe for a long time.
Secondly: All things pass. Eventually, what you think is going to kill you, doesn't bother you so much. With time and distance, an objectivity comes and with that an opportunity to look at the pain from a distance. I often ask my clients when they are heart broken and depressed over a break up, to tell me the name of their first love. Some of them can't even remember their name. I ask. Can you still feel how much in love you were? They all say no, but that they know they were. They can describe it but not feel it. I then ask, can you feel the pain of that break up still? They all say no, but they can remember it hurt. Voila. Things happen. At the time it feels life changing, sometimes for the good, sometimes for the bad. Regardless time heals everything. You can accept and step over what you understand.

Right now I'm caught off guard, that I am having to justify myself. I'm trying not to be angry, so I can talk, but while you two have been chit chatting behind my back, you both got this wrong. Your ignorance of what actually happened years ago and how I chose to handle it has prevented you from seeing the truth of the situation.

The rape was not my weakness then, and it is definitely not my weakness now. No, it is now part of my armour. It is a strength. It's as much a part of me as my skin grafts.

Those experiences, make me a more compassionate and understanding person. I'm not bitter and fucked up. I choose not to relive the blah details but rather focus on the choice of doing good and offering words of comfort to others who are struggling with their self worth due to similar experiences. I pride myself on trying to live a life of doing no harm to others and try desperately hard to be a good person filled with love.

As for my past being the reason for not leaping crazily into commitment. Only an empty person does that. I am not empty. I'm quite happy with my life. My messy, little life is ok. I do not have a void to fill urgently. I was getting to know you. I honestly do not understand why Di, you and some of my other friends, have not realised I have only been seeing you for a month. 4 weeks. 28 days. I'm being the sane one."

In my head, I acknowledged it felt like a life time but that was not the point and certainly not something I was going to share. Nor was it going to interrupt my argument.

"Finally, as to dating younger guys. I'm 48 years old. 50% of the dating pool IS younger than me.
My defense may condemn me but I'm going to say it anyway. I dated men before I met you. And I would like to think that anyone I formed any type of relationship, friendship or more are in my life, was because they are lovely decent people with a mutual respect not because I'm damaged goods."

I had probably finished my rant anyway, but Paul butted in.

"I don't think so Katherine. I believe this is not the attitude of a mature balanced person. I think you have serious issues and it's probably best as you said, for you to leave."

I had sat the entire time, my stomach pulling me forward, closer to my knees. I had felt paralysed up to this point, but now I was so angry. I could feel my left eye twitch. I forced myself to get up.

"Take the car. I'm not heartless. This is your choice. Your doing."

I didn't really care whose doing. I needed to leave. I was violated on so many levels. My skin was crawling and I had goose bumps. The hair on the back of my neck was sending shivers down my spine.

I felt like a robot as I moved. It took all my inner reserves to make my body respond. Just do it. Don't look back. Handbag in hand, I walked to the door, he turned the TV on and spat his final shot.

"So you are allowed to live with past ghosts in your head, but lose it at me for not removing a few items from my past that I didn't even notice were still in my house."

I didn't stop. I walked out the door.

# Chapter 22

I got in the car and slowly drove a few blocks before pulling over. I texted my good friend Steve. He had been out with us and it was now 3am. Who else was going to have a spare room and be awake?

"Can I come over?"

"Sure. Everything ok?"

"Not really."

"Lola is at her mum's. You can use her room if you need it."

"Ok."

It took 20 minutes to get to Steve's and when I arrived, I realised, that I had only ever picked him up from outside of his apartment building. I parked and texted.

"Haha. How do I get in?" I was probably still a bit drunk.

He came out to get me. He was genuinely concerned. "So what's happened?"

We went out onto his front balcony so I could smoke. There were two glasses and a bottle of red.

"Thought we may need it." He smiled at me. I love Steve, in the best most practical, bro' love way. My phone began pinging texts. They were from Paul. I wasn't in the mood to look.

I gave Steve the abridged version. "Paul still has dead girlfriend stuff in the house. Her name is Brooklin. She only died a year ago. It got nasty. Di has been messaging him and told him about Phil and some really personal things from my past."

Steve knows pretty much everything about my life, he knows my truths and sees me warts and all. I didn't need to go into all the gory details.

"Katherine, can I ask why you didn't tell him that stuff yourself?"

"Ah huh. Because people misconstrue things to their own advantage. Like now. Like, this is the perfect example of someone using an awful incident in my past to blame my current 'inexcusable' behavior. Yep I'm guilty as charged, Steve. I'm guilty of being rational and not leaping into "love." Putting myself in a situation where someone can hurt me emotionally, isn't my preference. We need look no further than tonight to understand why."

"Why would they be texting?" He was genuinely perplexed.

"I don't know, I really don't. Maybe Paul is more insecure than I thought."

"Do you think she is jealous? Is she making moves on him?"

"Steve, I really don't know. I'm trying to get my head around a few things to be honest."

We were finishing our first glass when his land line rang.

He went inside and answered it, and returned a few seconds later. He was talking to someone.

"No, she can't drive. If that's what you want, you can come and get the car. It's here, but, she's had some wine on top of everything we were already drinking tonight, and is in no state to drive your car."

He was mouthing silently to me. "PAUL." Then he was talking to the phone again. "Seriously, we are just friends. She is here because she's upset and you know there's not a bedroom in the shop anymore." Silence and then he said. " Look, it's between you two. Yep, sure. Do you have a pen? Oh, ok, we'll see you shortly then."

He hung up, walked over to me and picked up my mobile phone, opening the balcony door, he threw both into the centre of the lounge room and shut the door. Sitting down opposite me, he leant back in his chair and sculled the last of the little that was left in his glass.

"That was Paul, Katherine. He rang on my private landline that no one knows I have. My mother in England uses it. How did he get my number?"

"I don't know."

"More to the point, he has my address."

"Steve, I don't even know your address. I had to phone you from downstairs. Look my car is parked way down the end of the road."

"Well, he is coming to get the Maserati. Is there anything in it, because we will need to clear it out."

We went down and began to check the car for anything I had left inside. Steve was lifting the boot up. Instead he took a few step back and motioned me. He was staring at the number plate.

"Bet that hurts." Steve looked at me surprised and comprehending.
I joined him.

"BCPC"

I scrunched my nose as I took it in. I had only ever viewed it as a silver car. I'd never needed to know it's number plate and even if I had looked, I didn't know her name to even create what was now obvious. "Yep. Yep. Well, it makes sense now. I'm driving their dream. Their future goals. To be Brooklin Carter and Paul Carter. BCPC, Aw god, yuk and ewwwww. I'm so right. He hasn't let go of her."

"Wow, Katherine, WOOWW, and very ewwww. He always said he was completely over her and so focused on you. Why keep the number plates all this time?"

We emptied the car of my belongings and returned upstairs. The phone rang again.

Steve went inside and then left through the front door. A few minutes later he was back with me on the balcony.

"Paul was out the front. He just wanted the keys."

"Interesting turn of events. It's a bit dramatic don't you think? I am right though. I'll never be a third wheel. It's against my rules.
God Steve, here I am angry over a dead girl's belongings and he is acting like I have no right. Then he chooses her anyway. Ironically, it only proves why I stick to my rules. I think I was the rebound for a dead girl."

Steve was focusing on me intently. "It's certainly an unusual reason to break up, but you're right, if he was over her, he would have got rid of her stuff by now, even if it was only a year ago. Especially since he was in relationships with those other girls. I thought she died ages ago, too. He's certainly packed the girls in then, hasn't he. Ha! Didn't he tell us stories about traveling across America with a Canadian, and dating an Asian girl just before Christmas. Oh and Giselle, the model just after this Christmas. You remember, he told us that he gave her a laptop, and the boys from his work had to go pick it up, and he gave it to Oliver to use. Remember?"

"Yeah, Ollie gave it back to Paul because it was so heavily pass word protected. I know. This means he dated those three and me in less than a year. Is that right?"

"I thought they had been spread over 8 years. Seriously how did we get that so messed up? He told me when we were at the Long room so maybe I just misheard and when you said it, I thought that made sense. Whatever, right now though, I'm more concerned that he knew my number and my address. How did he find out so fast?"

I looked at him. "I don't know. I remember he once told me he had eyes everywhere, but that was more in the context of him being a well known business man. Something about a lot of people know him and do him favors, so I was to be aware of how I conducted myself in public to ensure I didn't do anything to damage his image by association. That sort of thing.
He once told me his last girlfriend, Giselle, went out and got drunk. Started kissing a guy in a club. A friend saw and called him. He broke up with her immediately. He told me as a warning that if I ever do anything he will find out. 'I have eyes everywhere Katherine.'"

"Do we really know who he is and what he does for a living?"

"Ha, I know right. Sometimes I wonder if he is a world class spy like the James Bond he would like to be, but, no, he's just a normal guy with dead girl issues and I have a girl friend who betrayed me by telling him things which he has used against me."

"I don't know Katherine. I'm confused as to how he got my number, and he was at the car, not the house. But in the meantime, he wants you to go get your stuff from his house tomorrow at 11 so I'll come and help. Let's just get this done."

I stayed in Lola's room, feeling awkward and embarrassed. The next morning we headed back to Paul's place and found all my belongings neatly folded in boxes outside the front door. Both of Paul's cars were in the drive.

We took everything left for me, and were doing our seat belts up to leave, when I asked Steve to give me two seconds.

"Don't make a scene, Katherine."

"No, it's all good Steve. I just need to return the necklace. I was with him because I thought he was wonderful, not for this stuff and I'm more a gold girl anyway. Can you help undo the clasp, it's impossible."

He leant in and eventually managed to remove it.

I pressed the buzzer at the front door, and heard Paul fumble with the locks. He opened the door and stood there defiantly. I handed him the necklace and his face visually crumpled into an ashamed sadness. Deal with it, I thought, and I turned and walked away.

Steve drove me to the shop and helped me unload my belongings. He wasn't happy about anything and nor was I.

"You deserve better than this."

"I'll be fine. Just lost to a dead girl. Sort of like a zombie movie where they never really die."

We laughed and he drove off, leaving me to settle in before work the next day.

It wasn't really funny. It was devastating. I was falling in love with this man, but on principle I needed to leave.

# Chapter 23

But, now I'm lying on a mattress, curled in a ball shivering with the flu and I'm remembering when I left Paul to voluntarily stay in the shop. I roll over, coughing phlegm and stare through unfocused eyes at the legs of the massage table. My present is blurry and shimmers. The back of my head aches and I can't get warm. I try to scrunch the blanket around me, but find I don't have the strength to grip it. My fingers are curled in towards my palms, rigid, like I've had a stroke. I can't make them move. I don't understand why. I'm sure I have actually been going in and out of consciousness, and feel that it's highly likely, I may die in this shop. No one knows I'm here, except the hitman. Irony.

Stupid memories. Stupid fights, stupid friends, wonderful friends, stupid me. I shouldn't have involved anyone. That whole week was embarrassing, but I need to remember everything, because up to now, as I relive it, what have I come up with?

He had a weather worn friend who had clearly lived a hard life, and a persistent preference to have everything his way on his time schedule. He was OCD about household order, and was utterly the boss of everything in his life.

One of my friends was betraying me, maybe trying to back door me, but that's my issue not Paul's. We'd just fought over something that was from my past, and the topic itself is more ugly than the fight. Again that was my fault not his.

He had a dead girlfriend, and I'd obviously misunderstood the time frame, which changed a few things. You can't really expect someone to have moved on completely within a year, but I didn't want to be around while anyone was still emotionally entangled with their past. Again this was my issue.

He was generous to my son, my friends and myself. In truth I was spoilt in a manner, I thought only existed in the lives of real Princesses.

As for Paul, well he was right as usual. We were perfect together. We were each other's everything, I just wasn't as quick to realise. I was sabotaging what was lovely, because I had misunderstood when she had died, maybe I was literally just not handling the amount of changes and speed everything was happening.

So far no one I met is red flagging the future events. Except me. So far, as Paul was constantly pointing out, I am the only problem.

But as I lie here with a death threat hanging over my head, I have to acknowledge, that it isn't true. This hasn't happened because of me. Just keep remembering. There must have been more signs. I know I will find the truth. I will understand how this happened.

I shut my eyes and retreated to memories of Paul. It's hard. This is a love story gone wrong, or so it seemed at the time of the fight. Lying here full of the flu, feeling like I am dying, conscious time no longer has any meaning, I'm aware that when you add the word hitman to any story, it is no longer just a love story. So what happened?

I willed myself back to the night of the argument. Back to me leaving Paul because of a dead girlfriend's clothes.

The next day I spent moving the shop around to accommodate me sleeping there, without disrupting work or have it noticed by the staff. I was also fighting with myself. I knew what I should do. Stay away, but I was pining for Paul.

Feeling miserable I phoned John and declined joining my friends for dinner. I told him that I had broken up with Paul. He already knew, which surprised me, but he explained that Paul had phoned Di and told her what happened, and Di insisted Paul still come out for dinner with them. Me not coming, would make things easier. They had wondered how they were going to manage with both of us at the table.

Well this is awkward. It hurt. A lot. It hurt that they would contemplate doing this. They had known Paul for a month, and me for ten years. The inner dialogue reminded me. 'Well, you are a loser, and he is definitely life's winner. Of course everyone would prefer his company. You aren't even in the race.' I missed him, and understood the attraction everyone felt to be around him. I was gutted at the turn of events.

My moral compass was failing, and I was contemplating contacting him and trying to sort it out. I was also trying to play the why game with myself, which had the inevitable result of just making me horrendously miserable, so I posted to my friends.

*Facebookers, Advice needed. My girlfriend found girls clothes and make up in her boyfriends house. The defense is its from a relationship that ended a year ago. What do we think?*

I knew no one, except Steve, would presume it was referring to me. As far as the rest of the world knew, I was in dating Nirvana and we had all thought Paul's girlfriend had died 8 years ago, so there was no reason to think it was me. I also expected everyone to give moral, sound advice. My friends are solid and sensible. Publicly I was surprised at the outpouring and I felt encouraged to be high horse principled as usual, even anonymously, and it gave me strength to stay away. Then I received two separate, private messages, which shook me to my core. Apparently I was also losing friends.

From Di, whose boys were still happily working for Paul.

*"U post one sided stories on FB to get support. Negative and destructive I won't be told who I can chose as friends. Paul is a good person and I wont dump either on a one sided opinion or be made to choose.*
*U only see yr. side & argue u r never wrong. Yr FB posts are viral*
*U r self destructive and continue to make bad choices."*

Wow. Yep guilty. I was referring to Paul. Um, not guilty about asking for any one to side. I was asking for advice, and some friends gave it privately, even when they thought it was about someone else. No one posted publicly presuming it was Paul, but yes 99% were straight to the point. 'The girl shouldn't stay. The guy has issues he needs to sort.'

I stand by this. It was the right choice. I hadn't said he kicked me out. I just needed help in staying away. If there isn't clearance for a relationship. If you aren't the priority, then leave. Normally for me, it's simple.

I read this message and remembered her cruelty at Easter lunch, and her smutty comment to Paul, which forced my hand to sleep with him earlier than I planned, and her devastating text regarding my past. Followed by the invite to Paul for dinner. Things were not looking good for our friendship, and now, here I was, again betrayed by her. From this point I no longer considered her a loyal friend.

From the same group. This one was worse.

My girlfriend Dee wrote.

*"Kathy the FB blob was appalling I don't know what you hoped to gain. I have seen half truths. I have seen twisted truths to suit your argument regardless how it implicates others U have become unhinged and you need to acknowledge this erratic behavior. If you need to talk I'm here. However I see thru the bravado."*

'Appalling: twisted truths: unhinged.' The words hurt to read but I had publicly asked for advice. This, though, was just personal criticism and I wondered where the link was. Neither addressed my post, just attacked me. These two cruel comments from friends, made me feel even sadder and somewhat isolated.

# Chapter 24

These memories are as ugly as I now feel. But in reliving the amazing good, the romance, the love, the hard times, maybe I will figure out what just happened. I'll piece everything together and understand.

I ache to go back in time. Back to when Paul was with me and we were blissfully in love. Not here alone in this shop, in the dark, feeling sick. Drugged up with cold and flu tablets. My brain foggy, playing this morbid nice cop, bad cop memory game. I don't have the strength to stop it. The images just keep washing over me like an opiate hallucination, the sorcerer's apprentice, the feed just keeps coming and coming. I need my brain to stop. My stomach is churning. I pull myself out of my nest and throw up in the beautician's bottom make up drawer.

Nice! Class act.

Oh god, I am so sick. When I finish, I can feel the sweat beads on my chest. I clean up my eyes and mouth with make up wipes, and reach for the upper drawer where thankfully we keep mints. I shove several in my mouth. They struggle to refresh my breath but I'm too achy to care. I retreat back under the blanket. To the nurturing peace of the past. Am I reminiscing or trying to piece things together?

Leaving him had been hard, but the right thing to do. It was two days later when he finally called.

"I would like to see you. Katherine, there are things that need to be said."

He came to the shop and sat on the couch beside me.

"Katherine, the more I have felt for you the harder it's been. I admit, I have felt guilty, and I was waiting till I knew you were the one. I needed to know you were worth the sacrifice, and every time you got upset over something, I would question whether my feelings were correct. You have to admit, you tend to be a bit irrational, ditzy, even volatile when you're angry or you decide you have been hurt. I hate seeing and hearing you like that. To be honest, that's not what I want in my life."

I sat there taking what seemed like the start of an apology, which had morphed into an insult, on board. My brain silently whirring. 'When? When have I ever lost my temper at you? Whenever something confrontational or hurtful happens, my first course of action is to hang my head and look down at my shoes or the floor. I retreat into my head. I know I have not raised my voice or stormed or made a scene. Me? I am the person who will not be with someone if they make me feel bad, because I don't want to feel rage. You on the other hand, say things because you're messed up about a dead girlfriend, and then apologise later when you realise you have been an ass.' I kept looking down as his words washed over me.

"Katherine, I don't want to make the mistake of falling in love with the wrong person, and then hurting because I must break up as a result of a poor choice. And I don't want you to be the right one, because every day I wake with this panic inside my chest, that you *are* the right one. I panic that you could be taken away and I could fall so deeply in love and then go through that pain of loss again. Princess, I know I couldn't cope with it happening twice. I've just been selfish. I am scared of loving and then losing you, so I subconsciously pushed you away. I know your rules. I knew that I should deal with her stuff, but we are always together and there never seemed to be a time to do it without you noticing, and then I was scared that this exact thing would happen and it did. You got upset over her stuff. Insignificant stuff I had forgotten about.

These past two days without you have been torture, and I realise I need to be with you. You have become my purpose in life.

Please don't romanticize my relationship with her. It was no where near perfect. I thought it was at the time, and the agonizing process of her death, devastated me. It deeply hurt to lose her, but I can look back and realise we weren't right for each other. There were issues. In all honesty, she was with me for the lifestyle I offered. She never did the little things which show you care. You cook for me. You include me in your life. You make effort. She never did. Just swanned around, cutting out pictures of cars, designer clothes and diamond rings. I don't even think she loved me. My God, we fought. We fought so loudly, we used to scream at each other. Looking back

I don't know why I thought it was so good, but at the time, I did. My grandmother wanted me to find someone else. There are things with her you don't know. Trust me, she had a very ferocious and vindictive temperament. You don't understand. I don't want to dwell on it. What am I supposed to say to people? "My dead ex girlfriend was actually a mean spirited, selfish bitch." You just can't go around saying that stuff. Regardless that it's true. I think that's partly why some of her things are lying around, because I just don't care enough to remove them. There is no emotional attachment to them, so I just don't notice them. I'm sorry I have misled you and your friends. Our relationship was no where near good. My family know the truth. Why do you think everyone has welcomed you into my life? Please don't be jealous. You are a million times her as a person.

I love you, and I hate that my inactions have hurt you. I'll sort it all tomorrow, I promise. I have no feelings for her at all. I've told you, after she was gone, I felt this enormous pressure lift off my shoulders, like I was free. Awful to admit, but as much as I was willing to stay and do the right thing, I was genuinely happy when I came back to Melbourne, and was free of the responsibility of her.

Please understand and stay the course with me. We are too wonderful together, to throw it away over pathetic memories. Part of me has been waiting to know that you are worth it. That you are the one. But, I know that now.

When you handed that necklace back, I knew. I knew you truly care for me, not my money. I have never felt like this before. You make me want to be a better man. I don't want to lose you, so please give me a chance to prove it. Don't go running away. You leaving like that, without a care. You didn't even turn around. It gutted me. I haven't slept since you left. I'm miserable. You have become my everything. My future needs you in it. Please talk to me so we can move forward. Start seeing me for who I really am."

"Paul, I do see you for you. Nothing else."

"No, you think I'm perfect and I'm not. Although being with you makes me act like a better person, and I thank you for it, you need to stop making things up in your head."

"Paul, beyond this issue, which I still want nothing to do with, I think you are the most amazing man I have ever met. I am happy with you. I understand and accept that you have a past. Everyone does. I just don't want to live in the shadow of it, or worse, with it."

"She isn't the ghost that haunts my dreams, Katherine. You shouldn't worry about her. She doesn't cross my mind, ever. My nightmares are made of other things. You need to know the real me. The part of me that sometimes thinks of driving off the road and into a concrete pole.

"Like what Paul? Seriously? What have you got to have nightmares about?"

"Well, I think the reason we feel so comfortable with each other, one of the main reasons we feel like soul mates from a lifetime ago is because we have more in common than you know.

Katherine, when you were talking about how your past has impacted you the other night, I wanted to reach out and hold you so much but I couldn't, because I was dealing with my own demons. Yes, you're not the only one. I know what it's like to think you're evil. To think that you are the devil incarnate. I'm sorry you thought my response was in reaction to you. It wasn't. Not really. You brought up things from my past, and I was incapable of dealing with them at the time. I didn't mean to be insensitive. I was just shocked by what you had to say, as I identify with it.

I have never told anyone except my dad, but when I was 11, we had a neighbor in Toorak, who took me in under his wing. He was in his 20's, rich family like ours, and he would take me out fishing, and invite my brother and I over to hang by the pool. My parents trusted him. They let him watch us, if they went out of town and then he did the unthinkable. Katherine, he raped me."

I had sensed where this story was going and as he went into brutal detail, I closed my mind off. I knew I should reach across the small distance, and touch his knee to reassure him, as he regurgitated the pain, the helplessness, the control, the violation, the detailed physical action. Detail by horrendous detail. But, I couldn't. I recoiled. Physically, I subtly removed myself by only centimeters, but I switched my head off. I looked present, but I wasn't. I let his words wash against me, up and over. I knew, my sanity required no reciprocal feelings. No common ground. No opening my past wounds.

I hated listening to it. It wasn't how I handled my own past, I never talk details and it didn't feel right. I let him tell his story. He finished.

"It's why you will see my dad kiss my head so often and tell me he loves me all the time. He feels guilty for not preventing it, and he wants me to know he doesn't think it's my fault. It's weird but it brought him and I closer. We have a special bond that he doesn't have with my brother."

At the end, he had tears streaming down his face. His eyes were blood shot, and he leant in for me to give a reassuring hug, which I allowed.

"Katherine, I think this is just one of those deep reasons, why you and I work. We know each other. Our injuries are the same. Please know I didn't mean to hurt you in any way, and I want you to come home with me. Please. Allow us to work. I think we really are meant for each other. Let me show you how awesome we are. Come back and fall in love."

He leant back, and pulled the diamond necklace out of his pocket. "But first, let me put this back on where it belongs." And he gently did it up around my neck.

"There. Perfect. Please don't ever take it off for anything. It belongs to you. I want you to always have it so you know what you're worth to me. Please."

Aware, that I don't like physicality when I'm hurt or upset, I tried really hard to work through my instinct to recoil. I sat there, not wanting to touch him, or be touched and raged an internal battle, to mimic support. The inner monologue rationalized. 'This is just you being you. Give him the support he needs. Let him make up to you. Your feelings right now aren't what most people feel, so do what they would do. Tomorrow you will want the hugs and touches, so get through the awkwardness of today.'

Logic won, and it felt good to be with him again. To be in his favor. We went home, and he took me out to dinner as a celebration. We went to The Press Club in Flinders St. It was my favourite restaurant.

The maitre de greeted me with a kiss on the cheek. "How is Oliver?"

As we were led to the table, I reassured him that he was doing well. I was aware that since "You're A Star" they had only seen him once. Before that, they had seen him every couple of months for a few years and had somehow adopted him.

Elegant table clothes had, unfortunately, been replaced with modern booths, but the food was literally out of this world.

As we sat down, he ordered a bottle of 1990 Ryas Chateauneuf-du-Pape and put a box in front of me. I opened it. A large shimmering bangle made from an intricate lace work of diamonds. I didn't know what to say. God I wish he had asked if I liked diamonds. Maybe it was his old girlfriend's thing. It's not mine.

"Oh my god, Paul, No."

"I bought it for you when I got the necklace, but now it's a beautiful, expensive apology. It's worth more than the two cars together, so don't lose it. Although if you do, it's insured."

He was putting it on my wrist. Again the clasp was like Fort Knox. There was no chance it could fall off. For all it's delicacy it was cumbersome and ostentatious. It really wasn't my thing. I felt he was confusing me with his dead girlfriend.

"I left the valuation in the box, so don't throw it out. Do you like it? Is my apology accepted?"

"Yes, Paul, but in future, perhaps you can just deal with what you need to do and then you don't need to apologize. And for the record you do not have my permission to bring the topic of my past up. It is not your story. It is mine and it is not necessary to my present or future. If I ever wish to discuss it, then I will. Do you understand that?"

"Yes, Princess, I'm so sorry that Di told me. I said horrible things that were spawned from your friend bad mouthing you. We need to disassociate ourselves from people who are not really our friends. I cannot apologise enough. I know you better than that. You are worth everything to me. You are my future. Everything I want to be happy, requires you to be by my side right now. Thank you. Thank you for coming back.

I ask one thing of you. Well, it's something I want to offer. Whilst we were apart, I spoke to a close friend from Hawaii, Jan, and beyond telling me to go get you back, and that I'm an idiot, she also invited us to visit, which led to the whole 'difficult to get to know my friend situation, with them spread across the globe.' Now I listened to her advice, just like you apparently heed your friends, and Jan suggested we merge our Facebook pages. Because you know it's the most used means of communication between distant friends, and I want you to truly know them before we travel. Then their homes will feel more comfortable when we stay. I'm allowing you to see my whole life. Full transparency, so you feel safe with me. Can we do that when we get home? I'm trying to live an honest and fully open life with you. I'm trying to let you in. Can you meet me half way? As part of us bringing our lives together?"

He looked plaintively at me. "Princess, I have such wondrous plans for us."

What could I say?

That night, he deleted his account, and my page changed from Katherine De Bois to Katherine Paul Carter. As much as I told him he couldn't do that. He laughed. "By the time Facebook allows us to change it to something else of your choice, it will be 3 months down the track, and you will be my wife by then."

Forever on Paul time.

As anticipated it took me silent weeks to shove my nightmares back in their chest, and crush the lid down tight. Long ago, I had discovered the power of the word, "blank". I use it over and over again when unwanted memories, with their elongated black fingers, try to drag me under. When images of past actions flash like reality and make me flinch. Repeating the word "blank" over and over, calmly, and slowly breathing, fills my mind with nothing. I don't stop until I'm in control again.

Unfortunately life doesn't always stop for this, so achieving peace of mind sometimes doesn't happen for days. Shadows lurking in the corners of my mind, physically groping my well being. I do not, and never will, deny the battle of sanity, of battling fear. My body shows the stress, but the reality is, it's a fear of something that can no longer hurt me. It's just a collection of stupid memories.

I now added Paul's past, and his association of evil, to my past, and dumped it inside the chest in my head. I hold no responsibility for what happened to me as a child, and I refuse to let it make me feel bad or impure. I don't want other's opinion of what they don't know, to impact me either.

However, I allowed myself to feel sad for Paul. It was tragic, that he felt bad about himself on such a deep intrinsic level. That he viewed himself as evil. The devil. His true self. It explained his constant desire to prove his worth and ensure everyone liked him.

# Chapter 25

I rolled over, pulling the blankets closer like a cocoon.

Blank
Blank
Blank

I have better memories to think about than that. I know I do. My friends had constantly reminded me of how lucky I was to be loved by this man. They had become his unofficial cheer squad, all trying to convince me to commit and give in to him. Be happy. I knew I was being obstinate. I couldn't help it. I couldn't believe this wonderful man could think I was wonderful too.

Paul was exceptionally attentive over the next few weeks. He realised he had over stepped boundaries and unfortunately he could see the damage. It shitted me that the shakes came back intermittently. I was embarrassed, but I knew to ignore them. They always go away, eventually, and I had Paul. Although a slight sadness now lingered in the back of my head, he went out of his way to prove his love, and remorse for opening my memory chest uninvited.

We had met friends for dinner and I had been embarrassed that he had told them, he had taken me shopping. Not just that, but how much he had spent on buying clothes for me that morning. I was mortified. I'd not felt comfortable with the shopping spree and now it was being broadcast. My favorite part of the morning had been when he produced a mars bar. I was ravenous. From then on I used to tell him.

"I'm happy with the little normal things, Paul. The mars bar moments are what makes me happy."

He had taken me to Witchery, and made a big scene to the sales staff about creating a new wardrobe for me. It sounds like every girls fantasy, but it left a nasty taste in my mouth. He was alway telling me about how his past girlfriends had dragged him into Versace, or how he had surprised his ex with shoes from Jimmy Choos, and here I was in Witchery. Second hand Rose. It wasn't a good feeling. I didn't want him spending money on me, but I also wanted the same treatment as the previous girls. I struggled with it in my head.

Made worse when he held up a cute little outfit and said. "I love that labels don't impress you. That you're not like those other girls and need to be spoilt in those shops."

Inside, I was asking myself, why? Why wouldn't you want to take me into those shops though, if I'm 'The One,' then why aren't I good enough? I felt second rate, and then the self awareness made me feel ashamed and guilty. But the truth is, I think everyone loves to be spoilt, and him wanting to buy me a stunning outfit from Prada or somewhere like that would have made me feel special beyond words, and I would have cherished it. Like silk underwear. No one knows, but you feel extra special. I think the value of being worth a label, was increased because I realised both he and I knew, I wasn't worth it. It was a confusing clash of feelings.

He had spent close to $2000. To me this is a lot of money, but I didn't want my friends to know. It made me feel awkward on many levels.

"Katherine, I can afford to do it. It is a sneeze. If I didn't buy you clothes and shoes, and pamper you, then that would be a problem. You need to stop having issues about my wealth. It's there and I don't want you feeling pressured to spend your money to look how my partner should. OK?"

"Paul, I'm not frightened by your money at all. I just don't wish to discuss it and I don't want it flaunted in front of my friends especially when some of them are struggling to make ends meet at present. They live in the real world like me."

I was aware of how nit picky I was being. I should learn to be grateful. He loved me and was generous with my friends.

But in truth, I did find it hard. The changes to my life, no matter, that they were an improvement; his generosity, him coming into the shop and finding a small invoice from a supplier and just paying it: It was in my face. I oscillated between being offended, protected and loved to insulted. I am my own worst enemy. He was generous. He paid for my friends when we went out, he had taken it upon himself to pay Oliver's rent and his gifts to me were at the least expensive, at worst ostentatious.

Once, early in the relationship, he had left me to pick up a few groceries on Chapel St, and had popped across the road, returning with a new iphone for me.

"Katherine, you can't go around with the broken one anymore. It doesn't look good. You're my little Katastrophe, but the world doesn't need to know. I can't have my partner using a phone like that."

Instead of being completely appreciative, I was internally conflicted. Mine was a new phone and one of the girls in the shop had sent it flying across the marble floor. Sad day, but it still worked. I had put contact over it. Who looks at my phone except friends. I just needed to get the screen replaced. I knew I should just be grateful, but I didn't have money to be carelessly spending on things. I am forever thinking, could that have been spent on something I need instead? This internal monologue always made me feel like a bad person. Just let him do it. He shows his love by giving things. Start being more generous and accepting of how he does things and what makes him happy. It was an issue both of us wanted me to work on.

During this new probationary period that Paul had inflicted on himself, we also celebrated his 48th birthday. It was the 8th of June, and he had a simple request for his present. He wanted to blindfold me. I internally cringed.

So, so sooo pathetically 50 Shades of Grey. Why are men obsessed about this stuff?

"Katherine I can buy myself anything I want. When you go to my warehouse and see everything that I have, you'll fully understand. You don't need to get me anything. Material things hold no interest really, so you buying me something is likely not to impress me, but giving me you, well, that is free, and it is all I want."

I knew I could say no. There was a fair bit inside that was insulted, and for no valid reason, scared. Scared of disappointing him. We had such an amazing sex life now. Constant passion; dining table, kitchen bench, shower, hotels, couch, the landing, and painfully, the floor.

"If that's what you really want."

"Thank you Princess. Can that be on my actual birthdate and then we can celebrate the following weekend with a few friends at Club 23, hows that sound?"

"Sounds lovely."

On the eve of his birthday, he sent me off to a day spa in Richmond because he felt guilty that with all the birthday lunches and dinners he had attended that I was feeling neglected.

I got home to a large brandy glass of tai maria on ice and on the corner of the bed there was a black box with a gold bow wrapped around it. I could see where this was going. Inside was a stunning lace bra and lingerie set. Delicate strings crossed at the hips and the bra reminded me of a beautiful spiders web. Underneath was the obligatory male fantasy. Suspender and stockings. Men are fairly predictable.

I got dressed in the ensuite, glad he had bought a new set for the evening, even though my entire underwear collection took up three drawers and I loved each piece. I had a feeling this one may not survive the night. When I was ready, and I knew I was presenting the image required, stilettos and all, I opened the door. He was still dressed. There was music playing from the bedside table.

"OMG, Princess. Oh, Baby, come here." He reached for my hand and instead of kissing me as I thought, he gently spun me around. "Trust me."

I was glad there was no mirror in front of me, as trust was not what would have been written across my face and then I felt the mask. His arms came over my head as I faced away from him. He pulled it across my eyes and gently pulled my head against his chest. I felt something slide tight around the top of my head and now he pulled carefully at the sides.

"Princess, feel the feathers."

I reached up as he tilted my head and closed a clasp under my jaw. I would have felt panic but he was still there holding me protectively. My hands reached up and I felt the satin mask that encased my whole head. It had feathers above my eyes and sequins. It felt that it looked pretty and delicate. It felt weird.

"Don't speak." He led me to the bed and slowly ravished me. His hands seemed to be everywhere, doing everything. As usual he was insatiable. Hard, fast, slow and tormenting. His hands one second squeezing a breast, the next second smacking my thigh. He alternated positions. He obsessed over things he normally didn't pay to much attention to. He milked my breast constantly, slurping and squeezing. The fact they still did that is crazy and weird and he normally avoided making it happen. He gently tied my hands, untied me, bent me over. Slid me down the bed, flipped me over. If I tried to speak he would just moan at me. He couldn't get enough. Every time I thought he was finished, he just started again. He had never been so loud. He focused on me then him, to the point of selfish, then back to me. He never let me cum, and it felt like it went for hours and hours. I was exhausted.

Finally he fell on top of me and rolled off. He was panting out of breath. "OMG, OMG OMG. Thank you. Thank you. Oh my god. I'm not even in this universe. I am floating. OMG!"

With much exhausted effort and shivers of delayed orgasm blasts, he managed to delicately remove the mask. He dropped it off the side of the bed and wrapped me into him, holding my head against his shoulder.

"Oh Princess, baby, THANK YOU. That was the best present ever. We were asleep in seconds."

In the morning when I awoke it was to an empty house.

There was a note on the kitchen bench beside my phone.

*"Thank you for last night. I'll never ask again but thank you for allowing me to live out a fantasy. I love you with all my heart."*


A few days later we went to celebrate his birthday at Crown Towers. He asked me to wear the new diamond bracelet. We had a scrumptious dinner at Koko's, where he had opened his gift from me. I had asked Oliver to buy a large box of chocolate covered salted caramels, as they were his favorite. Poor Ollie had ridden his motorbike in the rain to ensure they were there waiting at the table as a surprise. Later that night, we randomly bumped into his friend Belinda and a few of her girlfriends. I remember telling my clients about the night, and referring to them as the Katherine Haters Squad. At least I can say I tried, but I obviously wasn't these ladies' cup of tea.

The next day, whilst I was making us coffee, he had phoned Belinda. He ensured that I heard him, tell her, that the girls' behavior the night before hadn't been cool. Neither had hers.

I'm glad he noticed that I couldn't pretend not to see that she had been all over him. It had been awkward.

"I can't be your friend, if you act like that around Katherine. Your girlfriends were jealous and bitchy. It was not acceptable and I'm not sure where it came from. I'm really happy I have found Katherine and I thought you were too, but their attitude is a direct reflection of you. I think we need to reign our friendship in for a while, so I'll call you later. Take care Belinda. I'm really disappointed." He turned to me as he put the phone down. "See Katherine, that's what you do. We are a unit. I don't need friends being difficult and throwing obstacles in our way. I want you and I to focus on our happiness because I know we are perfect together. You have become my principle, my focus. My strength. I don't understand it, but this is what it is."

He came round and held me tight. Tilting my chin up, so he could kiss me.

He was truly wonderful, but even in exceptionally good behavior mode, he could be dogmatic and controlling. I understood and accepted it as part and parcel of being a successful business man. He was definitely used to getting his own way. It was probably this power and dominance that attracted me to him. I felt so protected and safe with him by my side. Nothing could harm me. He had my back.

So where are you now. Now that I need protection. You're last words were that you loved me.

What has happened to you? Why aren't you here, where you belong, beside me, loving me and making this all right again? I know it's where you would be if you could.

Then again, what do I know? A guy wants to kill me and I don't even understand why. Fuck what a fucking mess! It just didn't need to go this way. The universe is perverse in its cruelty.

I took some more cold and flu, and some pain killers. A sip of water with each swallow. I'm terrified of putting anything in my body as it's just more to throw up. My throat is raw and the smell of myself, so vile that it makes me gag. My abdomen aches from the constant vomiting. This is the purgatory they speak of. I'm in hell.

# Chapter 26

But up until a few days a go, I thought I was in heaven. I had felt blessed. Spoilt. Cherished.

We had gone away for the weekend. Paul had organised it as a surprise only a week after I had employed Joy. With my marketing and the two of us working long hours together, the turnover increased by 35% in 7 days. I deserved a reward. This was an amazing result, but it's not hard to achieve an improvement from plodding along.

He had booked a beautiful suite at the Sofitel Hotel, in the Paris end of Collins St.

We spent the first afternoon settling in and window shopping, down Collins St and through the lanes on Melbourne. Well, Paul's version of window shopping. Venturing into stores I would never have entered without him. Louis Vuitton, Armani, Versace, Chanel. We returned with so many bags, I thought we should get a taxi. There were suits for him. New shirts. Shoes. Ties.

"Just come in Katherine. I know labels don't impress you, so I won't make you try anything on. I promise, but I need a new shirt."

It had been a lazy ambling day and we finished it with Japanese for dinner at Koko's again. The food was as superb as their view, and it had become a firm favorite of ours. As usual it was another perfect night, more like a still crisp Autumn, than the cold winter it should have been. Our table was against the windows with a perfect view of the famous flames along The Yarra river. The city was lit before us, reflecting in the river 20 stories below.

We had been talking about what I would like to do, if money was no object.

"I'd like to give back. I wish I was in a position to look after struggling single mums who need a a roof and a bit of help."

He looked taken aback. "Have you been going through my Linkedin?"

I was confused. Where was the connection in that? For me It was a personal debt to society. I had been one of those mums.

"No, why would I? I didn't even know you had one."

His phone was already in his hand and he was looking something up to show me. He put it on the table and spun it around to face me.

"Read it Katherine. When are you going to get it? When are you finally going to see the real me?"

I scanned quickly, and had to pick the phone up to take it on board.
I read.

"Chief executive Officer for Uniting Housing Service."

The same organization that had helped me years ago, after I'd been burnt. I tried to hide the embarrassing associated memory. My mind clogged in confusion. 'He had worked there? A Christian based charity organization?

I looked at him, questioningly, and he explained. "I managed a team that sourced, renovated and repaired properties for the unfortunate people who needed our services. Our job was to ensure our clients' needs were met. When I went in, it was a shambles. I implemented new policies and procedures. Ramped up acquisitions. Increased their portfolio. To be honest I increased it a million fold. It was a real mess of non performing properties. When I left they had investments whose growth was naturally exponential. Found them reliable contractors. It was an inordinately satisfying job.

My head was reeling. I looked up at him. I could feel my eyes betraying me. They were getting moist. Threatening to leak.

"I didn't know." Was all I could say.

"Katherine, this is why I keep telling you. SEE ME. I have begged you to see the real me. Not my money."

"I don't see your money at all, Paul. It's, well, I just didn't know. You never told me you had worked in the emergency housing sector."

I'm painfully aware my life is extreme. My own personal story was dancing through my head, like scrolling through an Instagram account.

Struggling single mum.
Tough gig
Going well
Oliver at 10,
Autistic
My house
Stranger
Assault.
4 hour ordeal
3rd degree burns,
Emergency Alfred Hospital
Fresh skin grafts
Shattered
Tired
Hurt
Betrayed
Scarred
Scared
Needing help
Embarrassed
Ashamed
Ignored
Presenting too well
Unheard
Broken
Housed
More operations
Healing

I hadn't told many of my friends. Yes, housing for those in true need, is a very personal issue.

"I thought you knew, Katherine. I volunteered my time. I took two years out of my shallow life, so I could give back. I did it for me. This is a very important issue to me. To give back to those that need it. My job was to coordinate the houses and ensure they were allocated to those in need. I had a large team under me. Our aim was to minimise costs so we could provide the best accommodation to as many as possible. Even the contractors, who I found, are special people with big hearts. I'd like to think I created a team that gave generously out of their own pockets.

To be honest, it touched my heart so much at how many genuine people miss out on housing in the public sector, that I bought an apartment block in Sunshine. It only has 12 units, but I hand picked the families that now live there, and they do so for free. I think those most in genuine need are often, the ones that miss out."

"Yes, I think this is very true." I agreed. "So you were, and still are, helping the needy and homeless?"

My eyes scan further down the iPhone screen.

Brotherhood of St Lawrence. Capital works manager.

I knew he had worked in the disability sector. We had spoken about it, in relation to Autism. 'But this? He really was a nice guy. He was genuinely the beautiful man he seemed to be.'

He leant forward, across the corner of the table, and peered into my eyes. "Katherine meet Paul. This is me. A big part of me. I have charities, which is why I asked you ages ago if you would be comfortable having to dress in evening gowns, meeting strangers, making small talk. I sponsor children. Look." Again he turned to his phone and searched through some pictures. "Here."

He showed me a photo of an angelic, little Asian girl in a neat grey school uniform.

"This is Trinh. She is now 10. I look after her whole family in Vietnam. I met her four years ago, when I was traveling with my mates. Remember, I told you about the time I got Giardia. Never shitted so much in my life and was stuck in the hotel room most of the time thinking I was going to die. It was that trip, that I saw her and something just spoke to me. I told the guys to keep walking. She touched my heart. Her mother was a street vendor. They lived in abject poverty. Seeing her now, like this here, it's hard to believe how much of a dirty little scragamuffin she was. I bought them a house. Paid for her entire eduction.
Princess, I support her whole family and it cost less than $10,000 to buy them a home. Can you believe it? They are set for life. Trinh studies hard because she knows that if she can make something of herself, their lives change forever. She Skypes me once a week, I'm pretty sure you have been home when she has been online.

It's something I feel quite passionate about. I have found that the richer I become, the more guilty I feel. I would love you to join me in what I do. I feel wealthier for working in those places Katherine. I can honestly say, my self worth grew the most when I was the brotherhood and UHV. I know you understand what I mean."

I put my hand on top of his to hush him, and leant forward, gently kissing him on the lips. I pulled back slowly and looked him in the eyes.

"I love you Paul. I can honestly say I love you. You are a good man."

# Chapter 27

The next morning over breakfast, sitting in the club, reserved for VIPs, we looked down upon the roof line at the top end of the city. The treasury building was to my right. The gardens in front, with a few lower buildings between. My preferred church, St Michael's just out of sight to my left.

"So Princess, what do you want to do today?"

"Well, it's Sunday, and, if you don't mind, I wouldn't mind going to church."

He looked horrified.

"You'll be going on your own."

"You won't come with me for an hour?"

" No. I do not believe there is an omnipresent force dictating my outcomes. I believe in hard work. Seen too much tragedy to accept a God. Watched how slow and painful cancer can be. If he existed he would be an evil force."

I was surprised. For such a loving man, I suppose I had just presumed he would be some what religious, at least spiritual.

"Well, it's literally just there." I pointed. "So I have no excuse."

"I'll take you, and go for coffee until you are finished. Katherine, religion is against all my beliefs  You are in control of your life, no one else. No God would let innocent people die. Think of what my ex went through. Think of what I went through watching that. Let alone, all the others in tsunamis and earthquakes. All that suffering. That's not a God I want to have anything to do with. I believe in myself. I'm my own God, and I control my destiny, and as you know that doesn't make me selfish, I put others first."

"Paul, I fight with some of that myself, but I find that there is just a feeling in churches. Maybe the energy from prayer. I don't know, but it makes me feel at home. So, if you don't mind, I'd be finished by 11?"

I sat through the service which as usual was uplifting. Francis McNab, is an amazing minister and philosopher. I truly enjoy his sermons. Then I went to the prayer room. I walked through the pews and across the aisle. It was outside and around the back corner. I got to the big granite archway and suddenly realized for the first time in years, I was about to cry.
I rushed through the doorway, in a bit of an embarrassed panic to find the furthest darkest corner, managed to find a seat and then unexpectedly exploded into tears.
Copious tears.
I put my head in my hands, my elbows leaning on my knees.
I gasped and my ribs heaved. I was sobbing. I gave into it.
Another gasp. What is that on my wrists? I pulled a way and looked.
It had been so long since I had cried, that I had forgotten what tears on skin felt like. I put my head back in my hands with my eyes shut. I sobbed. I could literally hear the sound of my tears dropping into the little puddle directly in front of my shoes, on the granite floor. I opened my eyes and looked down in disbelief. I could still feel my eyes leaking. What the hell? This is ridiculous.
Silently now, my face literally was a slow sheet of distressed water, dripping off my nose, my chin, my fingers.
I started praying silently in my head.

"Please god. Let's this work. Please don't be playing games. Don't turn this into a disaster. I'm too tired. Don't give me a man who seems to adore me and then make him leave.
I am being the best I can. I've been trying for years, you know that. I try to live with love first. No harm. Please give me a break. I am so grateful to you for giving me Paul. He is wonderful.
Not dwelling, but he has issues. You could have perhaps not have given him a dead girlfriend, but hey.
Just let this work. Let me be loved. Please. Please don't turn this into one of your games. I don't need the down.

You chose to make him so over the top wonderful. Does he even out all the bad so far? Is that it? Ying, yang?

I don't need any more bad. Don't kill him off in car accident or a work injury.

Please let me and him be happy.

Please look after Ollie. Thank you for him. I'm so proud to have been allowed to get to know him. He is a good kid and I have tried my best. I know I'm not the world's best mum, but you do keep throwing things in my way. While I'm here, I do appreciate the "You're A Star" experience for him. He did a lot of growing up. It will be good for him in the long run. Bit shitty now, but I get that.
Please don't think I'm ungrateful. I get it. Things can always be worse. You have shown me that. I'm grateful. You have made me a survivor. I'm grateful for the shop, for Oliver, and now for Paul. Thank you. Please let this be ok.
Don't hurt either of them please."

I heard footsteps and opened an eye. I could see a practical pair of black, flat court shoes and slacks. A quiet voice.

"Take this. God loves you."

I looked up. A kind young Chinese woman was holding a freshly ironed handkerchief out towards me.

"Take it."

She put it in my hand, turned and left.

Here I was, in the middle of this crazy emotional face leaking episode of weakness, thinking that only in this church, would someone have a pressed handkerchief. Last time I saw one of these was in my childhood. I used to iron them as part of my chores.

Random. Kind.
The things that happen. That she would be there with a spare hanky. Not even a disposable tissue.

Oh my god. My face is a wet, sticky mess. So are my hands. Disgusting. And this is why you shouldn't cry.

Snot.

I finally wiped myself dry enough. Dab eyes. Blow nose. Wipe face. Dry hands. Wipe face again. Dab under eyes. They seriously have got to stop leaking. Seriously.

I've been scared for years, that if I ever let myself cry, I may never stop. I cried for 80% of every day for 18 months after the assault. It was 7 years ago. I thought I would never smile or laugh again. I never want to be that sad again.

I got up and steadied myself.

Ok, get it together you don't want Paul seeing you like this. He will obviously never understand your relationship with God, so pull it together.

Where did those tears come from? Such a waste of time. They don't achieve anything except swollen lids, blocked nose and a headache. Cannot believe that just happened.

Leaving the Mingary prayer room, I wandered out on to Collins St. It was bright. The sun shone through the leaves and was creating sunbeams down to the foot path.

He wasn't there. I called him on the phone. "Paul?"

"I'm just up a bit further."

I dabbed my face again. Can only imagine what my eyes look like. What can you do? I put my sunnies on and got into the car, leaning in quickly to kiss him on the cheek.

"Hello gorgeous."

I put my belt on slowly and then looking out the passenger window tried to make light chit chat about the beautiful day.

"Thank you for letting me go to church. What are our plans now?" I tried to chirp.

"Have you been crying?"

My face was spottly red. It was so obvious.

"No. Why would you think that?" It wasn't a lie, it was a joke. Clearly I had just cried enough for half a life time.

He had a confused smile. "Why would someone go to church happy and leave looking bereft?"

"I was actually thanking God, for you and Ollie, to be completely honest."

"And that made you cry?"

"Apparently."

"Why?"

"I don't know. You know crying isn't normally my thing. Maybe I'm just scared of losing you. Don't let that go to your head or ruin our day. It's over. Where would you like to go?"

"I booked lunch down by the water in Williamstown. I've told you about the place before. Been going for years. Perfect day for it and the whitefish is awesome."

It was only a short drive and after parking we strolled along the breakfront. A perfect 24 degrees, no breeze and cloudless sky. Does he have a deal with God after all?

'Can we have perfection surrounding Paul at all times please?'

We walked into the restaurant with it's uninterrupted views of the sea, and he greeted the owner like a long lost friend. Another lovely table. Another carefree lunch. Being together was comfortable, passionate and easy. We were so happy.

# Chapter 28

'Happy.'

There's an emotion.

I cannot imagine being happy ever again or laughing. Cannot imagine even smiling. I know I will, but I can't feel it. I also know deep in my soul that whatever life holds for me, that if it is to be without him, my life will always be a greyer, shadowed shade of what it could have been.

I open my eyes. I'm hunched over the table, partially curled in the old office chair. My nose has been dripping. God, I'm sick. I'm slow. My temples hurt. I try to tell myself to be positive. I'm not going to be sick forever. My head will clear soon. I lean forward and light another cigarette, returning my thoughts to the back of my mind.

The blessings continued, and I had so much to be thankful for. We were blissfully in love. We were comfortable with each other and now, only 2 weeks later, he had taken me away again.

I am so spoilt and cherished. I needed the break, and had I not met him, I would have taken some time off earlier. Being with him meant I definitely needed one. I had to ramp the business back up and find unknown reserves of energy to cope with the influx of new clients plus I was dating Paul.

He had initially organised a beautiful, private resort in Fiji for two weeks, then a week in Bora Bora, but each time he either chose to cancel, or we had to. Between us, there were time constraints and future deadlines looming. It got to the point that we could allocate only four days. He was apologetic as he showed me the surprise booking to Hamilton Island. He told me that he had let his travel agent, Natalie, arrange all the details. Part of me felt let down. I had kept hearing about all the things he used to do with other girls, and this wasn't at the same level. Again it made me feel second rate. It also made me dislike Natalie. I had friends who were travel agents. They were going to be tempting Paul with excellent business and holiday rates from now on. I knew I was being precocious and precious so I tried to step over it. To have said anything would have been totally ungrateful and I wasn't. The thought of just getting a break was joyous.

So we had flown up and arrived in time for a late lunch. We spent the afternoon strolling and finding a new bikini, as mine were all now in storage. Before we had left home, he'd actually pulled down some summer holiday clothes from the top shelf of our wardrobe, inviting me to rummage through and wear what I liked. As they were Brooklin's, I politely declined, and had to listen to a lecture about her being dead, and how not using the clothes was a waste. "You're a tiny bit smaller than her, so they'll fit. Katherine, they are expensive. Aren't you always the one telling me not to spend money extravagantly, and to stop being wasteful?" I had felt ungrateful, and then had to placate him to avoid a fight before we went away, but I wasn't wearing his dead ex girlfriend's clothes.

Wandering through the resort, looking at flip flops for him, and bikinis and sarongs for me, put Paul in his favorite element; shopping. I was happy too, having found the most flattering bikini, that I'd had in years. I fitted a child's size, and they were so much prettier than the adult ones and importantly to me, they were cheaper.

We then spent the rest of the day in the sun lazing and drinking, followed by a long, leisurely dinner at a beautiful restaurant on the water front with the waves lapping only meters from the table. It was balmy and still. As usual, perfect. He had made slow passionate love for hours, climaxing three times and still wanting more. I remember sleeping beside him legs entwined, exhausted from doing nothing all day.

Waking late the next day and taking forever to go down for breakfast, Paul noticed my left leg was swollen. Now that he mentioned it, yes it was sore. We must have spent the whole night wrapped around each other. We wasted the next day, lazing beside the pool and dawdling through the souvenir shops. It felt so good to unwind.

Then we took a walk along the beach as the sun was setting. Half way along, he had stopped and turned me to face him. Wow, is he going to propose? Good lord, there is literally no slowing him. It's only been 10 weeks!

I knew he had shown Oliver and Sarah a picture of a large pink, heart shaped, diamond ring, just after that, break up over the dead girl's belongings. It was meant to be a secret but Ollie was my only child and he was going to tell me. He said it would literally be too big for my small hand, and that it wasn't going to be my thing. Sarah said the ring was huge and stunning.

"Katherine, he loves you so much and the ring is just too, too beautiful. It made me cry."

Ollie pointed out it would get caught when I made the bed. I had had a large solitaire before. It stood proud and was a pain in the butt for an average person leading a normal mum life. God I love Oliver. He is so practical. He is my son and gorgeous.

They weren't meant to tell, but their loyalty was to me, and so I already knew Paul was thinking about it. He was always so fast paced. I would beg him to be still. Slow down. Relax. It's not a race. Breathe. Let me breathe.

So here we were. On the sand, along the shore, the waves lapping at our feet. Picture perfect. He held me by my upper arms at a distance, and then he raised my chin. I felt awkward.

"Katherine, look at me. In the eyes." He knew I hated it, but I concentrated on doing it. I know it's important for most people. He held the back of my head. His fingers through my hair. I knew it was to ensure I kept looking at him, and it's the idyllic pose of a couple on the beach together. My heart was starting to pound and I was beginning to feel anxious.

"Katherine, I want to ask, (Drum roll in my head), if I ever asked you to marry me, would you be interested? Would you say yes?"

I remember my face screwing up in the confusion of the moment.

'Wait.' I heard the pause in my head. 'This was a pre proposal? Was this the conditioning question, like you do when you are sussing out a prospective client? Was he ensuring that when he asked, that he didn't get a no? This is anti climactic. Even though I hadn't wanted it. Really? Who did that?' I was taken aback, and stifled an awkward little laugh.

Wow, I thought he knew I loved him. He asked me often enough. I told him all the time. I hadn't seen his uncertainty about my feelings coming. How could he doubt it?

"Yes, Paul, if you were ever to ask me to marry you, I would say yes."

"Thank god. I want to wait till we go to Hawaii in October, with my brother and Anna. It's where I'd like to propose. I just didn't want to go to that effort, put my heart on the line, and have you reject me."

As usual I felt on the back foot. Isn't your heart already on the line regardless of whether we are engaged or married, and why does he need a pre approval?
*And* now I know when it's going to happen. I'm not sure that's how it's meant to play out. I'm literally not sure, but it feels weird.

"So I have to wait that long then, ok, but it's so far away." I joked and hugged him. I said it to ease the uncertainty that he had just showed. I wanted him to know that I was keen. I was in love. I would happily say yes. I said it as a reassurance and because in honesty, I didn't want to be on holidays, with his brother when he proposed.

As he squeezed me tightly, he told me how happy it made him.

"Please don't mess this up Katherine."

"Why would you say that?"

"Because I need you. I want this to work out, and I don't want you to sabotage it. I have plans and they include you."

"Paul, I really thought you already knew how much I love you. Come on. I can't believe you really feel unsure about my feelings."

We began strolling down the beach, holding hands. It was romantic and made the sunset perfect. He was searching my face.

"Well, about three years ago I met a girl from Canada and we travelled around America together for six weeks. It was great. Fantasy road trip. Then I went back home to Melbourne and was tossing up how I was going to make the relationship work. Then I met my ex, and I started dating her. I had made the commitment that she was my girlfriend and you know how you do, I changed my focus."

I was looking at him as we were strolling back to the hotel along the sand, wondering why this story, now?

He could see my confusion. "There's a point to this. It's relevant. Anyway I got this phone call from Canada. Not the girl, but her friend. Apparently she had just disappeared. All her belonging were gone and she was off the radar. I had no answers.
It was when I was living in the Docklands and, you'll never believe it, but there was a knock on the door the next day. When I answered, there she was, kneeling in the doorway, proposing to me. Professing her undying love. She

had sold everything she owned and was here to move in and live together and get married. Oh, Katherine I will never forget the look on her face when I said no. I let her stay the night then marched her straight back to the airport. Bought her the only available ticket which was first class and sent her home. The point is, I never want to find out how much it hurts to be behind those pained, bloodshot, teary eyes. Those rejected, heartbroken eyes. So I just wanted to make sure that you were finally on the same page: same chapter. Same paragraph as me. Like you said at Huxtibles."

"Oh, my, god. Relax. I love you."

"I love you and need you more."

# Chapter 29

20 cigarettes and another 2 hours have passed. Hardly conducive to getting better. I have been day dreaming of how everything started. I groan. There is a cigarette in my hand, I have forgotten to smoke it and now I stare at it, in fascination. It has magically held its shape, imitating an unlit cigarette, yet turned to ash. I'm fascinated by the flakes of grey and white, tightly packed, sitting in air. In noticing it, I move slightly and it dissolves onto the saucer.

Now I sit and stare at the empty space that only a second ago was the cigarette.

The fragility of deception.

I don't know how long I again sat frozen to the spot, and I'm about to finally get up when there's a knocking on the shop door. I can see a tall silhouette through the sheer curtain across the door. It's my long time client, Deb. We have become girlfriends over the years.

I support myself with the table and chair, and raise my body on to stiff legs. With bare feet, and the clothes that I have slept in, and thrown up in, for days, I make my way, sloth like, towards the door. It hurts my fingers to move the locks.

She comes in the door, helping me open and close it quietly.

"God, Katherine, you look awful."

"I have the flu." I say trying to make excuses. "Thanks for popping in."

"Well, you weren't responding to my messages on Facebook, or text or my calls. You sort of left me no choice, and no, Katherine it's not just the flu. This is bad. You can't go through this alone. Joseph is home. Here is our key. Please come over. Have a shower and we will make a bed up. He will feed you. You can't stay here.
Katherine, I'm truly sorry for what's happened. I didn't think the universe would put you through anything this cruel after everything you have already gone through."

She leant in and gave me a long hug.

"I'd love that Deb, but let me get over this flu first. I don't want to give it to anyone. So in a few days? Surely I'll be over it soon?"

"OK. Two more days and if you haven't shown up, I will send Joseph to get you."

"Thank you for caring. I promise. I'll come, when I'm no longer contagious."

After she left, I grabbed my phone and cigarettes. My body thinks they are food and I'm happy to humour that, as it stops me needing to go out shopping for anything solid. I can't face opening the door and seeing humanity. Not because I'm a total fright but because I literally couldn't cope with humanity. If I can, I will go to the service station tonight, protected by the dark. I don't want to meet a living, breathing person. I don't feel safe outside. I'm jumpy. I have not forgotten the look on that man's face when he told me Vito wants to put me through a tree shredder. I limped back to the security of the office chair. My blankets are hung open, over the arms, waiting for me to enshroud myself again. I wrap myself in its dark hug.

# Chapter 30

I lower myself back into position by the table and rock gently as I light my cigarette. It takes a few attempts. My hands are shaking and it's hard to make the lighter and cigarette work together. They finally stay in contact long enough to meet, spark, flame, flare.

Everything has happened so fast. Dragged into falling in love, then wham!

The cigarette will end up snuffed out too. Smoking has become my latest analogy of life.

My head fogs, and I stare back into time. Where was I? Yes. Back when everything was normal. Normal within the parameters of it being Paul's awesome world. There must have been signs. This sort of thing doesn't just happen with no notice. Think. Think back. No, maybe just remember the good things. It might hurt less.

The night after he had conditionally pre proposed, we had gone out for a spectacular dinner at Bommie. Flamboyant menu and knowledgable, well trained staff. Perfect end to another perfect day. Fine dining with superb wine and we were celebrating being so in love that he had nearly proposed. I couldn't help but tease him.

We finished the evening on the balcony of our room with another bottle of champagne. Paul didn't seem to want the night to end. We could see the moon now glimmering across the ripples of the water, palm trees swaying and islands in the distance.

He leaned towards me and said.

"I know you have been finding things you don't like in the house. Stuff you don't understand, letters and things and you are being very patient with me, but I have to come clean. You don't really know who I am."

My heart sank. Married? Gay? Lover? Girlfriend? What else is there? I couldn't deny there had been some issues with remnants of his previous girlfriend. I understood and did my best to ignore them. Some of what I had stumbled upon turned out to infact be John's girlfriend's, from when they had stayed over the summer break. It had caused a bit of an issue at the time. Even the night we left for this holiday, I had opened the other bathroom cupboard, and inadvertantly found where he had hidden the make up, which he had so openly offered for me to use on that first morning at his house. This time, I had chosen to ignore it. He was going to slowly find, and collect all her bits and pieces in his own time. They had lived together, so the evidence of her life was everywhere. I did not want to ask him to remove it. She had died. It changed a lot of rules. Obviously I couldn't raise her as a topic. When someone dies, it literally becomes a taboo subject, and I certainly could not ask him to throw her stuff out. No matter how small and insignificant they were. I knew this was just not something to involve myself in. He wasn't aware of most of it anyway. Is this what he is talking about?

"What do you mean Paul?"

"Well, I don't really know where or how to start, but I have misled you."

My bra suddenly felt tight across my chest. "You're not married? I laughed. "Or gay? Oh are you really an illegal immigrant and you need sponsorship?" I was trying to make light of the suddenly sombre atmosphere he had created. I could feel my heart pounding through my sternum. Hard and fast. I was having a bit of trouble breathing. "Ok, so what do you need to tell me?"

"Well, nothing like that. You know, Katherine, sometimes people keep secrets. Good secrets. They are not always bad, you know." He laughed, showing those white teeth. His eyes crinkling at the corners.

Ah back to bright and breezy.

"It's just the truth is, I'm a bit richer than I led you to believe. I know you have issues with my money and it's caused us to fight before so I have been dreading this conversation to be honest."

"Well, I certainly hate talking about it but yes, you have made it clear that you're wealthy so it's really the same, same after a certain point isn't it?"

'No." He said. "I'm offensively rich. We can't spend as much money as I earn a month. It's just not possible. Even if we tried, and I've tried. Oh, except if you bought a house or a car, but general living, we won't be able to do it."

"Ah, well Paul that's yours and I really don't need to know about it. I mean I'm happy for you but knowing anymore than I already do is unnecessary."

"No. If you are going to become my wife you need to know the truth. In reality, it's hard being like this now. I didn't used to be wealthy. Not independently. You know my father had money and we had a pretty spoilt lifestyle growing up. I can't deny it, but, I've passed my father twofold and now it just keeps growing. It reaches a point where you can't keep up with it. Even I get surprised about the sources of money that I have found. It staggers even myself.

Remember when I told you about that first stock that just by chance turned into 8 million. That was 9 years ago. Well, I invested that in the hotel in QLD and sold the rights, and bought shares in the jet, and bought more property developments and nothing I've ventured into has failed. It's been ridiculous. I have the Midas touch. Investing everything into the hotel could have lost me everything. I can remember making myself so cash flow poor, that I was eating canned tuna by myself and freaking out about what I had done. I know how it feels to struggle like you and Ollie have. Trust me."

I didn't know where he was going with this yet, but I was silently acknowledging a small offense, at anyone, of wealthy descent, telling me that they felt the same monetary stress, as a homeless, single mother who had chemical burns, a special needs child, a cat, a parakeet, and couldn't get benefits as she fell through the cracks.

Asking for handouts from the salvation army to feed your child and worrying about whether you will get emergency accommodation for the night, when you can't walk and have splints on both legs, is entirely different to knowing mummy or daddy can rescue you, if you fail. It's not the same thing at all, and only the arrogance of insulated wealth lets someone think that it's remotely the same. One day I would raise this issue. I would like him to truly understand the difference. But he didn't know my thoughts, so he continued.

"At the time, my father was so stressed that he offered to lend me some money to help, but I turned him down. I can proudly say, that I am entirely self made. I realized I need professionals and that was my best business decision. I hired Westpac to manage my portfolio and invest wisely for me, and you saw the statement from that account."

I looked at him quizzically.

"You remember on the kitchen bench a few weeks ago."

Oh yes. I did see the bank statement. He had made sure. When I moved it across the bench away from me, because I saw it was personal stuff, he had slid it back and said.

"No, Katherine you should take a look at that." Then he had gone outside for a cigarette. It looked like it had been scrunched up as if it had been in the bin, and then ironed out with his hand. I glanced at it as I was getting my laptop out of my bag.

I saw it said $4,600 Interest. I didn't pick it up, just kept unpacking my things and organizing dinner.

He had come back inside and asked, "Well?"

I responded to his question. "So that's an interest bearing account?"

"Yes".

"Ok." I nodded comprehendingly. "So I bought chicken to have as butter curry and rice. Is that good?"

"There are other accounts as well."

"Ok Paul, it's not my business, but it's a nice, little income."

"Well, it certainly pays the bills. That's what comes in every month."

"Yes, it is good." I didn't know what to say. "It's good having a passive income. When Ollie was younger, and I had all the houses, I got about that amount as well. It's good knowing you can relax and your ATM card is going to pay for the shopping." I had smiled and turned to get the sauce out of the fridge.

"Really?" He laughed. "You were earning $46,000 a month?"

My head jerked up from what I was doing. "What? No! No, I earned about five and a half per month passively, after everything. It was nice." Wait? How much?? I couldn't help smirking. It was confronting. That was a ridiculous amount of money; nearly the average person's annual wage, and he was getting it a month? The statement was on the other side of the bench top, directly opposite where I was now slicing the chicken. I kept my head lowered and concentrating on not cutting my fingers off, moved my eyes to the paper and read it upside down. Westpac letter head, personally addressed to him. Details of changing bank account for the monthly interest, currently at…....OMG. There were more zeros on the other side of the crinkle in the paper.

I didn't think it was my business but he had made another outlandish claim and the proof was in front of me. Of course I was going to check. He wanted me to. Up until I did that, a part of my brain thought he may be joking or testing me. Well there it is.

Now sitting on the balcony together, I looked up, now I remembered. "Yes Paul, yes, I do remember that. I had forgotten. I seriously try not to think about your money. I'm aware it's there."

How could I have forgotten that evening. Probably because as usual I had changed the topic so quickly and moved on.

"Yes, I know Princess and that's one of the many reasons I love you. You are just so, so not interested in my money, unlike my last girlfriend and for the first time ever, I feel loved and appreciated for me. For who I am and I feel ashamed that I didn't tell you the entire truth at the start but I wanted to know you loved me for me. I've been living in fear that you would see the truth about me, before both of us were ready, and that your principles would wreck the future I want for us." He smiled hesitantly at me.

"Well, you are definitely loved for you. If you threw it all away and were still you, I would be as happy as I am today, with you forever. And that's the truth. I keep telling you. If it's fish and chips, or Italian or French just tell me. As long as I know what we can afford, I am happy with how things are. I just want honesty. So I know what's what and can understand. I love how you make me feel about myself, Paul. I love so much about you. You have made me come alive inside again and breathe.In all honesty, I still really haven't seen evidence of your money. Not really, and I prefer it that way. Ok? So, it could not exist and it wouldn't make any difference to me. We aren't the biggest spenders in the world.
If you were poor and were still you, I would love you just as much."

"Well, as I said, I'm far from poor. You know about all the businesses already." His eyes glazed and he held my hand. "I love the fact you aren't a name dropper, and you don't choose designer labels. When I met you, I was just so sick of spending all that money on those shallow girls. They constantly expected me to buy them only the best of everything. Versace this, Prada that. You on the other hand, expect nothing, you ask for nothing. I love that about you."

As he said it, part of me cringed. It's not as though I wouldn't like to own some spectacular brands, I just can't afford them. Another part of me hurt. He was forever telling me about how much he had spent on this or that girl at the couture houses. Why not with me? I felt cheap and then that thought made me feel ungrateful and ashamed again. No one likes second best.

He went on. "I'm not finished though Katherine. It gets worse. There's an inheritance."

"Yes, I know your dad gave you and your brother 10 million at the start of the year. He took his and you returned yours. Very noble of you." I smiled. I wanted to make light and hopefully move on.

"No. There's more. Lots more. I warned you, it's as if the universe wants to give it to me. I just need to know what to do with it.
I told you, my father is English and has worked hard, I learnt a lot from him. He invested in that land along Melbourne's Western growth corridor and sat on it. Cheap farm land, turned into a passage for power lines. And then he used that money and went into partnership with Gerry and formed Harvey Norman. He has kept life time friends from school. He worked hard and invested wisely. A bit of luck, his own inheritances and the rest is history. Now he just sits silently on the board of directors. Meanwhile, my mum had her salons to keep her occupied. Now, her mother, my beautiful Nonna, whom I adored, died last April. He wiped a tear from the corner of his eye.

"Yes I remember you telling me, how wonderful she was and you speak of her often."

"She died with nothing of her own. She came from the border of Trieste. Anyway, a couple of months before she died she handed me a letter from the Italian government and asked me to sort it. I couldn't understand a word of it, and she wasn't in a state to discuss it, so I paid for a translation. When I look back, I don't know why I did. I could have so easily just filed it away forever, but it was her dying wish to have me look at it.
It turns out that there was this worthless farm in the middle of no where. This hilly, non arable land. A couple hundred hectares across the border, with, of all things, a derelict chateau. Useless in every way. I had paid to translate a piece of paper to tell me, that basically, my brother, my cousin Lara, and myself have inherited a plot of nothing."

We both laughed. "Thank god Paul. I thought you were serious for a second."

"I am. Remember the Serbian war, when the government took everyones land?"

I nodded but really had no clue.

"Well this is the new government trying to return all the land to its rightful owners. Clearly my grandmothers parents are dead, as she is now as well. This leaves, my brother David, myself and my cousin Lara as the next descendants.

We've since flown over and seen it. There's a crumbling massive mansion, with squatters who are sort of living off the land. Totally worthless, so we decided to ignore it. Too much trouble and 50 years of back taxes.

Then I got another letter from the solicitor I used for the translation. It's so typical of my life. This worthless piece of land that no one wants. Suddenly the Yugoslavian and Italian government need to acquire it for a freeway they are putting through and basically, well there is now an inheritance of 36 million Euro up for grabs. So I have had to bank roll the back taxes and the solicitors etc. This is why I knew so much about the process of the compulsory acquisition of your shop, because I am going through it myself and my father went through it as well. Fortune favors the fortunate. It's ridiculous.

That's another 14 million coming my way for nothing which takes me well and truly past my 200 goal in cash assets."

I looked at him.

"Yes, that's the magical 200, I have been chasing. Now I can stop working. I was just driven to beat the number. Now that I have you, I have everything that I was chasing. I'm ready to retire and travel, not work. The inheritance comes in at the end of October. Then everyone's lives change. David's and Lara's. I'm hoping yours already has. Personally, I won't notice anything except, I'll stop working.

"So it's not fish and chips then." I lightly laughed at him.

"No, Princess, it's exquisite French served by a butler in the private jet, that you already knew I owned, flying to an island in the Bahamas."

"I needed to tell you Katherine. It's been worrying me so much. It's part of the reason we disagree. You alway say how much you hate money and I have so much of it that I didn't want you to know. I didn't want to lose you, but now that you said you'd say yes on the beach, I know you won't let money get between us. What we have is awesome.

We can do whatever we want with this money. I want you to know that half of that, is yours. I've been sorting all this with Randy, my solicitor. You remember, you met him. All the details of what would happen, when I marry you, what needs to happen if I die, and how you need to be 50% of everything. It's the right thing to do. I just can't have you go into this without knowing how much I am worth and therefore how much you are. And the responsibility that goes with it.

I interrupted. "I don't want to be responsible for any of that. Make sure the kids know what's what and your parents ok? I want to marry you one day, for you. Leave me enough so I am comfortable. I understand you need to plan so any future wife isn't thrown to the wolves of a family fighting over your inheritance however, just please sort it out and leave it at that."

"Princess, it's not that simple. You need to sign papers at some point and you need to know about the boys' trust funds, which I already put Oliver in. Also, I want to give you half of my share of the inheritance, to do with it what you want because I know you will invest it wisely. Sebastian will be there and the bankers. You need to learn, not just for your future. This all happens in October."

My head was listening to all of this but I was focusing on the last part. I was silent.

"Are you ok?" He was concerned.

I could feel my heart pounding.

"Princess, please, what are you thinking?" He looked terrified.

I was silent and I had been looking at the dirty grout between the tiles on the balcony floor. I looked at him. "Paul, I'm happy with what I have with you and you know that's the truth. If I wanted something from you, I'd have wheedled it out of you by now. I love you for you. I'm just thinking there are a lot of charities that are going to be very thankful, I am marrying you, if you ever propose."

He started to cry. "Only you would have given that response. That is perfect. It is what I expect from you. That you would think of others. I love you so much. I expect it would be Autism Advisory with your girlfriend Grace. God, I love you."

I was surprised he knew my friend's name, let alone the charity.

"Well yes, Autism Advisory, would be one." I was thinking of others, but was it by default? Was it guilt? The opportunity to say thank you. The Salvation Army. WAVES, St Joseph's church in South Yarra. So many places, that I could spread this opportunity. So many organization, and people directly need some help. I owe it to them and if I can give back then I just had to.

"Princess, you can create your own charity board. With me by your side, you can do anything. I'm going to change your life in ways you never imagined, if you let me."

"That would be wonderful." I couldn't speak any more. I was going to be able to help those, that had helped me. I understood why the universe had put me through so much over the last ten years, so I would end up here, in this position. Now it all made sense. Extreme suffering. Extreme reward. Giving me extreme ability to do extreme good.

"Katherine, are you crying? Really? This is what makes you cry?"

"Yes, Paul, if you call glistening eyes, crying. Apparently, gratitude and generosity make me cry."

We sat out there chatting about our future with rose tinted glasses. He painted it so perfectly. "You know we could try to have another child. Travel around the world. We can afford a nanny so it would be easy, not like when you were raising Ollie by yourself. We deserve it to be perfect. Try for the little girl neither of us have yet. We could go through IVF. I've heard it has a high success rate nowadays. I'm sorry. I regret the vasectomy now, but 17 years ago, I never thought I would find someone whom I wanted to have another baby with. I'd name her MacKenzie. That's a nice name for a girl, don't you think? God I cannot believe I finally found you. We are so blessed. I can be my true self with you. We can just constantly move around the world. Be global citizens.
You don't have to work you know. The boys can visit whenever they want. I promise, I will treat Oliver as my own. I've told you that. When we get married, do you think he would take my name?"

"Oh I don't know. I'm really not sure about that."

"Well it would be awesome. Then I would have three boys. When we get back I'll sort everything ASAP. It will need his signature as he is over 18. He needs to know he is as important as my boys, so I'll go out, and get him a BMW as well."

"Slow down Paul, he might not actually want one. I doubt he would want you to spend that much money on a car. I don't think it's his thing."

"Really? Well, we can sort it when we get back and my boys are getting $800,000 to buy a house each. I'm just waiting on this inheritance and dividing it up amongst those that need it. So Oliver would be included in that too."

"Paul, thank you, but I'd rather you help him to make prudent choices. I think if you give the boys everything to set their life up, this early, they won't be grateful to you or the universe. I don't think it's doing them any long term favors. What you do with your boys is fine. It's none of my business, but I'd prefer for Oliver to work a bit harder, so he understands, and is grateful for what he has."

Paul was staring at me with a concerned look on his face. "Are you ok? You don't look good Katherine?"

"No, I'm not feeling flash to be honest."

"Are you upset with me telling you?"

"No."

"I think we may have to call the doctor. You really don't look right. Your lips are grey."

"Just wait. We can go inside and lie down and keep talking."

"We went inside and lay on the king sized bed. I was having a bit of trouble breathing and was feeling dizzy."

"That's enough Katherine. I'm calling the concierge. We need to get a doctor."

I remember thinking it was an awful way to finish the night. It had already gone from perfect to the ridiculous. In a good way.

With my history for DVT, the emergency doctor had come straight out and jabbed me with Clexane to prevent any clots. He couldn't hear anything in my lungs, but wasn't prepared to take any chances. Now he was asking me to inject myself for the next three days, until we got home.

"No, sorry, nope, nope. No. No, I cannot possibly inject myself. I am a professional fainter. There will have to be an alternative solution. Why can't I pop into the hospital."

The doctor was trying to work with me. "Katherine, this is a small island. There is no hospital and tomorrow is a public holiday so no one is working in the surgery."

Paul surprised me by volunteering. "I'll do it for you."

"No, it's ok, I'll just go without the shots." My fear of needles makes me faint all the time, then throw up, which is not pleasant for anybody involved.

"Princess, I'm really good at giving injections. I had to give my neighbor injections for her IVF once a day for 6 months. Trust me."

Is there anything this man can't do?

He gave the most gentle injections I had ever had and as much as I threatened to faint every time, he never failed, and he never bruised me. We spent the next two days doing nothing, as I wasn't allowed to drink for the remainder of the trip, but it didn't impact us. We just lazed by the pool and went for shorter walks. We contacted my girlfriend Grace and chatted about helping the charity she had. It was a beautiful wonderful feeling, just as Paul said it would be, to tell someone you were going to help them.

By the time we went home we were both totally refreshed and loved up.

He was my world. I was his. Being together was all we wanted.

I prayed to the universe. 'Please don't ruin this.'

# Chapter 31

June 19th, 2014

We had only just got back from Hamilton Island and Paul was going to have to go away again. The business in Boston needed his attention.

"I think it will take a fortnight, Beautiful, I'm so sorry. I know everything has been a bit crazy. I can't go right away because of all my other commitments. I have a few board meetings with Marianne at T2, over us now parting ways, it's dividend time with the marketing company, and Randy has a mountain of paperwork for me to go through with him. Plus, I'm trying to finalise a deal that will change both our lives forever, so I can't leave for a few more weeks. It's actually exciting times. Everything is going to be awesome. I'm just annoyed I have to leave you here."

Apparently, the General Manager of Carbomac in the US, was acting like a petulant child, over comments a few staff members made, and was now threatening to quit.

"I've told you before, this GM has become a total pain in the ass, high maintenance queen. Makes for good designer flair but this blubbering down the phone is literally too much. It was ok at first, because the quality of work was excellent and I'm making money hand over fist as a result, but lately, I don't think it's going to work out. It's got to the point of 'fire or quit.' Shame, but it's like working with a spoilt brat. Their partner has been cheating, and fell in love, and is leaving or something. You know the story. Now I have to put up with this craziness. There's actually been tears down the phone. So unprofessional. The staff are making complaints to me so I have to go sort it out. I wish I could take you, but you are tied up with work. It's a bit of a clusterfuck over there right now. Apart from finding you, this year has been a disaster."

Trying to deal with it on Skype was not working out. Paul was annoyed, as the projects in Melbourne needed him. The four main ones, spread from Footscray, Bendigo, Brunswick and Fawkner, and were all at their crucial stages of fit off and as usual there were dramas. I listened to him have heated discussions with his staff and solicitor, he spent hours trying to soothe the waters overseas, but to no avail.

I often wondered why he kept that side of the business. It seemed it made him the least money and gave him the greatest headaches. Now was not the time to raise it. He said he liked to keep himself real. I hated hearing about the stress and listening to the loud discussions of deadlines, his brother's latest mistakes, contractors not turning up, and staff wage issues. It just went on, and being with him, on the phone, in the car, sometimes, would make my ears buzz with the increased volume of the discussions.

"In this business, you need to be there. No one has pride in their work anymore. You might be right Katherine. I should just sell it off. Maybe I shouldn't be giving the business to John. He isn't ready anyway. He should be supervising the sites. And those ringling brothers of your girlfriend, Ash and Sam, are just disasters. I'm sure they are doing drugs on the work site. Maybe I should just close the entire business down. Both here and in the USA.

God, Katherine I have so much to worry about right now. I hate stress, and I don't want to be worrying about you as well. It's winter and wet. I don't like you driving from the shop to here every day. It's too far. While I'm away, I just want to know you are safe. I'm worried about leaving you alone. You need a break and I should be looking after you. Would you like to go on a holiday for a couple of weeks? Hawaii, Bali, Tahiti, Fiji?"

I looked at him. Confused.

"No, I don't want to go on a holiday without you. I need a break from the constant whirlwind of being with you. You, who never slows down and is always planning our life at top speed. I need a break from the shop and all the legalities of the governments acquisition. From the accumulated exhaustion of the last few years. Yes, I need a break, I've been begging you for one. A break because life has just been crazy for too long, but, no, I don't want to go on a holiday without you.
No gorgeous man, I'll just stay here. We can go together, after you get back perhaps. Even just to Phillip Island for a weekend."

He seemed to accept that and changed the subject.

"I'll always be able to take you somewhere better than Phillip Island. So if not now, but sometime in the future, who would you like to visit that you haven't seen enough of, or want to party with? There's got to be some friends or family that you want to see."

"Why? Are you trying to organise a surprise Paul?"

"No just asking. Come on, who would you like to see?"

"Like anyone Paul, there are people all over the place that I'd love to see. I haven't seen my Aunt or Donna Lee in a long while, and there's Dianne in England."

"And where do the other two live?"

'Aunty Jenny is in Newcastle now. Retired off the farm. She is so down to earth and loving, and Donna Lee is the most beautiful person, from the inside out. She is so Christian it freaks most normal people out, but she means well and loves everyone unconditionally. She's in Tasmania."

"Why don't you ring her then, and see if you both want to catch up."

"Who? Which one? We would all love to see each other."

"Well this time how about a short easy flight so I don't have to worry about your DVT blood clots? Tasmania. I can fly you down there anytime, Princess. You could go while I'm away. Is Donna Lee, the friend who helped you after the assault? It will kill time, so you don't miss me so much, and Joy can look after the shop. Get Oliver in to help."

We were on the couch, and he laughed lovingly, as he leant towards me and literally slid me across his lap, so he could hold me tightly. He kissed me.

"When will you realise how much your happiness means to me? I would prefer to know you are with a friend than moping around this house by yourself for two weeks."

Suddenly the idea was appealing. I would love to be surrounded by the goodness of the most pure person I know.

He got my phone and tossed it gently to me.

"Phone her, Princess. I can't imagine how much you two have to catch up on."
It was fortuitous timing. Donna Lee was having a miserable time and would love to see me. It was perfect. Not her being miserable, that was awful, but I would be there with her and we could talk.

"When are you leaving, Paul?"

"I'm gone on the 5$^{th}$ of July, so I could put you on a plane on the 4$^{th}$. Does that suit Donna Lee?"

I relayed the question. She was ecstatic.

"Donna Lee wants to know how long we get to be together?"

"I get back on the 15$^{th}$, so how about I fly you home on the 16$^{th}$. Will that give you girls enough time to chat? I'll give you some spending money, so you can go have some pampering, sounds like Donna Lee could do with an escape as well."

"Paul, you are just too good. This is lovely. Really? You don't need to. I'm happy to stay here."

"No, I don't want you to be on your own."

He had booked the tickets before I was off the phone and it was suddenly all organised. Now all I had to do, was rearrange Joy and clients to cover my absence.

The count down was on. I was so excited. We seemed to catch up with so many people before he and I flew off in opposite directions. A wonderful Korean BBQ with my girlfriend, Louise and her husband, Darren. They were so excited about Paul doing their new house and it filled most of the conversation, as did how Charlotte, her daughter, was going with her cancer. Louise was definitely having a hard time accepting it and Paul again offered words from his personal experience and wisdom. He was wonderful. Paul and Darren had become friends and I was happy knowing I would have Louise in my life more.

We caught up with so many friends, for no reason other than we could, spending most of our free time socializing and enjoying the company and conversation.
It was so nice that everyone liked him and that our friends were happy for us. Thank god life was trundling along peacefully. We met my group of friends at The Long Room, saw Gab, Oscar and Oliver, even fitting in a film and dinner with his brother, David and new wife, Anna.

Then we went for dinner and met an old work collegue of Paul's from Anglicare, Keith, and his new partner Julie. The conversation focused a lot on her memories of an outer eastern suburb, Pakenham. Both Paul and she randomly had mutual friends, in particular a Paula Spaky and her family. Meant nothing to Keith and I, but they both just went on and on, focusing on the extraordinary wealth of the family, the fathers helicopter, her affair, a suicide and car accident, how absolutely selfish she was, and how neither knew what happened to her after the divorce. She disappeared off the radar. And now her family have literally disowned her. Keith and I listened, but had very little, if anything to add. The only time I was really involved in the conversation was when Paul pointed out, that this lady had crashed her car, resulting in smashed up knees with scars like mine.

Paul leant in towards Julie and whispered in a conspiratorial way. "I actually heard she wanted to kill her dad."
Keith and I were obviously awkward, but the conversation remained fixated on this family and their memories.
Julie still saw the family, and parts of the conversation clearly made her uncomfortable. Paul had nothing nice to say about them, and for the first time ever, actually seemed to revel in bagging these people out. It was an uncomfortable night talking incessantly about someone not remotely connected to any of us really, except Paul's and Julie's association.

He was telling Julie, "She's a spoilt home wrecker. Cheated for ages on that poor chump of a husband. Has no appreciation for the amount of wealth she comes from. Totally ungrateful. Always disliked her, and her father, Anthony, what a cunt! Tried to rip me off doing a 70 property development with him. He's a con artist and scammer. Deserves someone to put a bullet through his head."

Wow, that's embarrassing. Julie tried to laugh it off and the conversation again returned to Paula, who clearly was all we were going to talk about all night. Keith and I chatted between ourselves intermittently to fill the odd silence.

Eventually the night finished, and as we strolled together towards the car, Julie asked about the Maserati's number plate. Paul looked sheepish as he said, it was something he was going to sort, and all of us realised the night was just a total bust.

Grateful the evening was finally over, we drove home. Paul looked across at me and apologised. "God Katherine, I thought she would never shut up about that family. Sorry. Talk about an unpleasant blast from the past. No one likes those people. I tried to change the subject that many times, I just gave up."

"Oh well. A boring night that will never get repeated. It's not often you bump into a new person, and find that you know some mutual random, that clearly neither of you like. I just can't believe that's all that was talked about all evening. I never even learnt what they do for a living, or where Keith lives. This was one bizarre night."

"Well, one thing is for sure. I never want to hear Paula Spaky's name again, that's for sure. OMG what a fucking nightmare of a night."

We both laughed and hoping it would never be repeated, we spent the course of the next week, having enjoyable meals and cocktails with everyone else. I thankfully never saw the hostility, aimed at anyone else, from Paul again, and I wasn't sure what to make of that whole encounter.

# Chapter 32

3rd July, 2014

It was the night before I flew to Tasmania, which was the day before Paul had to fly to Boston, so he had organised a romantic going away dinner at the Sofitel. He had asked me to dress up, so I had chosen a white lace skirt and matching silk blouse. It was cowl necked and hung elegantly. I broke it up with back and white stilettos and black belt. My hair was slicked back into a smooth French roll.

He had booked a table at No 35, over looking the top end of the city and Collins St, way below. Lit up, the city looked magical. It was hard to believe it was the middle of winter down on the street, when we were perched like eagles up above, sipping Cristal and dining on an entire meal, which he had requested to be gluten free for me.

It was lovely. He talked about our future. He had never felt like this, with anyone before.

"Princess, I love you so much. You're so addictive, its like you are my heroin. I can't get enough of you. I hurt; physically ache, when I'm not with you. I do not know how I will survive this time away from you. Please don't do anything silly without me."

"Is that why you are sending me to Donna Lee's? Because you are afraid I will hook up with someone? Seriously? You know me better than that. You should know how much I love you by now."

"I'd hate to lose you Katherine. After losing someone I loved, I don't think I would survive losing you as well. You are a million times the woman she was and I cannot imagine a million times the pain, if I were ever to lose you. I am unbelievably lucky to have found you. I feel like you are my reward for all the angst I have been through. I'm alive in your presence, and you make me feel like a better person. You make me want to try being a better person every day. In truth, I am scared that I'm not good enough for you. That, if you knew the real me, you'd realise, you deserve better."

"You're the most amazing man I have ever met. Stop being silly. You're acting like a vagina again. You are an awesome human being, and I love you with all my heart."

We finished the scrumptious meal, with a delicate, dark chocolate mousse. My favourite. Then we went for a walk down Collin's St. I thought we were going to have some drinks at the Long Room. As we went past the stairs of St Michael's, he said.

"There's your church. It looks beautiful at night."

The lights reflected up the ornate walls and caught the branches of the bare winter trees. It was picturesque.

He led me up the stairs and we turned to look up at the light playing along the trees. The last stoic autumn leaves slowly flipping down the road in the slight breeze.

"Katherine, even though I don't believe in a God or church, I know it's important to you and what is important to you, is important to me."

He held my hand and slowly got down on one knee.
OOHH MMMYYY GGGODDD! I think he is going to propose for real this time.

"Katherine you are the one I have been looking for to spend the rest of my life with. I love you. I have waited all this time for you, and you know I have never loved anyone as I do you. I am blessed by your company. I am literally the happiest man on earth just being with you, and I cannot imagine being happier than I am, unless you agree to spend the rest of your life with me. So, will you? Will you be my wife?"

I knew he was going to propose sooner rather than later. He had been hinting since we had returned from Hamilton Island. I kept telling him that I'd say yes, when he asked me in another year. It was a funny response, but I was trying to slow him down. I was being logical and tactful, and stalling it to a further away time than his incessant speed dial plan.

Regardless, here we were 12 weeks after first meeting, on the steps of St Michael's and I didn't hesitate.

"Yes, Paul, I would truly be honored to share the rest of my life with you. You are a good man. The real gentleman that I have been looking for."

What could I do? He just doesn't know how to go slow. He is a powerhouse, who knows what he wants, kind of man. Take control and enjoy the now.

He pulled out a box and slipped a magnificent ring on my finger.

"Thank you thank you, Princess, I will love you like no other, and will try to always show you how I feel. You must always feel you are loved."

He stood up to kiss me, his eyes sparkling as he raised my hand higher so I could see it more clearly. It was an enormous high set solitaire.

"I'm giving you this ring, because this is how much you are worth to me." He scrunched his face. It's, ah, 3 and a half carrots, but by accepting and wearing it, you will always know and feel how much I treasure you. Promise to never take it off. I love you so much."

He held my hand up again and said, "Tell me, when you finally realise your worth." And then he kissed me slowly and passionately, on the steps of St Michael's, in the moonlight, through the winter trees.

Momentarily, my mind returns to the aching reality of the shop.

It had been perfect. We were in love.

The universe is cruel. It didn't need to take him away. Hating the present, I force myself back into happy memories.

He took his phone out and snapped a selfie, posting it immediately on our shared Facebook. "I want the world to know how happy I am right this very second."

We were blissfully happy and so much in love. As it should be.

Everyone commented. Congratulations. Friends and family, my clients were all so happy for us. What a romantic fairy tale. Paul stopped walking, so we could reply to them.

'Yes, she is amazing. I am so happy. She is my true love. My Princess.'

'Ha ha yes, so now I have a ring of diamonds AND a diamond ring.'

'Thank you, he is awesome.'

'Yes, I am so lucky. My Princess will soon be my future Queen.'

'Yes, she said yes. And yes Darrin, all the kids know. So it's your turn now, when are you popping the question to Maggie?'

So many people, many I didn't know yet.

His Aunt Bruna congratulating him, and his family joining in.

'Congratulations.'

'I'm so happy for you.'

'She looks perfect for you.'

His cousin, Trish.

'Another cousin. Welcome to the carter family.'

His family were genuinely over the moon for him to have found love again. I was still shocked that this beautiful, beautiful man thought I was enough for him.


These are wonderful memories, but are they holding the answers. Is there anything that explains why I'm now wanted dead. Why everything has gone so wrong?

I wrap myself tighter and pull into a ball.

# Chapter 33

The next morning, bleary eyed from celebrating with another bottle of champagne, Paul drove me to the airport. He kissed me goodbye and it felt devastatingly wrong to be parting after he had just proposed. He waited till I was boarding the plane and then my new fiance turned and purposefully strode away.

I missed him dreadfully. Being with him had become habit, but it was totally joyous to catch up with my girlfriend. It was like we had never been apart. Donna Lee is pure love and compassion. The kids, all five of them, had grown up so much but nothing else had changed.

Everyone was so excited and happy for my news, and we all got caught up looking at cakes and dresses online. Paul was sending photos of things he liked. I was surprised at how involved and enthusiastic he was. We all laughed. He had awesome taste. He told us that he wanted our three boys, Oliver, John and Andrew to be the groomsmen and left me to now find three age appropriate bridesmaids.

Obviously, I had thought of Donna Lee but realizing how young the boys were, decided that her beautiful daughter, Shaylah, would enjoy it just as much, and Donna Lee would still get to come to the wedding. Oliver's girlfriend Sarah, and my girlfriend Louise.

We spent the first two days gossiping and swapping stories in between the demands of her work and kids. Working as the manager of a Christian camp for kids meant they lived on site, so there was no escape. I managed to drag her away for lunch once. It was literally the only time we got away. We clung to the happiness Paul was bringing to my life. She felt this was God looking after me.

When Paul rang, it was to tell me he hadn't left Melbourne yet, as he needed to deal with a contractor, who had poured a slab and not used reinforcement. It was the deal breaker moment, and he now wanted nothing to do with Carbomac in Australia. He promised, he was getting rid of the business. Then I told him about how Dona Lee's Christian camp was struggling and needed some help. There were two fund raisers coming up. One was for

Shay who was a contestant in a charity pageant in Paris later that year. The other was directly for the benefit of the camp. It needed a lot of building maintenance work to be carried out. This all sounded like Paul was perfect for the job.

Without me saying this, he volunteered. "I know you love your girlfriend, and that she was there with you through some tough times, so I love her too. Can you find out what exactly is needed, and then tell me everything when you pick me up from the airport."

"What? When?"

"Tomorrow." I could hear his smirk through the phone. "It would just be awkward for me to meet them and ask." He laughed.

"I'm confused. Are you coming here? What happened to Boston?"

"I missed you too much, Princess. You are my world and I'll be honest, I don't know what you have done to me, but I just am not functioning without you here. So I booked my flights to wreck your time with Donna Lee. I wanted to surprise you. Baby, you are just more important than work so I cancelled and told them to all just do their job. My focus is you. I've just got engaged and I want to be with you. They are really happy for me by the way. They all knew my ex really well, it's as if she was part of the Woodmason and Carbomac teams. But they are just genuinely happy that I have finally moved on and found you. There were lots of 'well done, congratulations and about time' comments. They are looking forward to meeting you when we go over."

The next day, I picked him up and returned to Donna Lee's. There was a turn around of the Christian camps. One departing another arriving. It was a crazy frenetic day. At the end, we all went out for dinner to celebrate not only the engagement, but Paul's existence, and everyone finally meeting, and additionally, Donna Lee's son, Jed's 21st birthday. It was a great night, and then Paul handed over an envelope. Jed opened it and his eyes nearly popped out of his head. A cheque for $1000 to help towards his car. After the excitement died down, Paul asked Donna Lee to accompany him outside. She came back inside 15 minutes later, her face blotchy from crying. We all asked what had happened.

With tears freshly flowing, she emotionally stuttered. "Paul just offered to pay for all of us all to go to Paris for the Pageant, so Shaylah can defend her title and if that isn't enough, he is also donating $10,000 towards her charity fund raising. I cannot thank you enough Paul. You are truly a God send."

I could not have been happier for them. I was so grateful to Paul for being beyond kind to my friends. It was too wonderful for words to see my girlfriend and her family so happy and relaxed.

He took me back to the hotel, which he had booked for us to stay in for the next three days. We had raucous sex from the moment we got through the door, panting and ripping unnecessary clothes off, finishing against the wall near the lounge suite. We couldn't get enough of each other. A few days apart and the sex was phenomenal. We went to bed, and repeated the performance for longer, at a much slower and more sensual pace.

The next morning because Donna Lee couldn't spend time with Paul and I, we went exploring the local area.

"I hope you don't mind just cruising around, Princess, because in America, this is seriously how we will send most of our time, except in the sun. The more I think about it, the more I realise I should close everything down and just be with you. Clearly we don't work very well being apart. I was panicking without you."

We drove around, but there wasn't too much to see except Smithton, and as it was winter the tourist town was literally closed. We discovered a local supermarket back where we were staying and stocked up on supplies.

Once back at the hotel, we dropped the shopping and 5 bridal magazines on the counter and he bent me over and took me from behind. It was quick.

He was still fully erect inside me, and kissing my neck. His arm wrapped around me, his hand gently cupping my breast. His other arm wrapped around my waist holding me in tight against his body.

"God, I can't get enough of you. I thought at my age, this passion would have disappeared. It's the opposite, I have never been so aroused, so desperate to be with someone. I can't wait for you to be mine forever. Why don't we just do it now? Run away."

He left to clean up, and two minutes later returned.

"You are with me, Paul, and I wish we could, but we need to give at least a months notice and you know that."

I could hear running water. I gave him a quizzical look.

"I'm filling the spa bath. Thought we could spend the afternoon lazing. Afterwards we can download the forms, lodge them this week and get married by the beginning of August."

"Or we could take a little longer. The process is not that simple you know."

I laughed because regardless of everything that would need to be organised, I knew we would be getting married according to Paul time.

We made an enormous antipasto platter, and he moved furniture so we could rest it beside the oversized spa.

Two glasses and the champagne, and we were ready.

What a wonderful way to spend a cold rainy, grey day.

We lay there, slowly pruning. Chatting about dream weddings and honeymoons.

He had realized it would be a church wedding, but wasn't convinced we shouldn't just do that quietly, and then have a huge party celebration on an island, with our friends and family.

"Well, I think Bora Bora is out still." I joked. I still didn't know if there was a girl associated with his time there, but I didn't want to find out on my honeymoon. I had spent enough time sharing Paul with a ghost. I did not want another shadow on my wedding night.

"Ah, yes, well there is something you may want to know. It's not that important, but still."

I scrunched my face. Really?? There's more. What now? Surely if he had honeymooned with his wife he wouldn't want to go there with me.

"No seriously. Sometime there is so much to tell you. I've just led such a huge life, that I literally forget and then time passes, but if you are going to marry me, you need to know everything about me. Fair?"

"Obviously. So what is it this time and please Paul, just tell me everything. No more holding back. I don't want to be married and still having these surprise conversations."
I was smiling, but as usual I could feel trepidation. I was waiting for the day, he told me some deal breaker.

"You know I was married to Maggie and I've got the two boys. Now don't get upset, but, well technically I have sort of been married another time as well. I normally don't talk about it because it was such a short period of time, like not even hours, that no one even considers it valid, but when we put in our paperwork you are going to see, and you should know. I'm truly sorry. I just didn't want you to know about my failings. I don't want you to think less of me. I love that you love me."

I felt slapped. Shocked, and was waiting for his, as usual, rationalization.

Her name was Sonja. She worked in a jewelry store. It was after the divorce and he was letting off steam. She was young and beautiful.

"I dated her for two years and thought it was wonderful. We got married in Willimstown gardens and the reception was at Shellys, the restaurant you and I go to. It's why the owner knows me so well. I have been going for the best part of 15 years. I hold no grudges toward the venue for my failed marriage. If that's what we can call it. Anyway. On the way to the reception, we were having photos in the garden and slowly making our way over, when these two guys in suits started walking towards us. I can remember they looked agitated and one in particular seemed upset. I turned to Sonja and asked. 'Do we have a problem here?'
And she was saying. 'Oh my God, oh my god, over and over.'

The guy came up to me and knowing no better, I asked if I could help him. He said. 'You're marrying my fiance. I have photos here.' And he brought out his phone, saying. 'We've been engaged for a year.'

I looked at Sonja, in front of both our families and the entire bridal party, and she sort of just crumpled to the ground, still saying. 'Oh my god, oh my god.'

I took my ring off and dropped it on her dress. Turned to my groomsmen, David and Randy and said. 'Come on, we need to get drunk.' We left them to it. And that's also why I didn't want those two being in the bridal party for us.

Anyway, her mum was beside us, and I saw her walk across and spit on her own daughter. Called her a slut and the whole family walked off. I still partied the night away, but more as consolation obviously.

She tried to sort it out for months but I would have none of it. She said that she had broken up with him ages ago but he wouldn't accept it. I didn't believe her. I had seen enough of the photos to know he was telling the truth.

I got so drunk at the reception. It was one of the parties that I had there. I told you about it, just without the wife and failed wedding reception title, obviously.

I spent my honeymoon by myself in Bora Bora, which is why I want us to go there, because I know how wonderfully magical it is, and this time I'd like to actually share it with someone I love. You can learn to scuba dive, snorkel and hang in the water." He saw my face. "Seriously Katherine, I'm sorry. There are no more surprises. That's the last one. I just don't count it as a marriage. I mean it lasted what? An hour. Half an hour. She just doesn't deserve to count. I don't even count it as a relationship. No one does."

I remember looking at him and laughing. So much to take on board again. I can't judge for the universe throwing bizarre things. My life is full of totally strange coincidences and stories as well. My resume of life has some awful high and low lights.

"Come on Paul, how did you not know she was in a relationship of that level with another man for a year? It's not possible. There would have been signs."

"I don't know Katherine. I used to wonder. I'm not a stupid man. My friends aren't stupid. My family isn't stupid but we were all fooled. At the end of the day, I learnt people believe what they want to believe and hear and see only what they want to see. And people only let you see what they want you to see. It's natural, we choose to trust, and believe what we are told. I wasn't looking for any "signs," I was in love.

Maybe I should have known. Once she had a work function in the Hyatt and she asked me to grab something from our room. I went upstairs and her girlfriend Paula followed me, and fully made out with me until I pushed her away. Some of Sonja's friends were old money. This one was one of those. Spoilt, selfish and prepared to ruin her friend's happiness for a quick fuck. Her hands were down my pants. You know that sort of woman, isn't my type. I was in love with Sonja, and I wasn't attracted to her frumpy friend nor do I cheat. She was just a lonely, desperate, suburban housewife. I remember, she tried to justify it, by saying.

'Come on, you know Sonja is cheating. We should fuck here on your bed. She would.'

I man handled her out of the room. She was drunk. Well, that's what I thought at the time, but now I look back and realise that she really did know. I mean, they were best friends at the time."

I'd sat pruning in the spa bath, sipping my champagne and listening. Paul, never failed to surprise me. I have a failed marriage. Who am I to judge.

"I'm sorry you went through that. It's a bizarre story, but I had a girlfriend whose husband brought the bimbo he was having an affair with, to the actual wedding and reception, as a guest, so I know it happens. Their marriage only lasted a couple of hours as well. Shit happens. There is a reason that expression exists. It's because - shit happens. But truly, I wish you could just have told me before. You should be comfortable in telling me your truth Paul. I'm pretty well known for not judging."

"Well now you know Katherine. I don't talk about it as a marriage because it clearly doesn't count. She has since gone off fucking half of Melbourne, and is a coke head now or so I have been told. Goes to swingers parties and she won't change her name on face book from Sonja Carter. Can't believe it's the same girl I thought I loved. A true Jeckle and Hyde; a total mess. Her choic. She could have been happy with me, although it obviously worked out for the best. I realise she was a disaster in the making.

At the divorce she tried to take me for everything, but Randy ensured she got nothing. I let her keep the BMW I had bought her. That's it. After what she had done, she didn't deserve anything more. I don't like regrets, but she is one. She is an example of something I took too far. I wish I had stopped it earlier; that I had realized the outcome sooner. I feel my relationship with her, may still come back to haunt me. Like, the way I left things with her, that there's unfinished business. It's ok, Randy will handle it, and by then you and I will be long gone, so I honestly won't be around to face the repercussions, if she ever resurfaces. They can only try." He laughed, but it seemed somewhat sad.

"Again Paul, I'm sorry you regret your relationship with her. Your past helps form you into what you are now and you are a good man, so no one judges you. I don't. But you have to stop with these surprises."

"I hope not. I'm just sorry that I have to say I was married twice. I got it annulled, so it legally doesn't count. I cut my ties with her, and everyone associated with it, and moved on. Sorry sweet heart, I forget about her, so until now, didn't even think that you needed to know. It's been an honest oversight."

He stayed another two days, most of that with Donna Lee. He discussed the needs of the property, and how he could help the camp function better financially, as well as, focusing on the company and trust issues. He was full of advice. They even talked about him joining the committee in an executive role. He advised about the set up of charities and trusts to avoid tax and maximize thresholds. Totally over my head and Donna Lee's.

She was so grateful. "It's so complicated managing everything, this is why having you on a board, Paul, would be a God send."

"Donna Lee, I can honestly say, it would be my pleasure and privilege. I know being around you and your work would enrich me, ten fold." He hugged her tightly.

By the time he flew home, my poor girlfriend had a long list of things to find out, so he could help sort out the mess.

He left Thursday and we were on the phone that night. Between Jed, Donna Lee, Shaylah and the other children, it seemed everyone wanted to talk to him. He warned me that he had lots of international business calls and Skype to deal with, so he would call in between, over the weekend. He was under a bit of pressure because he hadn't gone over to Boston when he should have.

He rebooked me on to an earlier flight so I followed two days later. We just didn't like being apart, and now there was so much to organise. We were both ridiculously excited, and I wanted to come home and see Ollie and Sarah. I wanted him to be apart of this with us.

I didn't hear from him till just before I got on the plane. He had tried to contact me, but it was in the middle of the night and I had missed his calls. He had left messages. I couldn't wait to see him. I rang and left messages. Sadly getting more desperate. 48 hours with no communication was painful.

Before I got on the plane, Donna Lee pulled me aside.

"Katherine, I wanted to thank you for bringing Paul into our lives. He is wonderful. I am so happy for you. I prayed for both of you last night. You know, I woke this morning refreshed for the first time in years. I slept so soundly. I'm so relieved that Shayla can go to the pageant and defend her crown, and that he is making such a generous donation. I'm truly shocked. Thank you for this opportunity Paul is giving us."

# Chapter 34

Wrapped in blankets, pining for this wonderful man. Trying to put the pieces together as to how we went from there, to where I am now. Such a good man. None of this makes sense. You're no longer beside me, and I've been threatened with a tree shredder.

What have all these memories shown me? Anything? Is the key there, and I just can't see it?

So far, there is a charismatic, attractive, rich man with two wives, two children. His friends and family are happy he has me. My friends are happy. He has a haggard friend with a tarty girlfriend from the BBQ. Paul, himself is, polite, considerate, generous, loving, funny, gregarious, protective, stubborn, successful, busy, powerful, controlling, obsessed with me, compassionate, a joy to be around, classy, tattooed, multitude of friends from all walks of life, runs charities, sponsors children. Wealthy parents. Phone calls and meetings that I get to sit in on. Solicitor friend. Accountant friend. I'm now engaged.

There is nothing here.

What am I looking for? What am I missing? Who has caused this mess and why am I in danger? I need to keep looking. Where are you Paul? What has happened to you? Why aren't you here looking after me? Something bad has happened. I know that.

Forcing myself up, in search of warmth, I've shuffled, hunched over, wrapped in a blanket, hiding my light sensitive eyes from the world, and crossed the reception area of the shop. I can see my toes pushing the material forward as I make my slow way to the front beautician's room, I drag the oil heater from under the massage table where it keeps the staff's legs warm while they sit doing eye lash clients. Turning, I realise a second blanket has been caught in my moving cocoon. It has followed me like the black train of a morbid wedding dress. I feel saddened as I plug the heater in, beside my make shift bed.

The activity was exhausting and I curl up on the mattress, to continue my flu induced memories.

He greeted me at the airport and whisked me straight home to the couch where he literally ravished me. Again two days apart, and he was insatiable. By the time we went for dinner, he had cum five times. I was exhausted and chafed. He had obviously shaved all over, a few days earlier, and the stiff stubble destroyed me. This was something I had never dealt with before, but I didn't want to ruin my home coming, by being a whinge.

Over dinner at Nobu, we sat arm in arm, curled into the bench seat of the corner table looking across the river. He actually looked gray. It was clear he was under inordinate stress.

"Katherine, it's bad enough when business isn't smooth. Thankfully that isn't often, but I hate it when you aren't happy. That makes my existence unbearable. I used to think I had loved before, but nothing has prepared me for you. Sometimes it's like I'm drowning under a tidal wave of feelings. I physically ache. I don't understand it. I'm sorry you were stressed over the last two days. But just so you know, I missed you. I can't be apart from you ever again. I don't breathe. I need you. I promise that if I ever need to go away, you will come with me."

The next morning we woke to pandemonium. Whilst I was gone, Andrew had crashed his BMW. It had happened the day I left for Tasmania, and Paul had avoided telling me because he was so angry. Now, the panel beater had woken us. Apparently the whole underside was damaged, and the wheels on the left side were buckled in at the axle. Andrew had described it as a little skid and flat tire. Now, without coffee, Paul was being told that it was nearly a write off and that his son had deliberately lied. It hadn't been towed. They had to get a truck to lift it from the scene. Andrew knew this. It wasn't a good start to the day. Added to this, Paul had leant him the Maserati to see him through. Now Paul's generosity made him feel like a fool.

Standing in our dressing gowns, waiting for the expresso to brew, his phone pinged again. He had been opening emails.

"Fuck this shit." As he stormed down to the office, he turned, and over his shoulder, blew me a kiss. "Sorry Princess."

I stayed quietly in the kitchen.

He was multi tasking, and I realized, he was talking to Andrew. "No, you return the car now. I don't care. Don't lie to me."

I brought his coffee down and as I placed it beside him, I heard Andrew scream down the phone. "Don't you talk to me that way. You are no father to me. Parents don't act this way. I didn't ask for it, you gave it to me, to protect your own arse. Come and take it then."

I walked out of the room. God teenagers could be ungrateful. By the time I had my shower, Paul was seemingly calm, but it was just white anger.

"Princess, I have to go to Boston. The GM hasn't turned up to work. I have asked Natalie to sort our tickets out. We need to go for two weeks. We could have taken longer but you have the shop, and I want to come home and get married as soon as possible. Can you be packed for tomorrow, 5 am? I'm sorry. What a morning. I'm closing down the Australian businesses. I don't need mornings like this, and you don't deserve them."

"Paul, I don't think I can, I have to go sort the shop out. Joy needs a day off, and I want to see Ollie. Sorry, I'm not in a position to just drop everything this time. I wish I could."

"That's ok, Princess, I half expected it, but I didn't want to be the one to break my promise." He was turning and going back down stairs. He was already on the phone but he stopped at the landing.

"Natalie. Make that just for me. Business. Yes, and for only five days. Put me on a later flight so I'm not rushed tomorrow morning. Yes, back in five days. Leave me 3 days to sort out business. Email me."

He took a breath and turned to me again. "Since Andrew hasn't returned the car, I'll have to drop you at the shop on my way through tomorrow, or I can do it after dinner tonight. Up to you sweet. I know you hate mornings, but I don't want to leave you until the last second. God what an ungrateful shit. You're not going to be able to get yourself from the shop home. You're going to have to stay there or catch taxis. I'm so sorry.

Again he snatched his phone and called Andrew. They had another screaming match.

I wrote on a scrap of paper. *"Let it go. It's ok. I like the shop."* I pushed it in front of him across the kitchen bench, and walked away. I hate it when he raises his voice.

He sat beside me on the couch. "I'd prefer you in the house. You're meeting Sarah and Oliver tomorrow aren't you?"

"Yes. Someone wants to see the ring and it's important, considering the news, that I see him as soon as possible. I want him to be a part of this and share in the happiness and excitement."

"So do I, Princess."

Paul arranged brunch at a cafe in Brunswick St with Oliver and Sarah, as he wanted to be there when they saw the ring and he had something he wanted to discuss with Oliver. We grabbed a quick bite to eat and gushed over the ring. It was so exciting. It was lovely seeing Oliver be happy with me. When we finished eating, we all strolled up the street. Looking in at the window displays and popping into the cake shops, wedding organizers, looking at shoes, invitations,suits and dresses. I was increasingly aware that there was so much to choose from, most of it horrible. Clearly it was just a case of wading through bleached synthetic tulle, until you find something less plastic.

It was the 14th of July. I had been engaged for a less than two weeks, and he wanted us to try dresses on from random bridal shops.

"But Paul, you want Aldo Terrato to design the dress."

"I know, but we can get a feel for what will look nice. Trust me, you aren't going to find the dress today."

We went to Marianna Hardwick. They had some beautiful dresses. I tried on a crisp white classic meringue, and an ivory Grace Kelly inspired design. Technically the two dresses combined would be the perfect dress. Neither hit the mark. Let the pain begin.

Suddenly he had to leave. We watched him drive off, but this time it didn't twinge so much. I was home with Ollie and everything felt right.

We kept wandering and walked into another shop. Out of the corner of my eye, I spotted the same dress Sarah did. It was Champagne ivory. Full tulle. Love heart shaped corset and it had fine black trim detail. It was beautiful. So, so perfectly beautiful. She tried it on.

When the shop assistant left us unattended for two minutes, we whipped out our phones, and took photos of her. Oliver had tears in his eyes. "You look so beautiful, Babe."

I felt like I was intruding on their moment, and panicked that I had just sped up their relationship.

She stood in front of the mirror. "OMG, I want to wear this for my wedding." She was glowing.

Laughing I said. "I want you to wear it as my bridesmaid. It's perfect."

"Really? Really? Really?" She was giddy with excitement.

I sent Paul the photos and he immediately replied. "Get it. Get three."

At $3000 each, I was stunned. Sarah was visibly shocked. "I'm going to wear this?" She twirled.

We spoke to the assistant and told her when Paul had wanted the wedding. "Yesterday." I said in all seriousness."

She was horrified. "You need to order it today, and I will tell you when they can confirm delivery. You can't book a venue until I get a delivery date."

Ten minutes later she came back from the office. "We can get three in, by September 9th. That is the earliest."

I relayed this to Paul, who was about to board the plane. "They need a deposit now."

My phone pinged immediately. "I don't want to wait that long. xx"

Within 5 minutes another lady came out from the back room. "Maria, Maria? Where is your bride? Katherine, your fiance just paid the deposit for 3 of those dresses. I will need confirmation of sizes and measurements within 24 hours. This will be tight."

I couldn't believe the process had begun. I was marrying Paul Carter. I never thought that I could be this happy.

We spent another half an hour there. Getting Sarah out of the dress was a challenge because she looked so beautiful and was reluctant to take it off. I totally understood. She was radiant. I knew that I couldn't wait to see her eventually marry my son.

Then I had to provide details of the bridesmaids and myself. As usual everyone was shocked at the speed things had happened. I, on the other hand, had got used to reeling and living on Paul time.

# Chapter 35

Paul was only gone four days. He stayed in contact and bemoaned his tasks. He was interviewing replacements. He had lined up an agency, and plowed through potential manager after potential manager. He was over flowing with coffee, but on a good note he was enjoying the sun.

He posted photos of American sunshine, cafes, and donuts on Facebook, whilst we had winter grayness. Even so, I knew he wished he was home. His biggest whinge was not being able to sleep, because I wasn't beside him. When he finally got home he destroyed my body. His passion was out of control and I ended up having to tell him to stop.

"Paul. I can't cope." I laughed as I pulled myself away. "You're too much man for me. I get it. Seriously be gentle. Please." It was as if he needed to devour me. "Did you shave? Why would you do that, you know it chafes me."

"I haven't shaved since you told me to stop, baby. I know you're delicate. I try to be as gentle as I can. You are just so breakable and I'd never want to damage you. I don't want to hurt you." He flipped me over. "It won't bother you this way, Princess."

He needed what he needed.

It was wonderful to be able to sleep with him. Nestled in against his body. Him holding me so tightly. Every night the same thing. Cradling my head against his chest, pulling me in against his body and wrapping my leg over his large frame.

"This is my favorite part of the day, Princess. You are my everything."

"I love you too."

"I love you more.' He kissed my forehead and immediately dropped off to sleep.
Everything was back to normal.

Over the next few weeks, we leapt into organization mode.

He was relieved that the new GM was less expensive and more qualified. There was a fortnight before the last incumbent would leave and there was time for a hand over. Paul looked so much more relaxed.

'It's sort of ironic when someone doesn't realise they are helping plan their own demise, that they are being replaced. And helping you do it. Obviously they don't know they are organizing the company to wind down. I'll do the honorable thing. Keep it going for two years. Then sell it.

Right now, I'm more concerned about you. Princess I think you should close the shop. The government has their figures and you have pulled miracles in increasing the turn over, but now I think it's time to stop. Let's just organise the engagement and wedding, and us moving. There's so much to do, before we can be gone. Both starting our new lives before Christmas."

What a whirl wind. Engaged and then those next 8 weeks of organizing the wedding, engagement and our life. We focused so much on our future together. I didn't want a party. I wanted a marriage. Paul wanted both and everything.

We needed a planned exist. Three young, adult children needing to be told. Accept, feel safe and secure. Organised. Setup.

My visa. Sponsorship. My bank accounts. My financials. The shop. Meetings with his solicitor and mine, my accountant, finalizing my account books. Closing. Selling it piece meal. Packing. Moving all of me into Paul's house. Selling his unfinished penthouse. Cars. Sorting his properties, handing management of Carbomac in Australia over to Neville Meturst, his project manager.

There was just so much to do. The details of bridal parties were easy and simple in comparison.

Then two weeks before our engagement we went to a very special wedding. His father's.

# Chapter 36

I pull back from the memory. Some one got married, and it wasn't me. I think of the happiness of the day and it hurts. I light another cigarette. I can smell the acrid odor of my dirty, stressed, sick body. I have an ulcer coming up on my tongue. My mouth is the perfect bubbling acid bowl of anxiety and defeat. At some point I need to get better. Just enough to leave and be looked after by Deb. I need a shower. I need clean clothes. I don't feel safe. I'm waiting for something bad.

I shut my eyes.

We all looked so lovely that day. Paul in his brand color. Deep blue. Crisp white french cuffed shirt. Me in a classic tailored white linen shirt and black and white hounds tooth skirt. My favorite black and white winter coat with its black leather trim edges. I love that coat, and when Paul had bought it for me, I was so thrilled, I thought I would burst.

Paul's brother and Anna were there. Funny how two brothers can look so similar and yet one not quite match the other. David reminded me of a poor carbon copy. Designer blue suit but just not as crisp. Never as sharp when he stood beside Paul. Every time I met him, I wondered whether he was aware. Anna always looked beautifully put together. Maintained. I was envious of her ability to present so well. We had met for dinner several times now. I liked them. She wore the pants and David, clearly aware she was out of his league, doted on her.

We were standing in the foyer of the registry office waiting for the 80 year old bride and groom to arrive. Anna leant forward to Paul.

"You're looking lovely Paul. When are you taking Katherine and I shopping? So we can drape ourselves in Prada? Your brother stopped looking after me, the moment we got married."

"Yes, you nearly bankrupted me." David laughed and Paul joined in, but there was a cold look in his eyes.

"Seriously when? I was happy to wait till October when we were all going away together, but now that isn't happening. So when, when are you rewarding us?"

I was horrified. I never thought of Paul like that.

"You'll just have to make David work harder. Your clothes stopped being my problem a long time ago, remember." I saw a flash between the three of them. Paul rescued what ever the moment was. "Have you finished those changes on the kitchen? We can't finalise costs until you do. Your constant changing of details is slowing the whole process down. You could have been in before Christmas, but now my team will be pushing January to fit out.

David and Anna began making heated excuses for their changes and upgrades, and simultaneously retreated, looking for the room where the ceremony was to be held. Paul and I went out for a cigarette. Apparently the bridal party was going to be late for their own wedding.

He was making a funny face as he lit my cigarette. "You can't breed class, Katherine."

I looked at him confused.

"David cheated on his first wife. He'd always treated her like shit so it's no surprise. Not the way I would have conducted myself. My father was embarrassed. The writing was on the wall for a long time. I would go over there and act as go between during their arguments so I knew it was bad, but I'm still surprised that he started going to the strippers. That's where he met Anna. The strip club, Kittens. Bottom rung. Might as well be a Russian bride. His wife walked in on them having sex in the shower. The rest is history. She rightly made his life hell. Took the daughter away from him. Then again, would you want your child hanging around a stripper. I'm not supporting how they got together or any of what has happened, but she shouldn't use the child as a weapon to wound him. He loves his daughter.

They got married very quickly before her visa ran out. No one knew about it. No one still does. They don't want his ex wife to find out. Neither wears their rings in public, only around us. Clearly she is with him for the money. My parent's and friends, well everyone, is horrified. That's what he blew his inheritance on. You know my comment before when she spoke about me taking her shopping?"

I nodded. I was confused as he had never said anything bad about them except I knew David liked the strippers, and he was financially a disaster. Most of us are, so no judgement from me.

"Well, when they first started seeing each other, I was paying for him to fly her here and there, and then he came to me asking for even more help. He had maxed out all his cards. I saw the statements. Couture this, designer that. Labels, dinners. It was ridiculous. I paid them out clear, and cut them up. Told him to close all the accounts. That's why he doesn't buy her any nice things, because I basically bought her entire wardrobe. Once a whore, always a whore. My parents are mortified by her. Nothing any of us can do, except ask her to pull her skirt down."

Wow. Harsh. I thought she was a receptionist in an accounting firm. He could have left that alone. Maybe I would never have known. I still liked her. I liked David. I knew Paul and he were extremely close. God, families! They are all dysfunctional messes behind closed doors. I am not here to judge.

We were turning to go back inside, when his father and Grace arrived together, walking across the street. Tiny, frail old couple. She was constant laughter. The ceremony was short and full of laughter. They had dressed smart but casual, as Paul had predicted, but his father had embraced this new level of comfort, and taken it to a new height. He was actually wearing a cardigan and Grace was in a lovely nanna pant suit. We both chuckled.

Paul introduced me. The future Mrs Paul Carter to the future Mr and Mrs John Carter. It was exciting meeting them, but I was mindful that it was such a special day for them, and I was just an extra for the ceremony. They seemed over the moon to meet me, but I was conscious that Paul and I shouldn't be the focus. Neither got their vows right as they couldn't hear the celebrant clearly enough to repeat them. It was a riot. It took ages for them to stop laughing long enough to get through the ceremony. It was joyous and considering it was just the six of us in the room, it was loud. Paul, David and Anna chatted, heckled and interjected, the bride and groom laughed and laughed. It was the most raucous and genuine wedding I have ever been to. When the ceremony finished, we had a few photos as a group.

It was over so fast. As we wandered out to have lunch at the European, Paul held my hand.

"And that is why we won't be doing a civil service. Nothing special in that at all. But, there, you finally got to meet Dad and Grace. Told you she was loud. Not a typical Carter, that's for sure. Never stops enjoying life, and I'm really glad my Dad will get to laugh his way into his grave not mope around all miserable. The longest part of the service was them trying to hear their vows and say their own names. OMG. Let's get a drink."

I had thought it was lovely.

The next week, we went out for an early dinner with 40 of their extended family and friends. They were as excited to meet me, as they were for the new bride and groom.

I was introduced to all of them, and they asked us about our up coming engagement and wedding. Paul regaled them with his plans. The long tables generated so much noise you could hardly hear the person beside you. Our engagement being the next week was soon the focal point of all discussion. It was a happy, noisy family affair and the conversation seemed to just get louder and louder. Paul thought it was hysterical. "Bloody old people need to turn up their hearing aids. Shoot me before I have to shout to hear myself."

Being the only smokers, Anna, Paul, David and I spent time away from the table outside. Paul wanted to leave. "I warned you all, it would be like this. It's why I said I didn't want to come. They wouldn't even miss us if we left. They are all old retired farts. Come on. I hate being around them."

"Paul, seriously they are family." Anna admonished him.

"I know, but it makes me feel old. I hate seeing 'that' as my future. Come on let's get this dessert done, and we are out of here. I have too many things to do still."

I looked at him. He was genuine. He didn't want to get old. I wondered if he was ever going to have done enough to be happy.

# Chapter 37

And then there we were, suddenly the morning of our engagement. August 23rd. With the bridal party gathered together for the weekend, we had organised a tight schedule of partying, eating, and engagement and wedding issues. Trying on bridesmaid dresses and my wedding dress for a fitting. A relaxing lunch in the city with the girls and Oliver, and back to the house where everyone was staying. I worried that Oliver might be overwhelmed at being both Paul's Bestman, and giving me away, but he was handling everything wonderfully. Paul had gone with him and bought a Jonathan London suit. Swish, dapper and trendy for the engagement party.

The girls were wearing floor length evening dresses. Last minute details were sorted. Cakes delivered. Djs calling and getting lost. Caterers confirming. Thank goodness Paul and Ollie were on top of the logistics. He had been diligent in the organization of everything. Confirming, reconfirming. Ensuring the night was going to be the spectacular celebration that he envisaged.

Sadly in the morning we had a fight over jewelry. Tension had finally gotten the best of us. The ring he had initially wanted to propose with, had still not arrived because it needed to be resized for my tiny finger. Instead of giving it to me in a lavish display during his speech tonight, he now wanted to use it as my wedding band. I had vehemently said no. I wanted a simple band to show I was married, not a second engagement ring. I wanted the ring to be a symbol of love not a statement of wealth. He took it that I wanted a third ring.

"So you want the solitaire that's already on your finger, a gold band AND the massive pink heart diamond. Katherine, you can't be this greedy."

I think because of how opportunistic his ex had been, he found it difficult to hear my opposite desire. Less is more. I had an engagement ring. It was way more than I could ever have dreamt of. I loved it. Love, loved it. A simple solitaire. I needed no other.

I had to reassure him in front of the bridal party. Finally, I convinced him that my small fingers couldn't possibly hold another massive ring, and which ever diamond ring I ended up with, my wedding band needed to be just that.

I couldn't believe we were even having this discussion, as we had ordered the wedding bands weeks earlier. His was a gold band with a ring of platinum in the middle and a diamond, and mine was plain platinum to match my existing engagement ring.

In the afternoon, Paul and I had gathered our clothes, and departed for a hotel closer to the venue, where everything proceeded to go smoothly.

The night was spectacular and utterly perfect. It was wonderful to see everyone together and relaxing.

It was an evening that was over so quickly and I felt the anti-climatic exhaustion immediately afterwards.

God it's only been three weeks since we were all celebrating. Life is unpredictable. I was so happy, I literally couldn't have imagined being that happy. Ever. My friends were happy. Paul was happy, and even more importantly Oliver was happy. Life was perfect.

So much has happened since then.
I was tired then. Nothing like now, but I was certainly running low.

# Chapter 38

The week after our spectacular engagement, exhausted and gathering ourselves together for the next stage: Our wedding and immediate departure to a new fresh start in life together. New York here we come.

We were both so organised and calm. Nothing had been difficult. We decided to go down to Portsea for a relaxing weekend.

As usual, even though it was officially winter, the sun followed Paul closely. We spent both days strolling the town, along the beaches and drinking and eating. Over dinner, on the last night, he produced a thick file of paperwork. Not what I had ordered with my pesto linguine.

I cringed.

"Princess, you know it needs to be dealt with."

He had brought home a contract weeks ago. He kept talking about making sure he looked after me, if something happened, and as much as I didn't want to discuss it, I was worried that if he died, the family would shatter from fighting over it all. I just wanted it split up in percentages or something, so that didn't happen. I still didn't want to know about it.

Instead, it was an agreement that said I would receive $50 million upon separating amicably. Nothing if I cheated. (Bless. Fair enough, I wasn't going to cheat.) and the lot if he died, with pages of exceptions to account for children, siblings, and cousins, Trinh etc. It went on and on.

Apparently he and his solicitor, Randy Malkoon had been very busy. There was also contracts changing directorship of the companies. He wanted me to have 50% ownership of Woodmasons, the trusts that basically hid and protected everything, and Carbomac in the US.

"Katherine, this is our life together, on paper."

I would never leave him and he wasn't asking me to sign anything that protected his assets. It was just an acknowledgement of massive generosity from him to me, if he died or we split up. I knew in Australia, a pre-nup holds little merit and I hated what it all represented - us not being together. I didn't care if that was because of death or divorce. I didn't want to imagine either.

There were spots for me to put my assets and bank accounts, tax info, and a separate page for conditions. There was a spousal visa application for the US.

I had thought about it for a few days and finally I put blue sticky notes in it, where I wanted things amended.

My conditions.

I want to go on a date with my husband at least once a week, and have sex at least five times a week. We are not to be separated for more than two nights a month. We're to spend at least 3 nights a week in, with just ourselves and we are to create the charity for single mums.

Under my assets, I wrote NIL. Until I got the payout from my shop, all my money was tied up or non existent.

I had left it on the kitchen counter. The only change I noted as a condition for him was that if he cheated, I got it all. I pointed it out to him. "I'd feel the same if we were talking about you owning only a car. I don't want cheating to be an option for either of us. I want you to think about where you put that penis and how much she will cost you if I find out."

He laughed.

"I'm serious Paul. Otherwise, why are we getting married?"

"Princess.I'm fine with it. It had never crossed my mind that I was even an option on that clause. I will never, ever cheat on you. That I promise.

Here." He pulled the papers forward, and hand wrote the amendment in clear writing. If he cheated he gave it all to me. Initialled and signed.

The mere fact he did it made me feel better. I signed the document. We both let it hang around the house and disappear. I honestly loved him and I knew he loved me. If it ever imploded I think the way he looked after Maggie was a good enough indication he wouldn't leave me hungry and homeless on the side of the street.

But here we were, in this nice Italian restaurant and instead of food, I was looking at a thick folder.

"For the record, Randy laughed at your notes on the draft. Apparently your requested terms of regular sex of no less than twice, no more than 20 times per week" was the first time he had seen that. and let me see, oh yes, the clause stipulating "two home cooked meals per week," made him laugh. His wife can't cook. He asked me whether I wanted to negotiate that one.
Your other requests. That we were to spend no more than a night a fortnight away from each other, also made him chuckle. He says, eventually you will want me out of the house all the time.
Look Princess. You have to take it seriously. So look through this document with me. Its time for the signatures. Ollie can sign this week when we catch up for dinner."

I looked at him, sucked in my breath and bit my tongue.

192 million in the Westpac account. We live off the interest from that, Katherine. You saw the statement remember. This is now a joint account. Sign here." He pointed.

Then there's the 15 million property portfolio, here and in America. That includes some properties in Pakenham from a development I did a while ago. Remember when we had dinner with Keith and Julie. She grew up with Paula, that spoilt brat. Remember? Well these are the last of that development with her father. Good riddance when they are sold." He pointed to a line on one of the pages. " Sign here."

I nodded as I listened, and signed where he pointed.

"You will be 50% owner of everything. Remember that night with Julie and Keith, And she knew Anthony, her father. Apple doesn't fall far from the tree. Funny that they hate each other. Small world. He was the arrogant douche I went into partnership with. Parklee. Those properties are currently on the market. Some people are just plain greedy and shouldn't be in business. Karma will get that man. Pretentious know it all. Loud mouth. I made a huge mistake going into business with him. He tried everything possible to con me out of my share. You'll never know what I have had to endure to make money out of that partnership. I don't judge people incorrectly very often, but I called that one wrong. You remember how Julie said that whole family was messed up. Well, anyway, the investment with her dad is getting sorted, so you don't have to worry.

Ok, then there's the 50% share in the marketing company Redstrike and my partnership with Marianne in the tea company. You know I'm liquidating my interests in both. I don't need the headaches once we are no longer here. She has already agreed, so it's just a matter of her sorting the time frame for buying me out. It's nearly 10 million, but she is just so grateful I came to the rescue, when she was wanting to expand overseas. It will be spread out over a few years. We aren't in a hurry for it. I'm glad I could help her out. She is a great friend really. You have to meet her. I'm sorry she didn't make it to the opening of LUX that night. Hopefully soon though.

I digressed, sorry. So look, this spread sheet shows the Gold Coast hotel, that will stay. It's under management and I have an emotional attachment to it, being my first large project. I put everything on the line for that property. My father had watched me sink every cent I had into it, and sweat, not knowing if it was going to work. He offered to help finance me so many times but I have never taken any money from him and I never will. So, anyway, that one stays for the time being.
Then there's the portfolio of stock." He was flicking through the paperwork of stocks and balance sheets. " National Australia manage that. I have my own personal banker. I just get a statement of what's gone where and it just keeps growing exponentially. That can stay." He pointed agin. "You can sign here."

As you have pointed out, I don't want the boys and distant family and you fighting, so I have organised for Randy, to be power of attorney. It will be his job to look after all three of them, so you don't have to. You were home when I had that conversation with Randy the other day, remember?"

I looked at him a little more than confused. "Yes, yes, I remember that phone call. You got angry because he was shocked you were selling things off already. I got that. But which three?"

He faltered.

"My boys: John and Andrew, and Oliver. Don't look at me like that. I told you that I would treat him as my own. Love and protect him exactly the same. I meant it. Katherine, I love you. I am marrying you, and what's mine is yours and the boys. End of story. It would be wrong to go into this with any other attitude. I'll be honest, I have more hopes for my future, riding on Ollie, than my two little losers."

"Yes, but it's so soon and I don't like you talking about dying before I have even had the chance to really live with you. Plus I don't need to know all these details. Just let Randy look after me, the same as the boys." I had zoned out at the start of the conversation. The figures were too big to imagine, and if Randy was going to look after it, then I felt that I only needed the basics.

"Katherine I have more documents for you to sign before the wedding. We can do it in Randy's office as I want you to be able to ask questions. You have to sign these and become a director of my companies with me, so if anything happens, it would be a smooth maneuver for you. I'm trying to look after you. Please take this seriously."

I can remember just looking down at the thick folder and rolling my eyes. After a certain figure, it's all just irrelevant isn't it? It's just big.

So there's the cash, the stocks, the two companies, T2 and Strike. The hotel, and rental portfolio, Woodmason's: both of them and the trusts. The jet and finally the Carbomac Constructions business in the USA. Those properties are rehabbed and flipped, or we are doing side work on clients buildings. So as much as that brings in a lot of cash flow, the GM has been instructed that you will become 50% managing director and share holder, and if necessary, you would take my place. I feel that it would keep you occupied and it's a token title. You would be able to have as much or as little to do with it as you wanted.

And finally, there's the charity. We will organise it after we are married because I think you are overwhelmed. Seven million will be an awesome start. That will be all yours though. I'll be in the background, but for now we are sorted. Sorry Princess, I know you hate this side of things, but its not as though we are talking average jobs and assets here. It's a different world you're playing in now."

"Thank you Paul. Seriously Thank you." This was the only thing I understood. It was my purpose. Running a charity and giving back. I remember that was the part I was most grateful for. That I would invest my time in. I was excited and grateful that I was given this opportunity.

# Chapter 39

I didn't want Paul's life to change me.

But time changes. Feelings change. People change. Apparently everything can change.

It's all a life time ago. Irrelevant in many ways.

Now I sit rocking in the leather upholstered office chair. Looking at my unopened computer. The saucer is a disgusting, overflowing mountain of yellow, scrunched stubs and burnt scorched white butts. I'm offended by it and push myself up slowly. I notice there are actually butts, not just ash, on the floor. I have reached a new low, and I don't even care. I am slow. So slow, I have time between movements to be aware of how slow I am. My mind is fighting to make sense even as I shuffle to the kitchen. I am aware of every motion of my body. I ache and it's a concentrated effort. A tear slides down my hot cheek. This is beyond a fully blown fever. It's like nothing I have ever experienced, and I'm aware that right this second, I am upright so it's a window of functioning. I feel like my body is trying to die. At least the sickness helps numb my hurt. I reach the tiny kitchenette and dump the contents of the saucer into the bin. I grab a blanket from the bed and let it drag along the floor behind me. I wrap it around my body before sitting in the chair and curl my feet in under my bottom. The leather is still warm. I rock and light another cigarette. This is my world.

Black.

Numb. Just as I was five days ago.
Five insignificant days ago when I took that other phone call.
The second life changing phone call.

My memories are so fresh, it's real again. I'm there on the couch with Paul.

# Chapter 40

September 10th 2014

It's just after 6pm and I have the flu. The real flu. It suddenly started yesterday. One minute I was fine and within ten minutes I was sick. Paul's been looking after me and entertaining himself on his phone while watching TV. His phone vibrated and it woke me.

Now freshly aware of my own miserable state, I've managed to drag my aching body to the bathroom. My toe bones physically hurt and moving makes my body alternate between shivering hot, cold needles, to knife stabbing pain and aching to my core. Goose bumps and an axe through my nose from the back of my head. My eyes are throbbing in the light, and I'm oozing liquids from every orifice.

My mind is a befuddled mess. Earlier in the morning, Louise had rung and I thought she had asked whether Sarah was cheating on Oliver. Something about whether she was perhaps a bit crazy. And why was Sarah ringing Louise?

"I don't know. I don't have answers for any of that. It doesn't make sense. Don't think she would be cheating. I'm not sure why she rang you."

I asked her to call me tomorrow when I would feel better and we could chat then. Medicated. I was so mellow that Louise's version of that conversation may be totally different. My mind was AWOL.

I had told Paul and then snuffled as I curled back on the couch. My head on his lap. I had fallen asleep within seconds.

9 hours later, and I was gently making my way back to the couch, having just thrown up and gratefully feeling somewhat better. My phone is ringing so I detour to the kitchen. Paul, who had been watching TV while I slept beside him, has disappeared, presumably upstairs.

I pick up my phone and see my cousins name, Amanda, whom I hadn't heard from in 7 years. Shamefully, I can't remember when I last physically saw her. Ten years ago?

"Hi Amanda. Is everything ok?" I know I sound awful, but this wasn't a call I could ignore. My first thought was, this was one of those family calls. Our parents are of that age where death is not a complete surprise.

"Are you sitting down?"

"No, sweet. I've been lying on the couch all day. I have the flu and you caught me shuffling back from the loo." My voice was deep and husky. It hurt to speak.

"Well, sit down."

"Ok". Considering sleeping has been my only activity all day, it was only a matter of seconds before sitting would have become curling, then snoozing again anyway. I had already reached the couch and was cushioning myself into its soft corner. I wanted to get off the phone and just die, but this was a rare call.

I'm not sure why, but now I thought she was about to tell me that she was pregnant. I felt a surge of excitement. Anticipation of the long awaited good news. The thought of her happiness perked me up enough to smile.
What was she saying?

"Am I ok? Do I know?"

"Know what??"

"Are you on your own?" She asks again.

I say yes, even though Paul is now sitting on the other end of the couch. He doesn't seem to count. He is part of me. We are one. He tells me this all the time. So yes, we are alone.

"Katie, I have to tell you something." Her tone isn't so upbeat. It's actually tense.

"I've got some bad news." Ah, so it is one of our parents. Not really surprised.

I shouldn't have distracted myself with my own thoughts. I missed some of what she said.
She is just making sounds. I'm trying to make sense of it.

"It's on Facebook.
Someone is chatting to me.
Right now.
They are still on line.
Katie.
They have sent you messages.
Are you listening?
You aren't safe.
Get out.
He is a lying psychopath.
He is violent."

Well, that was a sudden turn around, The reality of the world I'm in, is moving away from me. I am struggling to be in the now of the lounge room.

She is still talking as if she has to get as much information across to me as quickly as possible. I don't have time to respond. I don't think I could have. I had no words. Each piece of new information was a body blow, taking me further from my perfect life.

"Paul's dead girlfriend isn't dead." WHAT?
"She is alive." WHAT?
"He has a wife." WHAT?
"She IS his wife." WHAT?
"Her name is Brooklin." WHAM
"Are you listening?"
"Do you understand?"
"Paul is married." WHAM
"He has a child." WHAT?
"They are living in the USA." WHAM
"She is waiting for him to join her." WHAM
"Katie? Katie are you there?"

My stomach is in my throat. My insides are becoming concrete settling into a lump of cold truth. Emotions are disappearing into a fog. I can literally feel the numbing denial move from my head through my chest cavity. I am empty. I hate the universe.

Paul is asking if everything is ok. "Who is on the phone?"

Amanda is still talking. What did she say? That she has rung three times, and Paul has answered and he said she had the wrong number. 'Don't call again.'

"Hold on Amanda." I turn to face Paul. "Paul?"

He looked up from his phone.

"Paul, did my cousin call my phone, and you answer it?" I'm in such a state of denial. I'm begging the universe to not have done this.

"You know it hasn't rung. You've been on the couch all day. You would have heard it. Why, what's wrong?"

I pull the phone from my ear, wipe my nose along the end of my dressing gown sleeve, and sniff. I am pathetically sick, and I'm seriously having to deal with this right now. I don't have the option of delicacy. I go into the settings on my phone and check the recent history. My blurry eyes making it difficult to focus.
I'm still hoping this is all wrong. That Amanda has got the wrong end of some bizarre story which has nothing to do with me. That my fiance whom I celebrated our engagement with only 2 weeks ago has nothing to do with what she is saying. This is a cruel joke. I'm about to get married in less than 6 weeks and he can't have a dead girlfriend who is not dead. Worse, he can't already have a wife. That my world is not about to implode, collapse, change. My dreams be shattered. That the man that I adore and who adores me, isn't lying to me on a grand scale.

Missed calls. None.
Answered calls. Three.
All from "Amanda cousin."

There they are. None longer than 7 seconds.
WHAM.
OMG.
My blood goes cold, as my heart physically sinks. A long breath leaves my body. A shiver replaces it.

I suppose wow, is an understatement.
Numb. Cold. Cope. Switch feelings off. Power down. I can physically feel my body react like a robot going into power saving mode. Emergency reaction only required.

This is really happening.

I can't look at Paul. I raise my aching body off the couch, aware of every movement. The phone is back to my ear, and Amanda is still talking, as I make my way around the lounge suite, past the dining table and into the kitchen, taking my place at the bench. I'm glad I just threw up. There is nothing left in my stomach. I shouldn't have to handle this right now. I am sick. I have the flu. My toes hurt. I'm trying to concentrate through a fog.

Paul is standing behind me, leaning over my shoulder, as I pull the laptop forward. He is asking what I'm doing. Who is on the phone?

"What, Katherine? What's going on?"

I can hear my cousin tell me to get out of the house. Her voice is muffled. My mind is trying to comprehend what she is saying, while Paul is raising his voice in an attempt to exert control over a landslide situation.

"Yes, Amanda, I'm here. Yes, yes, I'm looking." I am opening my laptop and searching Facebook messenger. Nothing is happening fast enough.

"Yes, I see something but I can't read the message."

"Katie, she says she has been blocked. She has been trying to contact you since yesterday morning, but Paul has blocked her. You share a page with Paul?"

There is so much information coming in, I am struggling to make sense of it.

"Go to the back end of Facebook."

"Ok, I'm doing it." Settings. Blocked list. I hate technology.

Paul's head is beside me.

"Yes, Amanda, I see. Sarah Lewis Dean. Ah huh. Give me a second."

"Paul," I swing slowly to face him again. "My cousin is on the phone. Have you seen any messages on Facebook from a, a ?" I have forgotten the name. I have no idea who it is.

Amanda repeats the name into the receiver. "Sarah Lewis Dean."

"Paul, have you seen any messages on Facebook from a Sarah Lewis Dean?"

He moves into the kitchen, putting the kitchen counter top between us.

"What's going on? You're sick. Go to bed. You're acting crazy. Is this another of your melt downs? Tell your cousin or whoever it is to call back later, when you are better. This is stupid."

Amanda is still regurgitating dates, times, names. Nothing is making sense.

"Amanda", I interrupt her flow. " Look, thanks for calling. Sorry you had to tell me this stuff. Can I call you back?" I know she isn't happy about hanging up, but it seemed an unspoken code.......
Please give me a few minutes,......... and she seemed to understand.

Her final words were blunt.

"You have to believe me Katie. You need to leave. Leave now. He is dangerous."

I hang up, still looking at Paul's face. He is going on about people interfering.

"Princess, I've told you before, everyone wants to stir up trouble. Why would someone say that I've answered your phone? I'd never answer your phone. It's not my business who calls you. Baby, you would have heard me if I'd answered your phone. You have been beside me all day."

For a millisecond this all seems rationale. It's true. I have been lying beside him in a half awake state all day, but I've just seen the proof. I know, for a fact, he is lying.

His words wash over me as barbed poisonous betrayal, prickling my skin, violating my world. The phone history was truth. Black and white.
Cold hard evidence versus Paul's words.

I cannot hold his gaze. I lower my head.

He never faltered just then. His eyes didn't flicker. He didn't hesitate. He lied to my face without guilt, remorse or uncertainty.
Technically not a life changing lie, but it meant the rest of Amanda's accusations could be correct. Why lie about a phone call unless there was more.

"Katherine, you need to go upstairs and have a shower. You'll feel better. I will get dinner. What do you want? Fish and chips. I think you can handle a small piece of fish."

He is acting like he is annoyed with me and that things are still normal. My heart is broken. I hate God. My life is about to go down the toilet again. It's just a matter of how far. How bad. How fucked up the universe is about to make it.

'Yes." I hear myself say. "Yes, that would be good." I am already on auto pilot. I know this feeling even through the flu. I know it too well. Survival instincts have switched on. I no longer have normal emotions. Hollow.

"I'll be back shortly. Have a shower and stop worrying about this. It's crap. I've told you before, to stop letting other people interfere. They all have their own agenda." He gently kisses me on the forehead.

"I love you Princess."Then he left out the back door.

It's nearly 7pm, and I feel sorry for myself, that I am so sick. My head is pounding through my skull, and I feel pressure through my nose and eye balls. My toes are still hurting. I pop three more strong pain killers and 2 cold and flu.
Seriously I'm just too sick for this.

I ring my cousin, who tells me she has been chatting to Sarah.

'Who the fuck is Sarah???????' My mind screams.

"He wasn't in America. Check your messages."

I'm doing as I'm told. She is still full of shocks. He didn't go to America? Of course he did. He posted on Facebook. He had photos. He was at the airport. His messages indicated his location. She keeps talking.

"Married ten years." WHAMMMMM
"The kid is about same age." WHAT? WHAM!
"His wife doesn't know about you." WHAM
"His family obviously does." WHAM
"She was here." WHAM
"In Melbourne." WHAM
"The week he proposed." WHAM!!!

"What? Wait. Amanda, he proposed that week of July 4th, then he was in Tasmania with me. I think this is all wrong. Seriously he was with me in Tasmania with my girlfriend and her family. I came home. He was only gone four days."

"Katherine, she says check his passport. He wasn't there. He is a liar.
He lies all the time to everyone.
He is a con man.
The wife didn't know about you.
Well, she does now. Literally right now. Sarah has just told her. They are messaging on Facebook.
Their son's name is Macky."

WOW HOLY MOTHER FUCK WHAM FUCK. That one hurt. A name. A non existent child has a name. The imaginary name for our imaginary future child. 'Perfect name for a girl.' I felt the barb. It wasn't in my heart. It was in the centre of my scrunched up forehead.

"Amanda, I have unblocked this 'Sarah,' but I can't find any messages. So Paul really answered my phone and hung up on you?"

"No Katie. He spoke to me. He told me I had the wrong number and to not call again. Hang on. I'm chatting with Sarah, who is chatting to Brooklin, on Macky's account. Sarah is still chatting to her now.
They have been married a while. She is waiting over there for him. Setting up house.
How could you not know? You didn't know, did you, Katie?"

"No Amanda, of course not! How can this be? He is with me, like all the time. We are never apart, unless he's at work. I don't get this. Why? I mean why would it be true?"

My mind wanders for a second. No, I was clueless,........Because, ..........because........... 'You'll learn, Princess. People only see what you want them to see: believe what they want to believe. They only hear what you want them to hear.' The conversation with Paul, in the Tasmanian hotel, the week he proposed, rang in my dull head. I didn't wish to share this with her. Remembering that conversation, those words, I realised Paul may have been mocking me.

"No Amanda, not a clue. He told me she had died. He told everyone that story in depth. He told the councilor, my friends. Oh god, he told my girlfriend, Louise and her husband, whose beautiful daughter has a brain tumor. Oh god how could he? Such graphic detail. He went on about how much he had loved her. How she was quiet, anti social. A lawyer. No one liked her, but he saw something special in her. She fought with everyone. It was her thing. Even her family didn't like her. I know I sound bitchy but it's what he said. Details of the slow painful death. Her smell. Rolling, bulging eyes. His faithfulness by her bedside. Speaking at her funeral. How he went to counseling. Her death made him a better man. Out of her tragedy, came greater good. He used to tell me I was jealous of a dead girl.

OMG!!! Oh my fucking god!

And she is alive?? Not dead? And he is really married to her.??
He told everyone, that he was relieved when she died, as it allowed him to move forward into a better life. To find me and, and,...I can't, I can't understand this. It's too much.

I thought he loved me."

I was pathetic. I crushed as I said it. The words caved me in on top of myself. Into the black. Sucking me inward. Hopeless darkness like a black hole in my soul.
The ever present record took up. Why would he? You're Useless. Ugly. Failure. Idiot. Stupid. Not wanted. Reject. Try hard.
Every insecurity I had ever fleetingly contemplated, became fact in that second. Surfaced like a skin. A sticky, gelatinous boil filled, slimy, unwanted skin.

"Maybe he does. Maybe he loves both of you." Her words disappeared into the abyss, becoming instantly void and unheard. "It doesn't matter though, Katie you have to leave. Sarah says Paul is violent. Has done things before. You need to leave now. Promise?"

"Amanda. I can't leave. I'm too sick. I have to throw up. I have to lie down. I can't drive."

I got off the phone and rang Paul. He had been gone an hour and a half. Obviously he was in damage control. He didn't answer, it went to voice mail. COWARD!
I hung up and texted.

*"Paul, I think you should come home and clean this mess up. LMAO."*

I didn't really think it was funny, I just wanted to make it sound less devastating. I can see the previous message from him, only yesterday.

*"I love you more each day."*

I fucking hate life. And God? Well he can go to hell as well. Our relationship has just taken a permanent nose dive. This is cruel. Unnecessarily mean. Why did this have to happen?

I don't know how I'm supposed to "unhurt" myself from this. I don't know how to undo the last few hours.

# Chapter 41

I was surprised when Paul opened the back door, I didn't think he would want to face this show down. He went straight to the fridge, and proceeded to skull the first of 5 beers over the next three hours. He stayed in the kitchen.

"Paul are you married?"

"Yes."

"Do you have a child?"

"Yes."

"Did your girlfriend die?"

"No."

I'm shocked he answered so honestly. I don't know how to handle this.

"Is there any sort of explanation for any of this?"

"I wanted to be happy Katherine. Is that such a bad thing? You made me happy. I was miserable before. Everyone knows that. No one was surprised when she left and then you were in my life. They welcomed you in. You went to my father's wedding. I just wanted the love, that my father had with mum and Grace. Then I found you. We were perfect. We are perfect.

I wanted you so badly, for so long. From the very moment you came into my life. I'm sorry. I never thought this would happen. I just fell in love. Crucify me. I love you. I'm sorry. I have done everything I can to make you happy. I have made enormous sacrifices.

Clearly she and I are not together. She is in America. I'm glad she left. We fought all the time and in front of Mac. It's been a war zone. I meant it, when I said you were the one. I have never, ever felt this way about anyone before. We work. We are perfect together in every way and you know it. Everyone knows it."

He looked directly at me, squinted his eyes and raised the can of beer towards me.

"And you know why you and I fight?

The only reason we have ever fought? Over her! She spreads her misery even now. It's her thing. Managing to cause fights from half way around the world, even as a dead person. She is just a bloody curse. You don't know how many times I wished she really was dead. She is a whinging, greedy, whiny mistake. All she wanted was my money, not me. A huge mistake. Always was.

I've wanted to tell you so many times before, but I just couldn't get the courage. I knew you and your ethics. Your principles, which is why I love you, so painfully much, I knew they, would be the very reason you would leave.
You would have to leave. You have told me. We have had these conversations where I have asked hypothetically, if I had been in a relationship with a girlfriend but it hadn't been working, would you have dated me. NO! You said it would have never started. That if I was with someone that you would leave. So I couldn't tell you, and I didn't want to lose you.

What do you think? That I would have gone this far if I didn't plan on getting a divorce? If I didn't love you? If I didn't want to marry you? Come on. What we have is close to perfect, don't you think?"

I was still sitting at the kitchen counter, laptop in front of me, looking at my cold feet. My pinky toes had turned purple. I glanced sideways towards him, not lifting my head. My response was little more than a murmur. "I had thought so, but this makes everything different. Doesn't it."

He came forward looking like a wounded puppy. The hurt across his face. "So I lied, and then I had to make others up, to keep the first lie true. I'm sorry. I have wished so many times that I could just go back in time and tell you from the start, but I would have lost you any way so I have known from the moment I met you that we were perfect for each other and doomed at the same time.

I don't want to lose you. I went to America to get a divorce."

"Paul, you used to throw me out over a dead girl. Do you realise how many times you returned me to my place, because I questioned a hair brush, a box of tampons, a yummy mummy coffee cup, hair products. You always had such believable excuses. You always made me feel guilty, and I always ended up apologizing. Over me trying not to question the changing time lines of when she died, how I didn't want to wear a dead ex girl friend's jewelry, over finding out I was driving a car with your combined initials, BCPC. Being upset that I was driving your dreams of a future together. A future fantasy. Only it just got worse, because it's not your future fantasy. BCPC is your present. OMG." I looked up. I felt the anger and hurt bore out of my eyes, and promptly looked back down at the floor. "How I wasn't allowed to be upset over the enormous tattoo of her name on your bicep, which you then got blocked out a month before our engagement party. The same time you changed the number plates of the car."

He interrupted me. "See, See Princess. Come on. Why would I block her name out if I was going back to her? I can't undo that. I did that for you and changing number plates cost money but again because you wanted me to get rid of the past, I did it. Replaced the custom ones with plain normal plates. Why do you think I have done all these things if not because I want you to see how much I love you? I've been trying. Can't you see that?"

But I didn't stop, I kept talking so he might hear me. I had often said to him that all I wanted was to be heard. Now more than ever, I needed to say everything aloud. My validation. My vindication.

"You have lied and made it all seem my fault. You said I was crazy. It was me being unstable and damaged. You made me worry that you would let everyone think I was psychotic, and you did. You told my friends that I was acting unbalanced. That I was creating the drama!! You let my friends message horrible texts, saying I was unhinged, jealous of a dead girl, sabotaging an adult relationship. You deliberately made me look bad to those I love the most. You went out of your way to convince them that you were wonderful and I was a charity case. Do you think this is how you treat someone you love? You have punished me over my confusion about how your story didn't always ring true. We just went to a councilor only two days ago, because you said I needed one."

With every sentence, a new truth was revealed. The truths he had spoken for months were now lies. I got up, and headed for the couch. I needed to be supported. He followed me at a respectful distance.

"I'm sorry about all that, baby, I didn't know how else to keep the story up. I begged you to let everything ride, and it would work out in the end. Now look. I'm not a very good liar, because I don't do it very often. That's the truth. It's not as though I go around creating stories just for the fun of it. I lied about her so I wouldn't lose you. When I met you, I didn't know what you were like, so I told you crap, thinking we might just fuck and that was that, but it didn't work out that way did it? How was I to know? I'm new at being single. Not like you.

Then it turned out you're wonderful. And then your bloody principles meant I couldn't undo what I had started. I fell for you so fast. It all happened so fast."

"Paul that was all your choice. I have said go slow the entire time."

"I know, but I just wanted to get this over the line, as soon as possible, so we could start our life together. It needed to go fast, so I could step out of this lie. So you and I could begin fresh as we deserve. So we could be happy. How often have I told you I deserve to be happy. You make me happy. I wanted to get through all this, get through till Christmas, be able to start my life new, because of you. It's all I wanted. All I knew and could focus on is getting us past this point and I could finally be happy on my terms.

You need to understand Katherine. I have been so insecure for all my life. It doesn't matter about the money. I always feel dirty. I never feel good enough. I settled for her. I was still hurt from Sonja. I accepted her for the limited things she brought to the table. I had been miserable and lonely for so long, and I tried so hard to make it work, but she is impossible. I didn't lie when I said no one likes her. Even her family hate her. I hate her. Towards the end she made my skin crawl. That's why I was looking for someone else. When she left before Christmas, I was so relieved. You realise she has been gone two years. And I started looking for someone. Least I waited till she was gone. I just never expected to meet someone as beautiful as you: an all round, perfect package. Katherine, do you understand what you are like? I see all those men waiting in line wishing they were me. You don't even see you for you. That's what's amazing. I'm not stupid Katherine. I struck gold when I found you. It's just timing. The timing for you was wrong because I never bothered to sort a divorce and then there you were. I didn't and don't want to lose what we have.
I didn't want you to find out. If I ever find the person who has done this, I'll kill them. I'll strangle them with my bare hands. They have wrecked everything."

"I think that you only have yourself to blame here Paul. Whoever they are, they are just the messenger."

"Katherine, we work. You and I, we work. Work with me now. I beg you. I know I don't deserve it, but work with me. See the forest not the trees. See the bigger picture. It's why I have kept saying it. I used to ask you to see the real me. Well, now you are. Here I am. I'm not perfect."

I was trying not to chain smoke as I sat on the couch listening to him. My head was reeling. His words were heard through blocked ears and a pounding head. My eyes weren't crying, they were shiny. I felt nothing. I was unmoved.
Auto pilot. Unfeeling. Dangerous. No regret. No compassion. I just wanted the truth so I could deal with it.

"Paul did you see her after you proposed?"

He was on the floor leaning against the corner of the couch at the further end. His legs were splayed out. He looked beaten.

"Yes, I phoned her weeks before I proposed to you, and officially told her that we needed to get divorced. She knew it was coming, there was no shock. My friends and family knew. Its all over Facebook. The staff all know. How has this blown up bigger than it is? I want to marry you. It's happening, and someone has turned it all evil. My lying is bad enough. But that's all it was.

She didn't care, obviously or she would have come back, don't you think? And you'd think basically, 2 months later knowing you and I were about to celebrate our engagement, that if she really wanted me, well she would be here? If this was reversed I would have been on the first plane. She doesn't want to be with me. I definitely don't want to be with her. There wasn't even any outburst. We were both resigned that our marriage was over, a very long time ago. Clearly she has been gone more than a year and obviously it was pretty awful for a long time before that, to get to the point that she left. She is so not interested in us, that she made me fly to her, to sort all the business paperwork and to discuss the divorce. We had lots of things to address, obviously. It's not as though I have a nine to five job. God, I was only gone a few days. I've been meeting with Randy and Sebastian trying to sort it all out with as little collateral damage as possible. There is no pre nup. I'm screwed. I'm telling you she was calm and accepting, but she is also calculating and conniving. Katherine, the women is ruthless. I can only imagine what she will do now.

I just want you. Obviously, look at the rock you have on your finger. You think I'd hand that sort of money out if I didn't love you: if I didn't want you and I, to have a future for forever? Katherine, I just stood up in front of all our family and friends, and announced how much I love you. My parents came. I organised the proposal. I had the ring for quite a while, and you know the other one is still coming. The pink diamond to match your earrings. Your wedding ring. Clearly I am committed to you."

I still wasn't touched. "So you went to America?"

"Yes, to sort a divorce so I can marry you, and because of the GM issues." I tried to avoid going there, and you know that. I stayed with you in Tasmania. You know this is true. You were here at home with me.

My brain is trying to ask the necessary questions, but there were so many I don't know which ones.

"Did you sleep with her?" I'm not stupid, but I needed to ask it any way. Hear the stab in my heart. Or hear the lie. Which one?

"No. She wanted me to, but she had her period. She tried, but, Katherine,." I'm trying to be honest with you. Ok? She did try, but I couldn't get hard over her. I love you. What you and I have."

I felt the spear. He chose the lie. A bad one.

"What! You couldn't perform? Find that very hard to believe." It came out of my mouth, and I immediately regretted accidentally stroking his virility and ego. A flash of jealousy remembering that he once told me that when he first met dead girl / alive wife, that they had amazing, hot, spontaneous sex. Clearly that hadn't lasted long, because she got sick so quickly and died. Now I catch myself. I'm still momentarily thinking of an enigma. Was it true? Dead girl. Alive wife. How much of each, is in the other?

"So you of, the, "I never cheat propaganda," you were in the same bed?" OMG, I felt my skin crawl.

"No. I was in a hotel. I went to the house for a few hours after school to keep Mac happy. I never cheat! I love you. I need you, if only you knew how much. Katherine, we had things to discuss and it was hard with Mac around all the time. Christ, Katherine, he's my kid and he is caught up in all of this. I was there less than two days. You know it. You were here the whole time. Have some compassion. He misses me. We are close. My entire future lies with him. She made a move on the couch after Mac went to bed.

Katherine, I don't know what you want to hear. That she has put on weight, has a bit of a pooch? That she is still making enemies, still focusing on material things? That she is lonely because she can't make new friends? Katherine, why would I want to go back to that. I'm in love with you. You - the exact opposite of her."

The words clutched at my heart but my head froze them away. He was getting progressively more drunk. His head was lolling to the side. I had never seen him drunk before.

I wanted to leave, but was just too sick. I got up. Paul looked like he couldn't even focus anymore. He looked how I felt. I made my way to the laptop at the kitchen bench. I was scared and anxious. Who was he? A married man with an extra child, who put so much effort into being in a relationship with me. A liar. A cheat.

I messaged my cousin. " Thank you. I'll talk as soon as I can."

She was instantly on line. "Please leave."

"I can't, I am too sick. I have to go to bed."

I glanced at my phone. Texts, Facebook messages, missed calls. Lots of them. What is going on? I scrolled through without opening them.

Armageddon.

Who the fuck is Sarah Lewis Dean? What is her beef? Why has she contacted so many people? Everyone. Clients, family, friends, random Facebook friend requests. Too many people, asking too many questions. They obviously all knew.

The general tone. "Are you ok?"

Paul was now unconscious. Drunk on the lounge room floor, snoring and grunting. More things he had never done before. A night of firsts. He looked like a common, outer burbs bogan. I didn't find him attractive like this at all. Thank you for helping me hurt less, I thought as I looked down at him. I don't like this person on the floor at all.

I went upstairs, taking more pain killers, and more cold and flu before dropping into bed.

My phone was lying under my pillow and as I propped myself up so I could breathe, it rang.

"Mum? Mum, I just got a message from a Sarah Lewis Dean."

Wow this bitch is getting around. She has got her message across.

"Yes Ollie."

"Are you ok? Is it true?

"Apparently it is."

"Mum. She says you need to leave. That he is a lying psychopath. Sarah and I tried to tell you months ago, when we couldn't google him. I knew that something was strange. No one just doesn't exist. So he was trying to hide that he was actually married. What a cunt."

The word was appropriate. There would be no correction.

"Ollie I want to leave, but I can't. I'll sleep and go first thing in the morning."

"Mum I'll come and get you, I'd rather you go now."

"No, Ollie I don't want you to come here. I don't want you involved and I'm full of tablets. I'm too sick. If I could drive I would, I promise."

"I'll call you first thing tomorrow. Mum promise me you'll leave."

I was gutted that I had let him down again. He will never be proud of me. I could not describe in word how much I hated Paul Carter at that second for involving my son. My son who had gone through so much in his young life, and who already thought men seemed to just cause so much pain and leave.

"I promise." I hung up, and Paul staggered in, as my phone rang again.

I answer it as a distraction and for protection. I am no longer sure of what Paul is capable of. I'm not sure why Amanda thinks he is dangerous.

It's a blocked number at 1.30 AM. A girls voice.

"Hello. Are you ok?" she asks.

My head reels. "Yes, why? Who are you."

"It doesn't matter. He is a pig, Katherine. We all hate him. You needed to know. I'm a woman. I'd want to know. He tells the boys things at work and they talk you know. It's disgusting. I wanted to tell you before. I'm sorry. Just leave him. Look after yourself."

Paul was leaning over me while this conversation happened, and I was too scared to ask probing questions.

"Thanks." I hung up.

Paul wanted to know who it was.

"I don't know.. She said I needed to know, so I'm presuming she's the one that messaged everyone on Facebook. The mysterious Sarah, I suppose."

"I don't think so Katherine."

He staggered out the door and fell asleep within seconds in Andrew's old room. I could hear him snore. I got up and slammed the door shut. I had just returned to the bed when my phone pinged in another message. I glanced at it. There were already so many texts and messages.

*Kara - lashes*

The name meant nothing to me. No idea. Except she was obviously a client of the shop, hence her name in my phone, synced to my contacts.

1.49AM September 11th

*"Hey katherine that's fine
I do hope everything works
out genuinely never picked
paul to be that person his
always been so good to us !
Dont feel foolish weve all been
lied to before ! I do wish you all
The best tho sorry to hear again"*

Followed with another that pinged in whilst I was reading the first one.

*"And as far as we all knew paul
isnt married only woman weve
know of is you sorry to hear
once again"*

Who is this? I quietly limped back downstairs.
I lit a cigarette and opened the laptop. Too much to deal with in this state.

I typed in Sarah Lewis Dean presuming she was the girl who just rang. She had said 'the boys at work talk'. Ok so where's the connection?
I can't find her. Ok, think. What would a smart person do? Go in under a clean account. I don't know what possessed me, but I created a hotmail and new facebook profile and immediately found her.
Her friends list has no privacy settings on it. Thankfully, there aren't that many people. I scroll. Ok….. She's friends with a Kara,……Kara Falcone.

So, who is Kara? Scroll through. Melbourne. Beautician. Friends…..

Tony Falcone. He is on Paul's and my Facebook page. We are his friend. I'd never noticed. Who are these people. Oh my God. Tony! Tony, as in Paul's apprentice?

Falcone. Ohhhhhhh
Paul has mentioned Vito Falcone. It's too unusual a name to not be the same family. Stalking, stalking. Yep. Vito is the father. I hadn't really pieced that together before. I'd heard the name and imagined it was spelled with an 'I'. Falconi.

Back to Sarah. Who is she? It seems to go no where. She doesn't actually seem to exist.

I look into Tony and Kara further. They are, apparently, friends with Ash and Sam, my girlfriend's sons, whom Paul had employed. Well, isn't this nice, and Andrew and John, and Tony. Of course they all know each other. They work together. Weird seeing them all linked to this Sarah, by less than 1 degree.

Ash is friends with Sarah Lewis Dean as well. I don't understand this.

I re-read Kara's recent message to me. On reflection it appears, she maybe the girl who was on the phone, who said I needed to know. So did she use this others girls FB account? Does that mean she is really Sarah?

Oh who cares.

But why did they do this now? Did they save me or destroy me?

I lit another cigarette and quickly scan through two dozen private messages. I didn't open any of them. They are all horrified, devastated friends, asking if I'm ok. Sarah Lewis Dean got around today. Whoever she was, she'd been very busy.

I'm too sick to answer all of my friends private messages, individually, so now I post on my wall, as an explanation to them all.

*"So the latest twist in my life. Turns out my fiance has a wife who is expecting him to join her in USA anytime soon. I.e. She is alive. Not dead. This is the girl he told me, my son, my friends that died an agonizing death from bone cancer!!! Obviously this means he didnt fly her back to the USA, (she wasnt even american, turns out she is australian. Nor speak at her funeral, nor go to the counseling to get over his grief.) Yes it was her clothes not sons girlfriends clothes in my wardrobe. Oh they have a nine year old. Well that's because the relationship wasnt 2.5 years but ten years. Yep I am a fool. Better a fool than be any of the arsholes who came to what now is a bogus engagement party. When they KNEW THE TRUTH. Why would any of them do that. His family and friends. 20 of you stood there thinking I was a "gold digger" clawing into a married guy, when I knew nothing about it. One of you could have had a shred of integrity to tell me he had a wife. I lose nothing. Nothing at all."*

I sat there. I want to cry. This is the time you cry. I don't though, so I light another cigarette.

Something was bothering me. Think. Think Katherine. There's so much to choose from. No, it's not the obvious. Think, think. What is it? Something you need to do.

I flicked through some of the things I had been looking at. My post had got some traction already. I glanced but didn't want to get involved. It was a public service announcement, I didn't want a gossip fest.
What is it that's bothering me?

Ah the word "we" jumps out from Kara's message. Again, it's there twice. "We'. Yes "We". In this case 'me and Paul' not them. "We" need to not be sharing a Facebook page. "We" need to get him off right now while I can.

Well done through all this fog, two flashes of genius. Now how do you do this?

For the second time, I clicked into the back end of Facebook, and managed to change the password. I immediately put it in the notes on my phone so I wouldn't forget it. That will keep Paul out of my business, while I sort this out.

I powered everything off and headed to bed exhausted, where I lay awake for ages jumping from one thing to another in my head. So, so many questions. I could hear Paul snoring.

I went and woke him. Standing in the door way to Andrew's room, I called his name. Quietly at first then louder until he woke.

He opened his eyes uncomprehendingly.

"What?"

"I want her number. If it's over. I want her number and I'll call her."

"Fine..here."

He grabbed his phone and scrolled with his thumb.

"I sent it to you."

My phone pinged.

"I'm sorry for everything Katherine. Go to bed. You are sick. It will all be better in the morning. I promise. I'll sleep here, out of respect. I get that I've fucked up, but know I was doing everything so we could be together. I love you like no other. You're what I want, but you know the truth now; that I don't deserve you. That's always been a lie. You are way too good for me. Please don't leave me. You deserve the life I can give you. I'm trying to be the man you deserve. Give me the chance. I promise it will work out."

I shut the door and went back to our room. Closing this door as well, I then put two pairs of his shoes and some books against the door.

I no longer trust you Paul. Least this way I will hear you.

I rang the international number and it went to a voice mail. An American professional office message. I did not leave a message. I would call again tomorrow.

# Chapter 42

Eventually I must have fallen asleep, because I woke to the sounds of the shower in the ensuite. I lay silent, incapable of moving. 'Good security work. He could have killed you and you'd have slept through it.' He got dressed quietly, just like any other day, behind the wardrobe door. I kept my eyes closed, and tried to look peacefully asleep. He came out, and leant down and kissed the side of my forehead. Quietly, as he did every morning, he whispered. " I love you Princess." But this time he added. " I truly do."

I didn't respond. I wanted to, but I didn't even know in what way. Is this positive? I don't understand. So I just stayed still. As if I was paralyzed. I knew if I moved I would have to face reality, both of us would and I wasn't ready. Maybe last night was a dream. A dream induced from the multitude of pain killers and cold and flu tablets I had been popping.

I crushed my eyes further shut. Suddenly I woke to the sounds of an empty house. Silent. I lay there listening. I got up. Oh god, my body hurts. My head was thumping. I tiptoed across the landing. My heart was pounding, and I peeked into the spare room. No, he wasn't there. Naked and exposed. I returned to the bedroom and silently threw a loose baggy long jumper on. I crept down stairs hand against the wall as I made my way towards the ground floor. I didn't want to make a sound. At the bottom step, I hesitated. I glanced in the study. Empty. Now what? The moment I move he would see me.
I stepped out confidently incase he was there.

No one.

I carefully walked through the lounge, peeking in the laundry, spare room and powder room. Empty. Every step resounded pain into my skull and left eye ball.

The back court yard. Nothing. I opened the back door into the garage. Slowly. The Aston is gone.

I spun around, grabbed my phone from the charger in the kitchen and flew up the stairs. I took the steps, two at a time. Adrenaline pulsing.

Where this urge came from I had no idea. Survival? The need for evidence that this is all true?

Self talk on overload. 'Why have you left me in the house? If I was you I wouldn't have.'

My phone rang as I get to the top landing, making me jump. It's only Amanda.

"No, I haven't left. I am by myself. Yes, I'll leave. No, I don't know where he is. I'll call later. No, he didn't deny it. Yes, yes he has a wife and child." I cannot get my head around it. "No, I don't know why he did this. He said he met me and fell in love. He lied to keep me because he deserved to be happy. Amanda, I can't talk. He says he was miserable and they both knew it was over.
Right now. I don't know anything."

She interrupted." I've sent you a message."

"What? Oh ok." I pulled my phone back and flicked to the messages. I groaned out load. She had sent a photo snap of two conversations she had.

The first was from Sarah Lewis Dean

*'Tell her to get out. He is dangerous. He has done some terrible things. Please tell her to get out. He is pure evil."*

Well, that was harsh. Seeing it in writing. I didn't know how to feel.

The second one was Brooklin using Macky Carter's Facebook account to message Sarah Lewis Dean.

Macky - *"This is Brooklyn. Just spoke to Paul who could no longer deny he was having an affair with our friend. My 9yo & I are shattered, and were expecting him to come & visit us in a week or two. Please contact me on my email to let me know all you know about this. He did the same thing when he met me and told me he was divorced but was still living with his wife.*

*He has all my money as I've been helping him out with his business & now he has abandoned us in Boston. He is a pathological lier"*

I stood there staring at the second message on my phone. The words, 'he has abandoned us.' What does that mean? Are they really separated? It doesn't sound like she voluntarily left then. Did Paul really want to leave her and start with me?

And 'our friend.' I'm not her friend. Apparently I'm supposedly, her husband's fiance. I didn't even know you existed. Why are you calling me your friend? Do you know me?

Do you know of me??

And finally, 'Macky.' I see the name and remember the conversation with Paul, in Hamilton Island, when he said he wanted a little girl called MacKenzie. The betrayal spears further into my heart. Lodged.

"Amanda, I'll call you later." It was all I could manage.

I hung up and began. I wanted answers. Proof of something. Everything. Nothing.

I opened the bedside drawers and found diaries of children I didn't know existed. I flipped through them, and wanted to throw up. They are on a holiday. They are writing every day like they are being told to. I felt the tension of making everything seem ok. Who are these boys? An entire diary in an adults hand, written on behalf of a child. I didn't understand. I felt sorry for these children but I didn't know why. Sleeping in this room for six months, I had never opened these drawers before. I never had the need. So these were from John, Andrew and the new child?

I looked further. Woman's books, '50 shades of grey.' 'How to find happiness.' 'Pleasing your partner'I sympathized with her pain and yet still felt violated, that I was now clearly in her space.

I was also angrily vindicated. This was why the dead girl wouldn't die. Because she was not dead!! I wanted to explode.

Omg. Omg Omg. I felt like a bitch for thinking like that, but she had been a ghost living in my shadow. Me in hers for 7 months.

Keep it together. My self talk should have driven me crazy. It was loud.

I pushed myself up off the floor and made my way into the ensuite, the walk in wardrobe, I even lifted myself up, standing on the edge of the drawers, and checked the back of the upper shelves.

I found jewelry boxes, empty. Little girl boxes of what, I don't know. Empty. A thick short vibrator with balls in his underwear drawer. I'm not

sure who that was for? Considering it was hidden there, he obviously knew of its existence. Sort of funny. His?
My mind is a whir of reality and conjecture.

'Continue, continue.' I could feel the panic rising, I was taking too long. What was I looking for?

I went into Andrew's room and looked at it with fresh eyes.

Lego creations. A full pencil case. Lots of caps, American. Nothing indicated whose it was, but definitely a young child's wardrobe. Folded neatly on the very upper shelf, a Thomas the Tank Engine doona cover, and small kids pyjamas. I took all this on board. Proved nothing yet, except I'm doubting an 18 year old kept all this stuff. I looked in the shelves. Nothing. The bed is a queen. It's not a child's bed. Was I meant to have thought there had been a child? Have I been blind? Paul had told me it was remnants of the boys, now grown up. I never looked in past a glance. I struggled with facing the mounting facts, against what I had believed only 12 hours ago.

The next spare room, empty. There were still furniture marks in the carpet. I thought I could make out the shape of a bed. See, so maybe this had been John's room where he just moved out of on the weekend before I moved in. The other room Andrew's?

Nothing else I saw was important to me.

I headed back down to the laundry. Now I see a built in cupboard in the corner. Even doing washing, I had never opened the cupboard in there. I hadn't even noticed it. All the detergents were underneath the sink or on the bench.
Inside was obviously storage. The place, we all have, where we keep sundry crap. I'd never needed to open it.

Now I did, and rummaged carefully through sewing kits, bathroom items, packs of unopened cheap shampoo - must have been on special. I was thinking. 'How domestic and organised Paul is. He literally can do everything.' I remember when he sewed the clasp on my engagement dress, when we noticed it was loose. He is so good at everything.' I caught myself day dreaming and wanted to smack myself out of my denial. "He isn't good, he is a liar.'

I regrouped, and looked further into the cupboard. There, leaning in the corner, a hockey stick. I picked it up turning it over.

There's a name in thick black texta.

"MAC."

I slumped to the floor.

He existed! OMG. He exists. His name is Mac.
A child denied to have been conceived. He existed.
I stared at it.

He exists. Therefore so does she.
My body tingled with shards of disgust at Paul. Up until that point, I had still hoped Amanda got it wrong. That everything was wrong. But no. No, this was real. I couldn't understand it, but I was looking at the evidence.

Come one. Get up Katherine. Keep going. There is more.

I continued to the spare room. My engagement dress was draped artfully across the single bed waiting to go to the dry cleaners. The spare TV and gaming stations sat in place staring at me. All the games in the drawers, that Paul had shown Oliver. He'd invited Ollie to take any that he wanted. They had belonged to John and Andrew, but they hadn't used them in a while. Ollie took two, and left the others. He said that he had many of them when he was much younger.

Paul had encouraged him. "Well, whatever you don't take, I'm throwing out. I have no need for them."

Now with fresh knowledge, I realised what a cold person he was. To be a parent, and dismiss your child like that. I never knew. The extreme opposite of how he had presented himself to me. I'm so soft. I have tubs of Oliver's stuff. I cry throwing away anything with memories. His books, his games. I still have them all.

Enough of that room. It provided little. I walked to the lounge, stopping to take a breath, leaning on the edge of the sofa.

Keep going, you are running out of time. The fear was physical: foreign and unexplainable. Beyond being warned to leave, I had no need to be scared of Paul. Angry at the enormous betrayal, yes, but scared, no. So why the panic?

I didn't know, but it was a driving force and it propelled me towards the TV cabinet. I had opened these drawers a thousand times but now I riffle through with fresh eyes.

Nothing.

Although I now noticed kids DVDs. I suppose when you don't think there is a child, you just don't see the evidence. I still have 'Horton Hears a Hoo,' so it's not completely unusual for adults to have some kiddy films. I was aware of my state of denial. I knew it was somewhat misplaced and stupid, considering the events, but I just couldn't take it all in. Numb. Fogged.

Sitting on the floor, I noticed a little cupboard to the left of the drawers. How could I not have seen this before? Simple. I had never needed anything to justify opening, or searching through anything. And it's not in my nature.

I opened it. There were three little blue and white canvases. The type you see out in the burbs; country shabby chic. Not my style.

There was a fine, solid film of dust in front of them. Carefully I lifted the three out as one so as not to disturb it. I didn't want Paul to know I had been here. I placed them in a pile in front of me.

They were the announcements of a birth. Macky Carter's birth.

He has siblings.
It's printed here. It must have been on his nursery wall.
Names, dates. I can't take it all in. I stare at the Macky one. It doesn't just represent an unknown, denied child. It's the evidence of a whole other concurrent, missing life.

I just sat on the floor. Goose bumps, trembling. Aching hot and then cold. I was internally miserable. My eyes were watering. Not with tears.

His parents: Brooklin and Paul Carter.

It was so in my face. The happy little family making a public announcement. 'This is us.'
It was unreal that the universe would provide such a loving pile of proof, so that it was undeniable. They existed, and at some point in time, Paul or Brooklin, or both, wanted everyone to know. At some point they had been a tight, proud unit. My musing haltered.

'Wait! Stop! The boys names. Not John and Andrew.'

Carter and, and Boston?

What?? WHAT?? I don't understand. I DONT UNDERSTAND.

I DO NOT UNDERSTAND!!!!!

I'm so confused. I stared at them. These would have been on a wall somewhere here. When did he pull them down. Years before I came along? Months? Days? Why leave them here? Why are their names different?

Wow he knew I wasn't a snoop. That I believed in trust. He used my own integrity against me. I could have looked here at any time. He left these here. Or did he trust my integrity so implicitly? Was he so blase? Didn't he care, if I found them? What would he have said?
Did he want me to find them?

I couldn't feel or think. I couldn't make sense. My head buzzed.


I remembered back to the first time I was left in this house by myself. He came home and asked if I had found everything I needed. I had told him, that I hadn't been able to do my work, because I needed some paper, and didn't want to go through his stuff.

"I know baby. You aren't a snoop. I know you didn't do that."

Holding the blue canvas, sitting paralysed, fused into the carpet, I was jolted alert again.

"How was he so confident? Are there cameras? Crap. Are there cameras???"

I quickly but carefully put the damming canvases back. I checked that everything looked untouched, in case I was being paranoid, and he didn't have cameras, I didn't want to advertise I did just snoop. Why should I have cared? I don't know, but I did. To my core, I cared. I could feel my body locking down. It was suddenly, so quickly, becoming hard to motivate myself to move. I was aware of how sick I was. Extremely sick.

I needed to leave. Regardless of lack of evidence, I knew instinctually, I was in serious danger, if I was caught here. I had to go.

Short on time, and aware there was an irrational deadline to get out, I still had a shower, being the first, since I became sick and I felt rank. I didn't remember the last time I hadn't had two showers in a day. It was less than brief but much needed.

I was acutely aware of the rising panic to leave, but not knowing where I was going to go, or who I would have to see, I needed to be presentable.

I wanted to press my face against the cold glass to slow everything down. I didn't. I washed body and hair simultaneously, both hands attacking different areas, and then fled out of the shower, hair whipped up in a towel, drying myself as I walked to the dressing room.

I pulled my loosest jeans over damp legs, and grabbed my baggy blue jumper dress. Ripping the towel off my head, I spun the wet, long lengths around my hand, and hoiked it up, secured with three bobby pins. My head was throbbing with all the movement and I couldn't put it lower than my body for the painful headache it caused. I knelt to grab some flats. Eight weeks ago I didn't even own flats. I had needed them when he sent me to Donna Lee's in Tasmania. My mind was jumping. Amanda's version of the timeline around Paul's proposal, still didn't make sense.

I grabbed several of my large handbags and filled them with breakables. Cosmetics. Jewelry. Loading myself up, I must have had seven hanging from me, as I lugged downstairs, and grabbed the Maserati keys. I hurriedly walked, skipped and partially ran down the drive to the car, parked outside to the street. I carefully loaded the handbags behind the passenger seat, then brought the car into the garage. Rushing, aware time was running out. I managed to get scrunchable clothes into Safeway, grey, plastic bags.

In Paul's words. "No fucks are given." I'm flying, tying the tops of the bags and anything that can bounce is thrown down the stairs. Hung items are stacked still on hangers and carried with herculean strength in piles one and a half feet high. The last box and I are coming down the stairs. Awkward and heavy. Shoes, boots, a few files.
I turn the corner, and walk as quickly as I can, to the back door and through the garage. I drop it to the ground and rearrange the boot. It has to fit. I'm desperate to get out. My hands are hurting and my elbow joints ache. I only notice again, now, how my body feels.

The car is loaded to the ceiling. Every available crevasse is filled. 'I can spatially organise a house into a container. I can do this.' Laptop. Files. Boxes.

One last check and I'm gone. I return inside to grab my phone and handbag from the kitchen bench just inside.

There is a man sitting at the dining table.

How the fuck?

His eyes, cold and strange, stare straight through me. He is on the phone. He hangs up and deliberately lights a cigarette.

Frozen to the spot. My momentum had carried me into the area between the kitchen counter and the dining table. The hairs on my arm stand up. I feel the fear.

He will see it.

He raises his large body up and comes towards me, looking me directly in the eyes, and I felt the hackles on the back of my neck rise and an electric pulse shiver through my body. Primeval. Instinctual. Fight or flight. I'd fight if I had a weapon. This person was clearly dangerous.

He came around the table, stopped a meter away from me and leant across the end of the kitchen bench. His actions were slow and deliberate. His hand covered an ash tray and picked it up. He turned, pulled up a dining chair closer to me, and sat down.

He looked up. Contemplative and calm.

"That was Vito."

This meant nothing to me. "Uh, huh." I didn't really understand what was going on. Why would that even be relevant right now?

"He wanted to know if you were a problem. He would fix you."

"And how would that be?" Even as I asked, I couldn't reconcile the terrifying reality with the beautiful life I had yesterday. Who is this person?

He held my stare. "Well, to be honest, I believe you may know, how hot headed Vito can be. I think you have heard many stories where he has had to be told, not to go off half cocked. At the moment, with what you have put on Facebook and people seeing it, well now there's a reputation to protect, that you have put certain deals in jeopardy. Vito understands that, and it is his job to sort it out. So he wants to take you out to a tree shredder on a pig farm. Nothing left. Nothing. You have become a liability."

"Is that a threat?"

"No, I'm just telling you what he said. I thought you should know. I'm just the messenger. Looking out for you, really."

"Well, I'll take that on board, but I'm not afraid of death."

"Yes that's what they all say until it hurts, then you find that everyone screams for mercy."

"Pain stops eventually." I had enough of a dark past, to know this, and have no intense fear of death. I have a total disregard for my own life. Pathetic but true.

I stared at him. So familiar. So similar, but different. A man in control, knowing his own power, making me feel his presence, but I didn't know this person. There was no feeling, no compassion, just danger and disrespect. I was definitely dispensable.

He meant this threat, and I needed to manipulate my way out safely.

"Katherine, there's a lot of plans underway, which you have just ruined, and now you are quite simply in the way. You don't even realise what you have done. The public, crazy activities of last night have seriously angered several people, and trust me, someone is going to pay. I'm going to suggest you voluntarily disappear. Go quietly. We are not likely to tolerate any more interference. Your public outbursts on social media last night need to be removed, as do all photos and evidence of the relationship. The family is in uproar. Not people you should have messed with.

Vito, Randy, and other vested parties, would like this solved today, but I'm hoping you see sense. You realise Randy is affiliated with the upper echelon of the Hells Angels. Not people to mess with. They are trusting my judgement. This is serious. Don't prove me wrong. Leave, don't look back. Don't cause any waves or trouble. Keep anything you know to yourself. Remember you are a mother and you wouldn't want to live with yourself knowing you were responsible for something happening to your son."

I was trying not to look confused and my thoughts were flying all over the place. No answers, just questions. What interference? I got told my fiance had an alive wife and child. I'm packed to leave. What is the problem? I'm not even making a fuss. Who the fuck are you anyway? I was trying desperately to not show anger, hate or hurt or fear, and I knew I wasn't good at verbal sparring. I wanted to leave before anything else happened.

'Happy to. I'm sure you'll understand when I say I'm borrowing the Maseratti until I sort myself out. It's packed with everything I need to leave 'quietly.'" I had some sparky attitude, that was misplaced in its timing and target.

"Use the car. If you don't return it, it will be reported as stolen. Do not be any more of an issue. Move on. You need to do that, regardless of how much this hurts you. I mean, I'm sorry for what you must be feeling right now. It wasn't part of the plan." He looked at me, with a face that was supposed to convey compassion for my current position. "Randy and Vito should be enough for you to understand this is serious and they will be more than happy to diffuse this situation. No option is pleasant, but you living is probably the one you should choose. You're already collateral damage, it's just to what degree you make that. You understand, otherwise I'll get Vito to convince you, and if you don't care about your own safety, think of your son. Trust me, I'll do what's necessary to protect our interests, no matter what it takes. You weren't meant to be found packing up and deserting. It is disappointing. I thought you were smarter."

I was looking at the ash tray as he had spoken. Keeping my eyes to myself. What was he talking about? What did anyone expect? Of course I'm leaving. Paul has a wife. What secrets? How have I disappointed anyone right now? And of all the shit I have heard in the last 24 hours, the threat to my son is where my brain snaps. I'm personally surprised that I'm physically capable of standing up, but now it's time to stand my ground.

"I'm leaving now. I am literally too sick to deal with this." I'm not being brave. I know I can't keep standing. I feel like I'm a few seconds from fainting and I'm terrified of being unconscious in this man's presence.

I side stepped towards the door slowly, and I would like to think, looking like I was somewhat in control, and not scared or hurt. I could feel my heart pounding and hear the blood course through my ear drums. As I entered the garage, I pulled the zapper out and clicked it. I was in the car and reversing as it finished opening. My mind in overdrive. 'I do not deserve any of this. I do not understand why I'm being threatened. I do not understand who Paul is. I do not understand who the fuck that was. I do not understand where that man just materialized from. I do not understand how Paul can have a wife. I do not understand why he lied to me. I do not understand how last night was a horrendous heart ache and now I'm also wanted dead. I do not know who Sarah Lewis Dean is, nor her beef. I do not understand what I'm supposed to know. And I do not accept threatening my son. You utter douche!

That is just not happening. Ever.'

# Chapter 43

Having left, I headed towards the shop, making it as far as the turnoff two streets down, where I turned the opposite direction, before pulling up a side street.
I couldn't make myself leave any further from him, and I had to come to terms with the fact, I really didn't have any where to go. What was I going to do? I sat and stared out the windscreen wishing I could at least cry. I just stared. I had shut down. I knew how this goes. I fossicked around my bag for some tissues. My nose was a mess. I couldn't find my sun glasses, and my eyes leaked in the bright sunshine pouring in the window.

Lighting a cigarette, I took a moment to breathe, and assess my limited options.

Leach off one of my poor friends? I'd rather not. I don't want company right now. I didn't think it was really what I needed ,and I'm pretty sure I'd be an awful house guest to put up with. Let alone, I'm already humiliated enough, without allowing them to witness the devastation I imagine I'm in for. I think the process before me is going to be painful.

Call my family? That's another no.

Run away? No funds.

Drive straight into a tree? Appealing but I realise God wouldn't let me die. He'd maim me severely, and leave me to pay off Paul's crashed car, for the rest of my life. Another strike.

I lowered the window a smidge so I could ash outside and continued to squint at the sky. Clear blue. It should be raining, grey, freezing, miserable. The universe doesn't care.

'Wow I'm homeless in a Maserati. Bet no one driving past, thinks that's even an option.

Ok what am I left with?' I wiped my leaking eyes from the sun and closed the tinted window.

'Go to the shop where there is at least my couch. I can make this work. It will be all right. What's not all right, is all of this.'

With me still frozen in inactivity, the phone kept pinging, ringing and buzzing. All the various forms of modern concern vying for my attention. Something I could do.

I looked at Facebook. I couldn't see very clearly too read. So many messages.
Ali, my old boss from many years ago, had left a message.

"*Shit, shit shit. Call me.*"

So I did. He was far enough removed, that I felt I could talk to him. It would still not feel real. It's not true, until you speak it.

We chatted for 40 minutes. He was trying to be philosophical, and upbeat, compassionate. Nothing was really going to help at this point.

I was back to numb. Slow. Devoid. Shock. He had so many questions.

"Did the wife know?"

"I'm not sure."

"How many kids has he got?"

"He has three. Two to his first wife and then this one to dead girl / alive wife."

"And already married twice?" His incredulity was apparent.

"Yes, well I knew of two. This is now three. I would have been his forth wife."

"Forth? Why did he propose to you if he had a wife?"

"I don't know.' I could see this was going to be a painful conversation with every body.

"What was he going to do?"

"I don't know."

"Marry you?"
"I don't know."

"How was he going to do that?"
"I don't know."

"How did he think he was going to pull it off?"
"I don't know."

"Why did he carry it so far?"
"I don't know."

"Why did he have such a lavish engagement?"
"I don't know."

"Why did his family come?"
"I really don't know."

"Do you think they knew?"
"I don't know."

"Why have you been threatened? That's so serious and nuts."

"Because I know things that can hurt Paul's reputation, because his wife didn't know about me, because I apparently now pose a threat to their business ventures, and his future plans? I don't know. I just don't understand how we could be in love yesterday and now this."

"How did you not know?"
"I don't know, but Ali, in my defense there were 80 people from my side at that engagement and they didn't know either and they had all met him."

I quickly realized. I didn't know anything. I could feel my brain swirling. Like a buzz in my head. Trying to understand it. Put logic in place. Make sense of it. The fog was getting thicker, as my morning flu tablets were wearing off, and reality was trying to force its way in.

"Ali, I've got nothing. I'm sorry. I just don't know. I can't talk any more."

"Call me in a few days, sweetie. I'm worried, and go to the police. You have to be safe."

"Yeah sure. Thank you for caring."

I hung up, and realised I had to call Ollie. I didn't want to. I had let him down.

He was relieved to hear my voice. "Good. I'm glad you left him. What happened?"

I told him what I knew, most of which was so random, so bizarre, it just didn't make sense.

"Dead girl - not dead.
Dead girl actually an alive wife.
Same name. Brooklin.
And a spare kid - Macky."

He was quick to digest it. "So that's three wives, not two, and this son, Macky- so that now three, with Andrew and John."

He knew both of the boys, having worked with them a few times for Paul. "Well, I can tell you now, mum. They hate him. I don't think he is anything like the person he makes out to be."

Over the last few years, Oliver hasn't liked me that much either, so I'm choosing to ignore this last bit. My denial is strong.

"So how did you leave?" I could hear he was worried.

"I packed my stuff into the car and just left. I'm going to bunker down in the shop." I didn't mention the threats. I needed to sort that out, and I didn't want him to panic. "I'm actually still near his house and I'm feeling sick again, can I chat later. I'm fine. It's going to be ok."

Having reassured him, I drove to the shop slowly. It was like it was raining, and the water on the windshield was blurring my sight. It wasn't though, it was just me. My eyes didn't want to focus. I couldn't get the car past 40 kph and even on the freeway I struggled to get above 70. My foot just didn't have the strength to push that hard. I burped a precursor to throwing up. I needed to lie down, as soon as possible. I don't think I'd ever felt so weak. I had trouble keeping my head up.

I managed a park right outside my shop, in the shade, and then I pulled out the handbag with my laptop, leaving everything else in the car. Regardless

of the flu sort of disappearing for that brief whirlwind of crazy packing, it was now back with vengeance. My eyes were running from trying to open in daylight. My head felt like an inflated ballon of lead and there was loud buzzing in my ears.
It's ok, I mused to myself, under the circumstances I would have felt like crap anyway.

I sluggardly, limped inside, trying to rush, resigned and accepting, that this was my lot. Dumping my bag and laptop on the chair near the door, I locked myself in, went straight to the little kitchen and threw up in the lower sink. The combination of standing up and heaving the entire contents of my stomach, made me wee a bit. Crap! None of this is ok. I turned the sink on and tried to force the mess down the trap, but only caused a blocked flood. It will have to wait. I turned, defeated and exhausted, and dropped the massive heavy curtains from their tie backs, to swish across the front windows, and close the world off. Dark. Quiet. Alone.

I made my way to the kitchen and found some painkillers and cold and flu. Thank god I work with girls. This place is a veritable pharmacy. I took four of each.

With my eye sockets pounding with every minuscule movement, and my bones aching through my skin, I wrestled a king sized blanket from a massage table in the back beauticians room and dragged it to the small front room where some of my things were still stored. My latex mattress being one. It was rolled up and had sticky tape holding it in place. Using small beauticians scissors, I cut the tape. The lower one, first, the top and then the middle one, which happily tore apart, as the mattress exploded like an emergency dinghy. It flopped open, crushing a box. A pillow magically landed on the corner in front of me. The mattress could only partially lie flat. Most of it is was up against the wall, and another third was caught leaning against a cupboard. I didn't care. I'm small. There's enough room for me to die in. I retreated to the couch, grabbing my cigarettes and an ashtray. Kicking my shoes off, I pulled the blanket around my body and lowered myself down. I got comfortable.

My mind pumped with cold and flu, and pain killers, I now didn't quite know what to do. What was my plan? What am I dealing with? I want Paul to fix this. It's my over riding thought. This has to be a nightmare. Paul wake me up. Where are you? Fix this. Love me.

I, at least knew why I had always felt like I was living in the shadow of a dead girlfriend, and this meant I hadn't imagined my discomfort. I had unwittingly been in the position of victim, and foolishly thought I was the winner. I feel humiliated, tricked and betrayed, but all those feelings didn't explain why I allowed Paul to manipulate me.

Paul has simply broken my heart. I am an idiot to think he loved me. That I am, in any way lovable. I am a joke.

By leaving, which I had to do, obviously on principle, and now I think by order, I have apparently awakened a new player. This new one wants to finish me completely. I'm not going to let that happen.

So, yes, this is the plan. I'm going to find out why my beautiful love story just became a suspense tragedy. I'm going to look back at every word, every look, every message, and I am going to piece it together, because it doesn't make sense that a stupid romance, the love of my life, has morphed and become so far removed from reality. I'm going to find Paul. And I'm going to flag every warning signal that I should have seen and learn from it. I don't ever want to feel like this again. I will tell everyone this story, so others don't fall for the same self absorbed lies, whether from Paul, or others of his ilk.

There will be patterns of behavior. I should have noticed. I will not stop until I understand what just happened.

But that's only half of it. I still need to understand why I'm wanted dead. It's a bit much to think it's just so dead girl / alive wife, doesn't find out about me. She already knows. Just like me, she will be reeling in shock. What's the connection between what I apparently know, and being told to keep quiet. Over what? I need to find out, what are all the secrets. How is Paul connected to these horrendous people? Was he going to leave his wife? Have I just over reacted and fucked everything up? Why has this all turned? Even this morning he kissed me, as he left the house. "I love you, Princess." I could have stayed and sorted it out.

But, then there is the reality check. Now I'm banished by a cold hearted cunt. I believe I am allowed to use that word. It is deserved. God, I'm so confused. It's too much. Just too, too much for me to make sense of.

My thick head couldn't think. It was too heavy with thoughts. I shut my eyes tight, holding my head under the pillow. I felt the sensation of being watched, and knew I was officially delusional. Hopefully, this is all just a drug induced nightmare; the worst flu, maybe I'm unconscious and this is all in my imagination, or perhaps I was indeed crazy and unhinged, as some of my friends had accused me of, only a few months ago. Maybe they are all correct and I'm wrong. Perhaps my strict adherence to rules, has forced me to play a hand that was utterly self sabotaging. The actions of a loser. Maybe he loves me. Maybe I am not a threat that needs to be dealt with. Maybe they are all realizing that now. Who ever they are. Maybe someone, somewhere is saying. "Hey, we got the wrong girl. Sorry about that. Business as usual. Go back and sort this domestic mess out." Maybe my obsessive desire to find the truth is part of a severe irrational mental instability. Can't I just walk away? Maybe I'm making this all up just to sabotage a relationship. Maybe I'm a woman scorned just seeking revenge. I'm clearly the unbalanced one.

I stared into unfocused space, my eyes glassy and sore. The phone rang, out of habit, I answered it without looking to see who it was. As it came up to my ear, I saw "UNKNOWN" and immediately regretted the waste of precious energy on a spam call.

"Hello." The man had a deep voice, heavily accented. European, if I had to guess.

"Hello." I responded with the little husky voice I had left.

"I'm going to suggest you don't cause any further trouble for our friend. We know where you are. The car's hard to miss."

"Ok." I groaned. "I have no intention of causing trouble. Paul and I are over. I get it."

I rolled over as I hung up, and threw up into a waste bin. Well, that clarified that. As long as I'm not hallucinating, I have to accept I'm in trouble. Bring it on. I can't get up and leave. I'm stuck here with my whirling crazy thoughts, feeling hurt and sick. That's how it is. Too sick to care. The only thing I care about, is that Paul isn't here beside me, protecting me from what's happening. He knows what's going on.

How could you do this to me Paul? How could you leave me with people wanting to kill me? Are you aware of what you have done? Why does it suddenly matter that I left you? Why has this angered everyone? Seriously.

Who is Paul that anyone would care whether I stay or go? This morning it seemed I angered these people because I chose to leave and immediately they demand I do it quietly. I don't even understand if I'm in more trouble being with him or leaving. FUCK!

I finally dropped off to an uncomfortable flu induced sleep, already aware, that for every memory, dredged up with hindsight and perhaps some increasing clarity, I now had more and more questions.

Why did he take it so far? Did he love me? And for all the pain that I felt, I was aware, that I hurt in a manner I never dreamed possible. I knew that I would never love, or be loved like that again. Was I just a babysit fuck, killing time till he returned to his wife? Who are these angry people?

I lay there pining for Paul's arms to wrap around me. The very person who betrayed me, was the man I needed to take the excruciating pain away. I craved his protection, and in the same breath knew there was no logic in that as a solution.

Nothing else would work.

Except the truth.

And that's what I focused on. I became determined to find the truth and use it as my armour. I would build a new wall with it, and it would encompass my son. I was not willing to be anyone's collateral damage. How far am I prepared to go to heal my own heart, and how much knowledge do I need to be safe? I don't understand any of what happened.

What is it that they think I know? I will find out. I'm good like that.

I shut my eyes. The phone was ringing. I ignored it. There's an accumulation of texts and messages. I'm aware I can't protect myself just yet, I'm too weak physically and mentally.

I don't care. Tomorrow. Tomorrow, as soon as I can get up. I am going to begin piecing it all together, I'm going to look back on everything I heard and saw, revisit my relationship with fresh eyes, and hopefully I will understand what happened to my life and my beautiful Paul Carter. I will be able to see the truth, that he had a second life, with a wife and child, and I will unravel the lie and extricate myself from this hurt.

As the phone pinged one last time, I fell off to a nightmare fueled sleep. I didn't see it for days.

*"I love you. I'm sorry for everything. This has got out of hand. Katherine, your facebook posts have put everything in danger. Come back. I'm leaving everything behind. I need a fresh start. I need you with me."*

# Chapter 44

Literally, sitting under an umbrella, watching crystal clear, waves lap gently along the shore, I realise my life has mimicked art. It seems a tacky ending. I still live in the twilight of a romance thriller, and appropriately I have ended up in balmy paradise at the end of a mystery suspense. I see the corniness, but it is the truth. It's the truth, because that apparently *is* the place to run, when you need a cheap place to hide.

I now know how far I went. From the safety of anonymity, I look back and realise those weeks of lying in the shop being sick and heart broken, scared and shocked, were only the beginning of a horrendously, painful and confronting journey, that so far has lasted three tumultuous years, as I deconstructed my relationship and my beautiful Paul's life, in the hope of reclaiming what I had, and struggled to maneuver my way through heart ache to safety.

I have been in hiding. I live with guns. I do not answer my door. I'm never where anyone thinks I am. And yet I have been threatened. My friends have been contacted. I have been called numerous times, and reminded to remain quiet and forget Paul.

But being quiet doesn't protect me, and it doesn't hold the guilty accountable. The truth needs to be told. How did a wonderful love story end up such a twisted mess?

Perhaps if I had been allowed to live in complete peace, I would have let things go, but that wasn't how they wanted the game to play out. Apparently none of them were finished. I was going to be dragged further in, before I could dig my way out.

I can wish my journey had been less painful but it wasn't. It was, what it was. Sadly, not completely surprisingly, and admittedly pathetically, I wanted Paul back. I craved his love. I wanted answers, and in flickering back and forth through the remnants of my relationship, I uncovered lie upon lie, and it didn't make it easier that they all had the same theme. She doesn't exist. I love you.

I hear his words.

"She died a horrible death."

"Her leaving allowed me to grow. My life is better with her dead."

"Princess, my future happiness requires you to be in my life."

"We are together for a reason."

"I need your goodness."

"Katherine she is dead. You are sabotaging what is best for you."

"I'll love you like no other."

"She was a malicious, vindictive person. Not like You. The polar opposite."

We are getting a divorce. We just had an engagement party. My parents came. I want to marry you. I love you."

The layers were not peeling, they were shedding. Over the next few weeks, weighed down with being catastrophically ill, I would become angrier by the day. More hurt, and more confused as to why, but beginning to see the how.

# Chapter 44

But I didn't know, as I lay curled up in the shop, that it wasn't just a love story gone wrong. That would have been so simple. The messages accumulating on my phone that I would soon read, would open an entirely new world to me. Each had a piece of a much bigger puzzle. A puzzle I was going to solve.

I didn't know that by the following March, I would be talking with Vito, discussing how he was going to kill me. I couldn't have dreamed that instead of being happily married, I would then be on the run, with no idea what happened to Paul. Everyone was looking for him, but no one would find him. It would be left to me.

I didn't have a clue that my life was going to spiral out of control, and that what I was going through now, in the shop, was actually, by no way, going to be the worst part. I couldn't imagine it getting worse. But it did. A lot worse!

And for everything that was happening, I still couldn't regret being loved by him. I hankered for him, even in the throes of his betrayal.

She wasn't a dead girlfriend, she was an alive wife.

I still wanted him to come, and be a buffer between me and the fear of being in danger. I wanted him home with me. I knew it wasn't rationale and that it's shameful to admit, but by now there was so little of me left, when Paul was no longer by my side, I ceased to exist.

But back then, lying in the shop, day after day, I didn't know any of this, I only knew this was not how the story ended. I knew there was going to be more. I had no idea to what extent, and from what direction anything was going to come from, but, there was one thing I did know.

I knew that Paul and I were not over. I knew because our names were now in the same book but they were not yet together in the last sentence.

There was going to be unimaginable, collateral damage, before that happened, and as I drifted off to more unpleasant memories of love and betrayal, flickering through my head, I willed my beautiful Paul to come and rescue me.

Once thought to be a love story, don't miss the climatic and unimaginable ending to this true life, psychological thriller. The story continues in ....

## What Happened to Paul Carter VOL II. Collateral Damage.

Up to this point, my reflections are of confusion, betrayal and hurt, but it was just a love story gone wrong. However, from here things got so much more complicated, so, so much worse. I look back on all of this, with increasing sadness and shame. I'm still awed by some of the events. Puzzled and confused.

I'm aware that when you add the word hitman to any story, it is no longer just a love story. So what happened?

Nikolai, leant forward across the restaurant table. "At the moment, you say you have no idea what panicked this scumbag in the first place. If people are prepared to hand you information, then take it. Don't disclose anything about yourself. Keep safe. Don't let anyone know where you are. Let them think the wrong location, as often as possible. I'm sorry you are now spending your money but while you are here, you are completely safe and can relax. Vito is a professional and his associates are thugs. I'm glad you're out of the shop, I have had discussions, and we need to face certain facts. I'll meet you here tomorrow. I want to discuss where you are going to move to. You realise you have to leave until this has an end, do you understand."
He looked at me very tenderly. "Darlin, look at me. You're in danger. Vito has been hired to kill you. You understand. He has been paid to kill you."

Looking in the mirror. I saw a pathetic, shallow version of myself. Dark grey bruise with small spottles of purple smeared under my eyes. I gingerly touched the bridge of my nose. It killed, making my eyes water. Won't be doing that for a while. I stared at it. If it's broken and stays like that, I'm going to be lucky. It's pretty straight.

I was in such limbo. Would someone come to my door and blow me away? Would Paul come back? Not knowing exactly what it was that he was afraid of, meant I could see, I was always going to feel this way. A daily attack of suspicion, confessions, anonymous phone calls, Face book messages, cries for help from strangers, betrayal, shock, hurt, broken pierced heart, shattered soul, destroyed beliefs, deception, subterfuge and straining my brain trying to ensure justice would be done. I could see no way out except to control the ending myself.

Collateral Damage, the second Volume unfolds, exposing the raw truth and simultaneously, unimagined pain, morphing Katherine and Paul's beautiful love story into a dramatic psychological suspense story. Only to Katherine, this wasn't a story, it was all true. Continue reading to help figure out, what really happened to Paul Carter?

Made in the USA
Lexington, KY
13 February 2018